泄密的心

爱伦·坡短篇小说精选

名家导读有声版

英汉对照·插图版

朱振武 主编
冯德河 蓝云春 副主编
[美]爱伦·坡 著

華東理工大學出版社
EAST CHINA UNIVERSITY OF SCIENCE AND TECHNOLOGY PRESS
·上海·

图书在版编目(CIP)数据

泄密的心：爱伦·坡短篇小说精选：英汉对照·名家导读有声版 / 朱振武主编. —上海：华东理工大学出版社，2019.2
（经典短篇双语阅读）
ISBN 978-7-5628-5472-2

Ⅰ. ①泄… Ⅱ. ①朱… Ⅲ. ①英语—汉语—对照读物 ②短篇小说—小说集—美国—近代 Ⅳ. ①H319.4：I

中国版本图书馆CIP数据核字(2018)第098521号

策划编辑 / 信　艳
责任编辑 / 赵楚月
装帧设计 / 风信子
插　　画 / 秦姝妤
出版发行 / 华东理工大学出版社有限公司
地址：上海市梅陇路130号，200237
电话：021-64250306
网址：www.ecustpress.cn
邮箱：zongbianban@ecustpress.cn
印　　刷 / 上海盛通时代印刷有限公司
开　　本 / 890mm × 1240mm　1/32
印　　张 / 8.375
字　　数 / 318千字
版　　次 / 2019年2月第1版
印　　次 / 2019年2月第1次
定　　价 / 39.80元

扫一扫，听有声导读

走进上海师范大学

博士生导师朱振武教授的

文学课堂

聆听该音频，你可以获知：

1. 爱伦 · 坡的国际影响力及其传奇人生。
2.《泄密的心》深度解读。
3. 学好英语的二字箴言。

经典阅读的当下意义

朱振武

有个学生要考我的研究生，我回信给她说，考我的研究生，要能够静下心来读书，不枉过三年，不要只顾蝇头微利，不要陷入琐碎，不要流于肤浅，立足在眼前，但立志要高远，至少要做一个文化人，而不是个只顾眼前利益的小市民，渐次达到人生较高的境界。这个学生很坚决，她回信说，读研的目的不仅是学习更多的知识，更重要的是充实人生，完善人格，提高自己的精神境界。回答得很好，正是我要的答案，后来她得偿所愿，心无旁骛地读起书来，再后来表现出很强的后劲。

要否读书，读书重要与否，重要到什么程度，这些在不久前被看作是只有白痴才会问的问题在当下还真成了问题。我们的孔老夫子曾说，不读诗，无以言。十七世纪英国哲人弗朗西斯·培根说得好，读书使人充实，不常读书者须欺世有术，始能无知而显有知。人之才智但有滞碍，无不可读适当之书使之顺畅。读书，首要的是读什么书呢？当然是读经典著作。什么是经典？常念为经，常数为典，是为经典。经典就是经得起反复重复的文本，其之所以得以如此就在于其丰厚的文化蕴含，就在于我们每次对之重温都能从中开掘出熏染和涤荡我们灵魂的东西。

同样一篇文章或一个理论，能经得起人反复咀嚼。经典还具有不可超越性，更不是我们眼前这些急功近利的东西所能替代的。著名电视导演张纪中说：“经典是不能超越的。你可以在他旁边再垒一座山，却无法超越这座山。”经典就是这样的一些作品，常读常新，且不会过时或落伍。历史文化学者易中天说得好，经典就是最有价值、最有意义的著作。他还引用中国那句老话教育大家，“取法其上，得乎其中。取法其中，得乎其下。”“取法其上”，对于我们读书人来说，当然就是阅读经典。

有个读者在网上留帖子说，没有读意大利的伊塔洛·卡尔维诺的《为什么读经典》，那是旷世奇憾。旷世不旷世不敢说，遗憾是肯定有的。卡尔维诺对经典的阐发确实深刻，他认为，经典作品是一些产生某种特殊影响的书，他们要么本身以难忘的方式给我们的想象力打下印记，要么乔装成个人或集体的无意识隐藏在深层记忆中，经典作品是一本不会耗尽它要向你说的一切东西的书。他还认为，经典作品是这样的一些书，它们带着先前解释的气息走向我们，背后拖着它们经过文化或多种文化（或只是多种语言和风俗）时留下的足迹。这些话说得真是深刻，我曾经在一次关于经典阅读的讲座上稍事夸张地说：经典文学是这样的书：

它是使没有头脑的人变得有头脑，没有文化的人变得有文化的书，是使肤浅之徒变得稳重、呆板之人变得诙谐、迟滞之人变得睿智、短视之人变得远见、丑陋之人变得俊拔、狭隘之人变得宽容、妒忌变得羡慕、贪婪变得节制、吝啬变得慷慨、苛刻变得宽容、卑微变得高贵、猥琐变得雍容、空虚变得充实、奢靡变得简朴、情调低俗变得品位高雅、百无聊赖变得丰富多彩的书，是那些让你得到调整、使你得到憩息、能够与你沟通、可以帮你排遣郁闷的书，是能够为你提供生活坐标的书，是可以让你放松身心、宣泄激愤的书，是使你保持坦荡荡免于长戚戚的书，是使你高出只掌握某种一般技能的人的书，是使你摆脱生存尴尬、尽享人生乐趣的书，是使你懂得一个人为什么要活着的书，是使高级动物有别于其他动物的书。

有个听众问我什么时候读经典，我戏谑地回答说："当你神情抑郁、兴趣寡淡的时候，当你情场失意、官场失落的时候，当你挫败连连、股市大跌的时候，当你参透人生、看破红尘的时候，当你失业下岗的时候，当你屡试不中的时候，当你穷得只剩下钱的时候，当你辗转反侧、夜不成寐、茶饭无思、百无聊赖的时候，当你不知道人为什么而活着的时候，当你不知道你到底有什么用处的时候，当你在充满喧哗与骚动的都市里无处逃逸的时候，不要想入非非，不要萌生他想，尽情享受经典阅读带给你的乐趣吧！"

为什么要读经典？易中天说得好，就是因为能从经典中读人生，读智慧，读社会。我颇以为然，所以，每天没有不看书的时候，没有不接触经典的时候，否则就觉得怅然若失，缺少了根基，没了底气，丢了自信。

这套四卷本的"美国名家短篇小说精选"所收作家作品就是前面所说的那样的经典之作，很具代表性，基本上让我们看到了美国短篇小说的整体面貌，而且这些作品仍与当下有着很强的意义关联，因此，其读者群也比较宽广。画龙点睛般的导读、简练严谨的注释和紧扣源语的译文为读者体会作品主旨意蕴、创作技巧和学习、欣赏原文文本提供了很大便利。

这套书的撰译者都是在高校里专门从事英美文学教学和研究的人员，主编是上海师范大学的朱振武，副主编是上海师范大学的冯德河、蓝云春，山东大学的高静，三峡大学的陈月红、杨鸿雁、黎智林、任慧芝以及上海大学外国语学院的张惠英。大家在多年的教研实践中达成一个共识：一个不读经典作品的人是不完整的人，没有一定的英美文学经典作品的阅读量，一个人的英语水平是不可能达到较高层次的，他在这个方面的整体文化素养肯定是有缺陷的。因此，我们向各位读者奉上这套“美国名家短篇小说精选”。

朱振武

2018年春

关于爱伦·坡

埃德加·爱伦·坡(Edgar Allan Poe, 1809—1849)是美国十九世纪诗人、短篇小说家和文艺批评家，是在文学的几个领域对欧美文学乃至整个世界文学都产生了深远影响的文学巨匠。

1809年1月19日，爱伦·坡出生在巴尔的摩。爱伦·坡的祖父原属爱尔兰籍，后随家人迁居至此。爱伦·坡的父亲大卫·坡(David Poe)二十岁时加入了弗吉尼亚的一家剧团。1806年4月初，他与这家剧团的知名女伶伊丽莎白·阿诺德(或伊丽莎白·坡)(Elizabeth Arnold)在里士满结为伉俪。婚后两人共育有三个子女，长子亨利·坡，次子埃德加·坡和小女罗莎莉·坡。由于在演艺事业上壮志难酬，再加上生活的拮据，大卫·坡自1810年10月起销声匿迹。爱伦·坡过早地失去了父爱，这在一定程度上造就了他"苦难天才"的双重特质。另一方面，变幻无常和恃才傲物的秉性又让他动辄陷入文人之争的泥潭，成为同时代人蔑视和摒弃的对象。丈夫的失踪使一家人的生活更加窘迫，1811年10月，伊丽莎白不堪重负，一病不起，于是年12月撒手人寰。双亲一个早早撒手人寰，一个则如泥牛入海，音信全无，兄妹三人一个先他而去，一个为他留守终身，使得人世间最真挚、最纯朴的情感在爱伦·坡身上演变为可望而不可即的奢侈品。于是，他带着慈母的幻影，带着对亲情的渴望，开始在人生历程和创作生涯中不断寻求心灵的慰藉。

爱伦·坡幼年失祜，旋即成了曾经救助过他们的爱伦（Allan）夫妇的螟蛉之子，这也是爱伦·坡名字的由来。养父约翰·爱伦（John Allan）平时不苟言笑，不太容易让人接近，所以，爱伦·坡在家中享受的关爱更多是来自养母。1815年，爱伦一家前往英国居住。到达苏格兰后，爱伦·坡被送入当地一所文法学校念书。学校开设的书法课要求学生去附近的坟场临摹墓碑上撰写的铭文，从而也让爱伦·坡对死神有了更进一步的认识。在伦敦，爱伦·坡奠定了深厚的古典文学基础。他在斯托克·纽因顿学校学习的经历为他创作短篇小说《威廉·威尔逊》（*William Wilson*, 1839）积累了宝贵的素材和丰富的灵感。通过这次英国之行，爱伦·坡不仅接受了英国正规教育的熏陶，领略了大洋彼岸的旖旎风光和异域风情，而且也收获了对哥特城堡、公共墓碑和历史遗迹的认识，为他描绘现实以外的世界寻觅到了可供临摹的模本。

1826年2月，爱伦·坡成为弗吉尼亚大学的一名学生，在这里接受一流的教育，为今后的创作生涯蓄积了大量的知识储备。不过，由于这所新办的学校风气不正，爱伦·坡沾染上了酗酒、赌博的不良习惯。当年年底，对爱伦·坡非常失望的爱伦不准许他再回学校，并把他安排在自己的商行当学徒，但爱伦·坡仍以读书、访友为乐，被养父冠以“游手好闲”“吃闲饭”的骂名。1827年3月，爱伦·坡决定离家出走。4月，爱伦·坡化名为亨利·里·雷恩特（Henri Li Rennet）去了波士顿，不久就邂逅了一家小印刷厂的老板卡尔文·弗·斯·托马斯（Calvin F. S. Thomas）。他愿意在自费的条件下帮爱伦·坡出版一本名为《帖木耳及其他诗》（*Tamerlane and Other Poems*, 1827）的诗集，这也是爱伦·坡正式问世的第一部作品。出版这本诗集使爱伦·坡再度陷入了经济危机，于是他把注意力转向了军队。5月，爱伦·坡以另一化名埃德加·A. 佩里（Edgar A. Perry）的身份应征加入美国陆军。对于爱伦·坡而言，这段戎马生活有得亦有失。一方面，身处部队的他不仅可以解除衣食之忧，腾出更多的时间和精力写诗，而且也能利用深入祖国边疆要塞的机会，寻求日后创作的素材和灵感。其中，《金甲虫》（*The Gold-Bug*, 1843）中宝藏的埋藏地就是设在人迹罕至的沙利文岛上，《长方形的箱子》（*The Oblong Box*, 1844）中"我们"登船离港的出发地选在查尔斯顿港，而在《气球骗局》（*Balloon-Hoax*, 1844）和《梅岑格施泰因》（*Metzengerstein*, 1832）等几部小说中同样也能觅得这段生活的些许踪影。但是漫长的服役生活也带给爱伦·坡难耐的孤寂和无限的愁苦。1829年3月，养母溘然长逝，飘零无助的爱伦·坡愈变孤苦。先前不支持他退伍的养父现在同意他提前退伍，去上西点军校。

为了赡养家人，爱伦·坡逐渐将精力投入更具收益性的领域。短篇小说《梅岑格施泰因》在费城《星期六信使报》（*Saturday Courier*）的匿名发表是爱伦·坡正式由写诗转向小说创作的标志。不久，他的《瓶中手稿》（*MS. Found in a Bottle*,1833）在巴尔的摩《星期六游客报》（*Saturday Visitor*）举办的小说竞赛中一举夺魁。他也借此机会结交了在当时的文学界享有盛誉的约翰·P.肯尼迪（John P. Kennedy）先生。1834年3月，约翰·爱伦在里士满病故，爱伦·坡难以维持一个四口之家。关键时刻，肯尼迪将他介绍给里士满《南方文学信使》杂志的主编托马斯·怀特（Thomas White）先生。怀特曾为爱伦·坡登载过短篇小说《贝蕾妮丝》（*Berenice*, 1835），他毅然向爱伦·坡发出邀请。1835年8月，爱伦·坡回里士满出任《南方文学信使》助理编辑，从此开始不停地撰写书评杂文，创作短篇小说，为自己诗歌的再版奔波忙碌。当年年底，他就被荣升为杂志编辑。但是，由于薪水不高，经济的窘迫不时折磨着爱伦·坡，他经常醉酒误事，于1837年1月被解雇。在《南方文学信使》工作的一年多的时间里，爱伦·坡共发表了八十三篇评论，六首诗，四篇杂文，三部短篇小说以及一部未完成的剧本。1836年，还在《南方文学信使》工作期间，二十七岁的爱伦·坡与不满十四岁的表妹弗吉尼亚结了婚，这段婚姻生活幸福而温暖。

离开《南方文学信使》后，爱伦·坡来到纽约，但受到当时经济危机的影响，一直没能找到工作。利用闲居纽约的这段时间，爱伦·坡下了不少功夫研究密码。他在破译密码方面的天赋和功力在其后来创作的推理小说《金甲虫》中得到淋漓尽致的展现，该小说在1843年6月还获得了《金元报》短篇小说征文头奖。这一时期，爱伦·坡创作了中篇小说《南塔特克的亚瑟·戈登·皮姆的故事》(*The Narrative of A. Gordon Pym of Nantucket*, 1837)，发表在《南方文学信使》上，这是爱伦·坡创作的小说中篇幅最长的一篇。1838年8月，爱伦·坡一家再次迁居费城。几个月后，爱伦·坡迫于生计向《博顿绅士杂志》(*Burton's Gentleman's Magazine*)主编博顿毛遂自荐，并且受到博顿的欢迎，正式到《博顿绅士杂志》上班。爱伦·坡的编辑工作使他结交了一批文坛挚友，其中有梅因·里德、乔治·利帕德、托马斯·邓恩·英格利希以及鲁弗斯·格里斯沃尔德。这些朋友对他的文学创作和生活产生了很大的影响。1839年9月，爱伦·坡在《博顿绅士杂志》上发表了恐怖小说《厄舍古屋的崩塌》(*The Fall of the House of Usher*, 1839)。10月，爱伦·坡又发表了短篇小说《威廉·威尔逊》，这篇小说被后人誉为意识流小说的雏形。1840年费城当地的出版商利和布兰查德出版了爱伦·坡的小说集《怪异故事集》(*Tales of the Grotesque and Arabesque*, 1840)，其中收录了《厄舍古屋的崩塌》《威廉·威尔逊》《莫雷拉》(*Morella*, 1835)等25篇短篇小说。

1840年春，乔治·R.葛雷姆买下《博顿绅士杂志》，并把它与自己原来的《卡斯基特杂志》合并，改名为《葛雷姆杂志》(*Graham's Magazine*)。次年，爱伦·坡成了新创刊的《葛雷姆杂志》的助理编辑。这一时期，爱伦·坡先后发表了《人群中的人》(*The Man of the Crowd*, 1840)、《摩格街谋杀案》(*The Murders in the Rue*

Morgue,1841)、《大漩涡底余生记》(*A Decent into the Maelstrōm*, 1841)、《仙女岛》(*The Island of the Fay*, 1841)、《艾蕾奥瑙拉》(*Eleonora*, 1841)、《椭圆形画像》(*The Oval Portrait*, 1842) 等一批颇具影响力的作品。《人群中的人》说明爱伦·坡在一百多年前就敏锐地觉察到现代社会的弊病，睿智地预见到现代人孤独的生存困境。《摩格街谋杀案》开创了侦探小说的先河，爱伦·坡也被公认为侦探推理小说的鼻祖。1841年5月，爱伦·坡在《葛雷姆杂志》上发表了恐怖小说《大漩涡底余生记》，6月，又发表了小说《仙女岛》。秋天，爱伦·坡创作了小说《艾蕾奥瑙拉》，这是爱伦·坡的作品中文笔最流畅、辞藻最华丽的一篇。

1841年春夏之季，鲁弗斯·格里斯沃尔德拜访了爱伦·坡。他是爱伦·坡后来的遗稿保管人，然而，也正是他编造了一系列诋毁爱伦·坡声誉的世纪流言，并讹传至今。对于朋友的背信弃义，爱伦·坡大为恼火。1842年1月，弗吉尼亚得了严重的肺病，她每一次咳血都令爱伦·坡痛苦万分，这不禁唤起了他内心深处对童年时母亲口吐鲜血的记忆。两种场景跨越时空，相互交融，不时在爱伦·坡的脑海中闪现。受此启发，爱伦·坡创作了另一篇代表作《红死魔的面具》(*The Masque of the Red Death*, 1842)。1842年3月，英国著名作家狄更斯访问费城，与爱伦·坡相识。狄更斯颇为赞赏爱伦·坡的作品，回国后向英国出版界推荐，然而正统保守的英国文坛根本接受不了爱伦·坡的那些离奇怪诞的作品。长期以来艰苦的生活和坎坷的经历使这一时期的爱伦·坡开始将创作的注意力转向人类的下意识，转向人类的病态心理和邪恶欲望。《泄密的心》(*The Tell-Tale Heart*, 1843)、《黑猫》(*The Black Cat*, 1843)等几篇恐怖小说就是爱伦·坡这一时期的代表作。《泄密的心》讲述的是一位心理扭曲、人格分裂的病态人，《黑猫》中的主人公也是这样一位理智崩溃、心理反常的病态人。

1844年4月，爱伦·坡和妻子重返纽约，仅仅一星期他就创作完成了《气球骗局》，并发表在《纽约太阳报》(*New York Sun*)上，引起了巨大轰动。更令人叹服的是，爱伦·坡这篇科幻小说竟然真的预言了人类百年后的首次气球越洋飞行。1845年1月，经过一遍遍的反复修改和字斟句酌的仔细推敲，《乌鸦》(*The Raven*, 1845) 一诗在《纽约明镜晚报》上发表。该诗具有严格、华丽的形式美、音乐美和高度统一和谐的效果，是爱伦·坡高超诗艺的最佳体现，不久就被传诵开来，人们都说，"这只乌鸦简直会取代作为国鸟的鹰"。1845年7月，纽约威利普特南公司出版了包括十二篇小说在内的《埃德加·A.坡故事集》(*Tales by Edgar A. Poe*, 1845)。同年11月，该公司又出版了爱伦·坡的诗集《乌鸦及其他诗》(*The Raven and Other Poems*, 1845)。

1846年，除发表在《戈迪斯淑女》(*Godey's Lady's Book*) 杂志上的短篇小说《一桶白葡萄酒》(*The Cask of Amontillado*, 1846) 外，爱伦·坡在文学创作上的收获甚微。1847年1月，弗吉尼亚病逝，这一打击对爱伦·坡来说是致命的。这一年，爱伦·坡除了创作出一首怀念弗吉尼亚和他们忠贞爱情的诗《尤娜路姆——一首诗歌》(*Ulalume—A Ballad*, 1847) 和一首阐释自己对人生和宇宙看法的诗《我发现了》(*Eureka*, 1848) 外，几乎就再也没有写出什么作品。直到1849年5月，他才又写出了令人称颂不绝的诗作《安娜贝尔·李》(*Annabel Lee*)。这首怀念亡妻之作最初发表在10月9日的纽约《论坛报》(*Tribune*)上，两个月后《南方文学信使》又予以刊登，引起很大反响。此时的爱伦·坡脆弱不堪，玛丽·休夫人守候在他身边，对他关怀备至。1848年春末，爱伦·坡前去拜访休夫人。休夫人家住在一座教堂旁，时时可以听见从教堂里传出来的钟声。受此启发，爱伦·坡创作了《钟》(*The Bells*, 1848) 一诗。此诗是爱伦·坡审美统一性、音乐性、总体效果性理论的杰出实践代表。爱伦·坡在诗中对钟声的描写正是他对自己人生经历的最好总结——最先度过的是快乐而短暂的童年，接着经历了半生的痛苦和磨难，最后带着一颗伤痕累累的心走向人生的终点。

同奥斯古德夫人的感情一样，爱伦·坡与休夫人的恋情也经受了社会舆论的压力。人言可畏，为避免这些无聊的中伤，休夫人与爱伦·坡逐渐疏远，最后中断了与他的来往。爱伦·坡对此非常痛苦，但痛苦之余他还是满怀热情地到处寻找他生命中的知音。继奥斯古德夫人和休夫人之后，坡又与简·厄米娜·洛克、埃斯特尔·安娜·刘易斯、安妮·里奇蒙、莎拉·海伦·惠特曼夫人以及谢尔顿夫人等多位女性发生过恋情，但都是无花之果。爱伦·坡心力交瘁又得不到抚慰，只能借酒浇愁。1849年10月3日，酒后的爱伦·坡被送到华盛顿大学医院。10月7日凌晨，爱伦·坡说了声“上帝保佑我”便猝然而卒，一颗耀眼的文学巨星就这样告别了人世，年仅四十岁。

爱伦·坡在其小说创作中总能凭借各种手段制造出其预设的各种效果，这自然与其转益多师、博采众家之长并对之大胆融化创新密不可分，但爱伦·坡以其高度的文学自觉和超前的创作理念在创作上兢兢业业，惨淡经营，精心营构自己的效果美学，或许是其作品产生良好的美学效果的又一重要原因。正如波德莱尔在称赞爱伦·坡时说，爱伦·坡之所以赢得众人的赏识，在于“他对美的爱，对美的和谐条件的认识”。可以说，或许正是因为这份独特的气质和超前的创作理念，爱伦·坡不仅没有在文化土壤贫瘠、实用观念高于一切和支配一切的国家里随波逐流，反而以追新求异的探索精神为美的事业竖起一面特立独行的大纛，在新生的美国文学发展过程中独辟蹊径，一改对欧洲文学特别是英伦文学的顶礼膜拜之风，凭着自己的那份执着、努力和才情使美的实现成为可能，为美轮美奂的诗歌和小说等文学样式植根于新大陆进而实现本土化做出了一份贡献，也为他身后的文学家们提供了诸多可供摹写的范本。

目　录

Edgar Allan Poe

1809 – 1849

Edgar Allan Poe was an American writer, editor, and literary critic, who is generally considered the inventor of the detective fiction genre and is further credited with contributing to the emerging genre of science fiction.

The Tell-Tale Heart
泄密的心

“我”和老头住在一起，“我”很爱老头，但是却无法忍受老头的眼睛，特别是那种目光，于是“我”便把老头杀死、肢解，结果老头的那颗心脏泄了密，“我”只好招供。这就是《泄密的心》(*The Tell-Tale Heart,* 1843）的故事情节。情节简单，但意蕴却深远。人类虽然历经千年万年的时间，历经千种万种的形态，其内心潜藏在一切意识最深处的潜意识，却是大体相同的。这种潜意识，按照荣格的观点，不是个别的，而是普遍的，“具备了所有地方和所有个人皆有的大体相似的内容和行为方式”。以传统的批评眼光看，我们只能概略地说这是爱伦·坡的又一部恐怖、惊险故事，有的把它归为侦探类，实在过于勉强，因为它连侦探小说的基本要素都不具备。坡在小说中所着力描写的诸种细节读了确实令人不寒而栗，但让读者想得更多的可能还是小说的标题“泄密的心”。这篇小说对宿命、神秘特别是“心”和“眼”的描写的确意味深长。

读《泄密的心》，其中有两处反复出现的意象是无法忽略的，一处是激起“我”去谋杀老头的原因：老头的眼睛（eye, 这个词重复了 11 次）；一处是使“我”得到报复的原因，也就是老头那不死的心（heart, 这个词重复了 8 次）跳声。不管爱伦·坡是有意识还是无意识地描述，这些意象却实在是意味深长并且触目惊心。其实这篇小说的非常之处，就是心跳声的不合常情。首先是老头受到惊吓时的心跳声，二是老头虽死却心跳不止。到了作为报复形象出现的心跳声时，作品中充斥的几乎就是这一意象了，光是“声音”(sound)重复了 8 次，说“越来越大”（louder）就出现了 13 次，说恐惧或声音等加剧或增强(increase) 就重复了 7 次。这些意象在段落中顽强地潜伏在一个紧逼一个的节奏中，形成了一种重压。这些反复出现的意象不能不使人抛弃文字的表层含意，而去追寻它的深层意蕴：究竟是什么使“眼睛”成为一种蛊惑呢？又是哪种力量使得报复来得如此迅速和必然？“我”无法承受的是什么？其中有没有回荡着亘古不变的旋律？

关于“鹰眼”的描述确实应引起人的注意。鹰是猛禽，在飞鸟世界中它代表不可一世的力量。原型批评大师弗莱曾对之有如此描述：“动物世界以妖怪和猛兽等意象来描绘……所有的统治者都和怪兽等同。”据此，我们有理由将鹰眼视为一种象征：它代表了权势。它的邪恶或者它的强大的力量正是“我”爱它又天然地反对它的真正原因。这种心态是集体的、一般人类心理共有的。再回到故事内容得以展开的结构，“我”不满于一种强权，想扼杀它，但却最终得到了强权的报复。在原型批评理论中，这些貌似蔑视真理的现象却是原型的最直接的表现。这时，《泄密的心》已经不再是一篇恐怖心理小说了。它所表达的是西西弗斯式人类生存的某种困境：世界充满了违情悖理和徒劳无益。正是在对人类这种悲剧状态的关注中，读者获得了对小说的普遍同情——对自身境地的潜意识认识被唤醒了。整篇小说里两个主要人物，“我”和老头应该说是魔幻型意象中替罪羊和暴君的分别对等。“我”不是单纯的受苦受难，暴君也不是完全地强悍有力。当然我们并不是要挖掘出人对命运的无可奈何而后悲天悯人，这也不是原型批评的最终目的，我们对作品进行原型批评，很明显的一个作用是找出了作品的深层结构。在这种找寻中也容易地把握住了人类普遍存在的集体无意识，明确了心灵受到震撼的最初原因。可以说，《泄密的心》在一定程度上泄的是人类的集体经验和深层无意识的大秘密。当然，这部作品能给我们很多启示，我们可以从更多层面对其进行多方诠释，这也是经典作品的真正价值所在。

True! — nervous — very, very dreadfully nervous I had been and am; but why *will* you say that I am mad? The disease had sharpened my senses — not destroyed — not dulled them. Above all was the sense of hearing acute. I heard all things in the heaven and in the earth. I heard many things in hell. How, then, am I mad? Hearken! and observe how healthily — how calmly I can tell you the whole story.

It is impossible to say how first the idea entered my brain; but once conceived, it haunted me day and night. Object there was none. Passion[①] there was none. I loved the old man. He had never wronged me. He had never given me insult. For his gold I had no desire. I think it was his eye! yes, it was this! One of his eyes resembled that of a vulture — a pale blue eye, with a film over it. Whenever it fell upon me, my blood ran cold; and so by degrees — very gradually — I made up my mind to take the life of the old man, and thus rid myself of the eye forever.

Now this is the point. You fancy me mad. Madmen know nothing. But you should have seen *me*. You should have seen how wisely I proceeded — with what caution — with what foresight — with what dissimulation I went to work! I was never kinder to the old man than during the whole week before I killed him. And every night, about midnight, I turned the latch of his door and opened it — oh, so gently! And then, when I had made an opening sufficient for my head, I put in a dark lantern, all closed, closed, so that no light shone out, and then I thrust in my head. Oh, you would have laughed to see how cunningly I thrust it in! I moved it slowly — very, very slowly, so that I might not disturb the old man's sleep. It took me an hour to place my whole head

① passion, 名词，本意是“酷爱”或“酷爱的事物”，这里译成“觊觎”。

真的——紧张——非常紧张，极度紧张，以前，现在，都是这样。可你为什么硬说我疯了呢？这毛病反倒把我的感觉弄得更灵敏了——没失灵——也没麻木。特别是听觉，最好不过了。天上人间的一切声息尽在我的耳鼓里，我还听见地狱中的许多事物。那么，我疯了吗？听着！你看我气色多好——多么镇定自若地把这一切给你和盘托出。

这点子最初怎么进入我的脑海的，是说不上来了，但这点子一出现，就日夜萦绕着我，没啥目的，没啥觊觎。我喜欢那个老头，他从没伤害过我，从没侮辱过我。对他的金子，我更无非分之想。我想是由于他的那只眼睛吧！眼睛，就是这东西！他的一只眼睛酷似鹰眼——一只淡蓝色的眼睛，覆以一层薄翳。只要这只眼睛看到我，我就不寒而栗。于是，渐渐地——一来二去——我便拿定主意要他的命，这样就可以使自己永远摆脱那只眼睛。

你看，这就是问题的关键。你以为我疯了，可疯子是啥都不懂的。可惜你没看见我，可惜你没看到我干得多漂亮——那么审慎，那么周详，伪装得多么巧妙。杀死老头之前的那一周里，我对他是体贴备至。每天夜里，大约午夜时分，我转动门闩，把门拨开——噢，极轻微地！然后，我把门推开，推到我的头那么宽，再放进去一盏黑乎乎的提灯，灯遮得严丝合缝，光一点都透不出来——然后我再探进头去。噢，要是看到我有多么巧妙地探进头去，你定会发笑的！我慢慢地探进头去，慢慢地，非常慢地，唯恐搅了老头的美梦。用了一个钟头的时间，我才把头探进门缝，刚好能看见他平躺在床上。哈！——疯子有这脑瓜吗？接着，等我的头全进了门，我就小心翼翼地打开提灯——哦，十分地小心翼翼——小心翼翼（因为折合之处会发出声响）——我把提灯掀开一条缝隙，一道细细的灯光

within the opening so far that I could see him as he lay upon his bed. Ha! — would a madman have been so wise as this? And then, when my head was well in the room, I undid the lantern cautiously — oh, so cautiously — cautiously (for the hinges creaked) — I undid it just so much that a single thin ray fell upon the vulture eye. And this I did for seven long nights — every night just at midnight — but I found the eye always closed; and so it was impossible to do the work; for it was not the old man who vexed me, but his Evil Eye. And every morning, when the day broke, I went boldly into the chamber, and spoke courageously to him, calling him by name in a hearty tone, and inquiring how he had passed the night. So you see he would have been a very profound old man, indeed, to suspect that every night, just at twelve, I looked in upon him while he slept.

Upon the eighth night I was more than usually cautious in opening the door. A watch's minute hand moves more quickly than did mine. Never before that night had I *felt* the extent of my own powers — of my sagacity. I could scarcely contain my feelings of triumph. To think that there I was, opening the door, little by little, and he not even to dream of my secret deeds or thoughts. I fairly chuckled at the idea; and perhaps he heard me; for he moved on the bed suddenly, as if startled. Now you may think that I drew back — but no. His room was as black as pitch with the thick darkness, (for the shutters were close fastened, through fear of robbers,) and so I knew that he could not see the opening of the door, and I kept pushing it on steadily, steadily.

I had my head in, and was about to open the lantern, when my thumb slipped upon the tin fastening, and the old man sprang up in the bed, crying out — "Who's there?"

落在了那只鹰眼上。我就这样一连搞了七个长夜——每天夜里，就在午夜时分——但我发现那只眼睛总是闭着，因此也就没法做那活儿，因为这样他就不是折磨我的那个老头了，折磨我的是那只可恶的眼睛。每天清晨，天刚破晓，我就大摇大摆地走进他的房间，仗着胆跟他说话，亲热地叫他的名字，问他这一宿是怎么过的。所以你看，这老头并非老谋深算之辈，他万没想到我会每天夜里，就在十二点，趁他熟睡的时候去窥视他。

第八天夜里，我更加小心翼翼地打开了门。钟表上的分针都比我的手移动快。这天晚上我才生平第一次感到自己本事如此了得——有如此脑瓜。就要得手了，我几乎不能自已。想想看，我来到门前，打开门，一点一点地，而他连做梦也想不到我有如此秘密之举或非常之想。想到这里，我竟暗自发起笑来。可能是给他听到了，因为他在床上突然翻了个身，像是吃了一惊。你或许以为我会就此打住吧——可是我偏没。他的房间里漆黑一片，伸手难见五指(因为百叶窗关得严严的，以防强盗)，所以我清楚他看不见门开了个缝，我就这样一点一点地往前推着门。

我探进头，正要打开提灯，拇指刚滑到那个锡钩，那老头从床上一下子坐起身来，大声喊道——“哪一个？”

I kept quite still and said nothing. For a whole hour I did not move a muscle, and in the meantime I did not hear him lie down. He was still sitting up in the bed, listening; — just as I have done, night after night, hearkening to the death watches in the wall.

Presently I heard a slight groan, and I knew it was the groan of mortal terror. It was not a groan of pain or of grief — oh, no! — it was the low stifled sound that arises from the bottom of the soul when overcharged with awe. I knew the sound well. Many a night, just at midnight, when all the world slept, it has welled up from my own bosom, deepening, with its dreadful echo, the terrors that distracted me. I say I knew it well. I knew what the old man felt, and pitied him, although I chuckled at heart. I knew that he had been lying awake ever since the first slight noise, when he had turned in the bed. His fears had been ever since growing upon him. He had been trying to fancy them causeless, but could not. He had been saying to himself — "It is nothing but the wind in the chimney — it is only a mouse crossing the floor," or "it is merely a cricket which has made a single chirp." Yes, he has been trying to comfort himself with these suppositions: but he had found all in vain. *All in vain;* because Death, in approaching him, had stalked with his black shadow before him, and enveloped the victim. And it was the mournful influence of the unperceived shadow that caused him to feel — although he neither saw nor heard — to *feel* the presence of my head within the room.

When I had waited a long time, very patiently, without hearing him lie down, I resolved to open a little — a very, very little crevice in the lantern. So I opened it — you cannot imagine how stealthily, stealthily — until, at length a single dim ray, like the thread of the

我静静地站在原地，一声不吭。整整一个钟头，我纹丝没动，但同时也没听见他躺下。他还坐在那儿，在听动静，正如我以前一样，夜复一夜地，倾听着墙缝里报死虫的叫声。

不一会儿，我听到一声轻微的呻吟，我知道这是极度恐惧才有的呻吟，这不是疼痛或悲伤的呻吟——哦，不是！——这是吓得魂飞魄散时从灵魂深处发出的那种压抑的低吟之声。这声音我很清楚。多少个夜晚，就在午夜时分，当万籁俱寂之时，这声音就从我自己的内心响起并越来越大，伴随着那骇人的回声，加剧着那使我狂乱的恐怖。我说这声音我很清楚，我清楚这老头的感受，也同情他，尽管在心底发笑。听到他在床上翻了个身，我清楚他自打一听到那轻微的声音起就一直警觉地躺着。老头内心的恐惧不断增长，他曾尽量把这些恐惧想象成子虚乌有，却做不到。他曾对自己说——“不就是烟囱里的风嘛”——“也就是个耗子穿过地板吧”，或者，“不过是蟋蟀发出一声叫罢了”。是的，他尽量用这些猜测之词来安慰自己，但他发现这都白费心机，全都白费心机，因为死神在逼近老头时，已带着自己的黑暗之影向他悄然逼近，罩住了这个冤魂。正是这种未曾察觉的阴影的忧伤之力让他感受到——尽管他看不见也听不着——感受到房间里我的头的存在。

我等了许久，非常地耐心，还是没有听到他躺下，便决意打开一点——把提灯打开一个非常非常小的缝儿。我就这样打开了一个小缝儿——你想象不出我是多么神不知鬼不觉——直到，也就是那么一丝微弱的光，像蜘蛛拉出的细丝，从那道小缝中投射出来，照

spider, shot from out the crevice and fell upon the vulture eye.

It was open — wide, wide open — and I grew furious as I gazed upon it. I saw it with perfect distinctness — all a dull blue, with a hideous veil over it that chilled the very marrow in my bones; but I could see nothing else of the old man's face or person: for I had directed the ray as if by instinct, precisely upon the damned spot.

And now have I not told you that what you mistake for madness is but over acuteness of the senses? — now, I say, there came to my ears a low, dull, quick sound, such as a watch makes when enveloped in cotton. I knew *that* sound well, too. It was the beating of the old man's heart. It increased my fury, as the beating of a drum stimulates the soldier into courage.

But even yet I refrained and kept still. I scarcely breathed. I held the lantern motionless. I tried how steadily I could maintain the ray upon the eye. Meantime the hellish tattoo of the heart increased. It grew quicker and quicker, and louder and louder every instant. The old man's terror *must* have been extreme! It grew louder, I say, louder every moment! — do you mark me well? I have told you that I am nervous: so I am. And now at the dead hour of the night, amid the dreadful silence of that old house, so strange a noise as this excited me to uncontrollable terror. Yet, for some minutes longer I refrained and stood still. But the beating grew louder, louder! I thought the heart must burst. And now a new anxiety seized me — the sound would be heard by a neighbor! The old man's hour had come! With a loud yell, I threw open the lantern and leaped into the room. He shrieked once — once only. In an instant I dragged him to the floor, and pulled the heavy bed over him. I then smiled gaily, to find the deed so far

到老头的那只鹰眼上。

那只眼睛睁着——很大，睁得很大——我凝视着，怒火中烧。我看得再清楚不过了——一团暗淡的蓝色，蒙着一层可怕的薄膜，令人胆战心寒，我全然不见老头的脸或他整个人，因为我好像本能地把光线分毫不差地投在了那个该死的地方。

噢，我没跟您说过您错把我当作疯子，其实那只是我的感官过于敏锐而已吗？——现在，跟您说吧，我的耳边传来一阵低沉、单调、迅疾的声音，像是裹在棉花里的手表发出的声音。这声音我也很清楚，这就是那老头的心跳声。这加剧了我的怒火，正如咚咚的战鼓激励着战士的勇气。

即便如此，我还是克制着自己，一动不动。我连大气都不敢喘。我稳稳地持着灯，看看自己能多么稳当地把光线照在那只眼睛上。这会儿，那可恶的扑通扑通的心跳声加剧了。这跳声一下快过一下，一声高过一声。老头的恐惧一定是到了极点！跳声越来越大，跟您说吧，一声高过一声！——弄明白我的意思了吗？我跟您说过我紧张，我是紧张。而此刻在这死一般的静夜，在这古屋的可怕的寂静中，声音如此莫名其妙，使我产生了一股无法抑制的恐惧，但我还是又克制、又静立了几分钟，可那跳声越来越大了，越来越大。我想那颗心定是要爆炸了。现在，我心头生出一种新的焦虑——这声音会被邻里听到的！这老头死期至矣！我发出一声喊，唰地打开提灯，噌地跳进屋内。他只尖叫了一声——就一声。我旋即把他拽到地上，拖过沉重的床压在他的身上。活儿干得这么利索，我轻快地笑了起来。不过，一连好几分钟，那颗心脏都带着压抑的声音跳动着。这倒没激恼我，这声音隔着墙是听不到的。终于，心跳声停止了，老头死了。我挪开床，查看了他的尸体。是的，他已经死了，死

done. But, for many minutes, the heart beat on with a muffled sound. This, however, did not vex me; it would not be heard through the wall. At length it ceased. The old man was dead. I removed the bed and examined the corpse. Yes, he was stone, stone dead. I placed my hand upon the heart and held it there many minutes. There was no pulsation. He was stone dead. His eye would trouble me no more.

If still you think me mad, you will think so no longer when I describe the wise precautions I took for the concealment of the body. The night waned, and I worked hastily, but in silence. First of all I dismembered the corpse. I cut off the head and the arms and the legs.

I then took up three planks from the flooring of the chamber, and deposited all between the scantlings. I then replaced the boards so cleverly, so cunningly, that no human eye — not even *his* — could have detected anything wrong. There was nothing to wash out — no stain of any kind — no blood — spot whatever. I had been too wary for that. A tub had caught all — ha! ha!

When I had made an end of these labors, it was four o'clock — still dark as midnight. As the bell sounded the hour, there came a knocking at the street door. I went down to open it with a light heart, — for what had I *now* to fear? There entered three men, who introduced themselves, with perfect suavity, as officers of the police. A shriek had been heard by a neighbor during the night; suspicion of foul play had been aroused; information had been lodged at the police office, and they (the officers) had been deputed to search the premises.

I smiled, — for *what* had I to fear? I bade the gentlemen welcome. The shriek, I said, was my own in a dream. The old man, I mentioned, was absent in the country. I took my visitors all over

就了。我伸出手，放在他的心脏上，在那搁了好几分钟。没有心跳了。他已经死就了。他那只眼睛不会再烦我了。

你要是还以为我疯了，等我把藏匿尸首时的精细审慎描述一番，你就不这么认为了。夜色阑珊，我麻利地忙活着，当然是悄无声息地。我先是把尸体大卸八块，割下头，砍下手，卸下脚。

然后我又从房间的地板上掀起三块木板，把肢解的尸体都放在间隙中，然后又把木板放回原处，极为利落，极为巧妙，人的眼睛——就算是他的那只眼睛，也看不出任何蛛丝马迹。没什么要刷洗的——没有污迹，没有任何血迹，我干得一丝不苟，一个大桶全装下了——哈，哈！

这些活干好后，都四点了——天色还是黑如午夜。正在时钟报点之时，大门外传来了敲门声。我漫不经心地去开门——我现在还有什么担心的呢？进来了三个人，他们温文尔雅地自我介绍，说是警局的警官。邻里半夜听到一声尖叫，怀疑发生了暴行，便向警察报了案，他们（警官们）便被派来查看究竟。

我笑了——我还有什么担心的呢？我对几位先生表示了欢迎。那叫声，我说，是我自己在梦中发出的。我谈到那老头，说他到乡下去了。我带着他们三位把房子搜了个遍。我让他们搜查——好好

the house. I bade[1] them search — search *well*. I led them, at length, to *his* chamber. I showed them his treasures, secure, undisturbed. In the enthusiasm of my confidence, I brought chairs into the room, and desired them *here* to rest from their fatigues, while I myself, in the wild audacity of my perfect triumph, placed my own seat upon the very spot beneath which reposed the corpse of the victim.

The officers were satisfied. My *manner* had convinced them. I was singularly at ease. They sat, and while I answered cheerily, they chatted of familiar things. But, ere long, I felt myself getting pale and wished them gone. My head ached, and I fancied a ringing in my ears: but still they sat and still chatted. The ringing became more distinct: —it continued and became more distinct: I talked more freely to get rid of the feeling: but it continued and gained definiteness — until, at length, I found that the noise was *not* within my ears.

No doubt I now grew *very* pale; — but I talked more fluently, and with a heightened voice. Yet the sound increased — and what could I do? It was *a low, dull, quick sound — much such a sound as a watch makes when enveloped in cotton*. I gasped for breath — and yet the officers heard it not. I talked more quickly — more vehemently; but the noise steadily increased. I arose and argued about trifles, in a high key and with violent gesticulations; but the noise steadily increased. Why *would* they not be gone? I paced the floor to and fro with heavy strides, as if excited to fury by the observations of the men — but the noise steadily increased. Oh God! what *could* I do? I foamed — I raved — I swore! I swung the chair upon which I had been sitting, and grated it upon the boards, but the noise arose over

① bid, 动词，过去式 bade 或 bid，吩咐、邀请、请求。

搜查。最后，我把他们领到了他的房间。我把他的细软给他们看，东西都安然无恙，完好无损。我信心满满，竟把几把椅子拉进房里，请他们坐在那歇歇腿，而我自己，则由于自己的杰作而肆无忌惮起来，把座位就放在下面藏有老头尸首的地方。

警官们颇为满意，我的举止已令他们信服。我是异常轻松。他们坐着，聊着家长里短，我则是对答如流。但不久，我就觉得自己面色苍白起来，盼着他们走。我头疼起来，觉得有股耳鸣之声，但他们还是坐在那，还谈着。耳鸣声越来越清晰——这声音持续不断，越发清晰了。为了驱除这种感觉，我越发恣肆地说着话，可这声音还是不断，更加分明了——终于，我发现那声音并不是源于我的双耳。

无疑，我已面色惨白——但我越发滔滔不绝地说着话，还提高了嗓门。而这声音却有增无减——我该咋办？这是一阵低沉、单一、迅疾的声音——特别像是裹在棉花里的手表发出的声音。我喘着粗气——但警官们并没有听到这声音。我说得更快了——越发激越了，可那声音仍在加强。我站起身，态度激烈、手舞足蹈地为琐事争论着，可那声音越发加强了。他们怎么就不走呢？我迈着重重的脚步在地板上来回踱着步子，似乎是被他们的言论激怒了——可那声音仍在增强。哦，天啊，我该咋办？我吐沫飞溅——我胡言乱语——我赌咒发誓！我晃动着我坐下的那把椅子，椅子磨在地板上吱吱嘎嘎，但那声音却盖过了这一切，在持续增强着。声音越来越大——越来越大——越来越大！而那几个人依旧在海侃神聊，还在嘻嘻哈哈。他们可能听不到吗？万能的上帝！——不，不！他们听到了！——他们猜到了！——他们知道了！——他们在拿我的

all and continually increased. It grew louder — louder — *louder!* And still the men chatted pleasantly, and smiled. Was it possible they heard not? Almighty God! — no, no! They heard! — they suspected! — they *knew!* — they were making a mockery of my horror! — this I thought, and this I think. But anything was better than this agony! Anything was more tolerable than this derision! I could bear those hypocritical smiles no longer! I felt that I must scream or die! — and now — again! — hark! louder! louder! louder! *louder!* —

"Villains!" I shrieked, "dissemble no more! I admit the deed! — tear up the planks! — here, here! — it is the beating of his hideous heart!"

恐惧取乐！——我当时如是想，现在仍如是想。不过没有比这更痛苦的了，没有比这种奚落更折磨人的了！我再也忍受不了这几个伪君子的嬉笑了！我觉得我得喊出来，要不就会死于非命！——这当儿——又来了！——你听！越来越大！越来越大！越来越大！越来越大！——

“坏蛋！”我尖叫道。“别装腔作势了！我招供！揭开这几块地板！——这儿，这儿！——这就是那颗可恶的心脏的跳动。”

The Oval Portrait
椭圆形画像

《椭圆形画像》(*The Oval Portrait,* 1842) 讲述了一个受伤的贵族在古堡中避难的奇妙遭遇。喜欢短篇小说的人总有一个疑问：什么是短篇小说？什么样的小说才是好的短篇小说？率性直白的胡适先生早在《域外小说》刚被引入中国时就说过，并不是短的就是短篇小说。他还借用宋玉的话给好的短篇小说下了个定义："增之一分则太长，减之一分则太短；著粉则太白，施朱则太赤。"这话实在太精妙了，用来形容爱伦·坡的小说再贴切不过。他的作品《椭圆形画像》就是如此。小说的叙述手法极为简单，主要由两部分组成。一是对主人公深夜借宿的描写，采用的是横剖面的描写手法，即按照时间顺序娓娓道来；二是借引文的方式来讲述画像的来历。通常来说，短篇小说总要使故事的中心冲突沿一条线向高潮迅速推进，越接近故事的末尾，推进的速度越快。所以短篇小说常常采用纵剖面的写法，就像树的年轮，以截面来隐射整体，耐人寻味。而《椭圆形画像》的成功却有赖于爱伦·坡对两种手法的并用。横剖面的手法在故事的前半部分营造了一个"听故事"的环境，这与后面令人窒息的"故事中的故事"形成对比；而纵剖面的手法则能省去许多赘笔，使故事达到迅速推进的效果。童话故事般的白描手法简练明了，使得读者完全关注于故事本身，最后画家完成画作，而他美丽的妻子在那一刻死去的事实令人惊愕。此刻，故事的寓意已是无足轻重。好的故事就是这样，如一件小巧的艺术品，没有瑕疵，没有任何多余的边赘。它不花哨，也不啰唆，平淡得就像流传在不同国家里的同一个传说。它是人类智慧结出的奇异果实，也是人类智慧永不枯竭的源泉。

The chateau into which my valet had ventured to make forcible entrance, rather than permit me, in my desperately wounded condition, to pass a night in the open air, was one of those piles of commingled gloom and grandeur which have so long frowned among the Appenines, not less in fact than in the fancy of Mrs. Radcliffe. To all appearance it had been temporarily and very lately abandoned. We established ourselves in one of the smallest and least sumptuously furnished apartments. It lay in a remote turret of the building. Its decorations were rich, yet tattered and antique. Its walls were hung with tapestry and bedecked with manifold and multiform armorial trophies, together with an unusually great number of very spirited modern paintings in frames of rich golden arabesque. In these paintings, which depended from the walls not only in their main surfaces, but in very many nooks which the bizarre architecture of the chateau rendered necessary — in these paintings my incipient delirium, perhaps, had caused me to take deep interest; so that I bade Pedro to close the heavy shutters of the room — since it was already night — to light the tongues of a tall candelabrum[①] which stood by the head of my bed — and to throw open far and wide the fringed curtains of black velvet which enveloped the bed itself. I wished all this done that I might resign myself, if not to sleep, at least alternately to the contemplation of these pictures, and the perusal of a small volume which had been found upon the pillow, and which purported to criticise and describe them.

Long — long I read — and devoutly, devotedly I gazed. Rapidly

① candelabrum, 枝形大烛台，带有几个臂或枝状物的大型装饰性烛台， 其复数形式为 candelabra。

男仆不忍让身受重伤的我在野外露宿，贸然闯入了一座城堡。这座城堡阴郁而堂皇，是一直以来耸立于亚平宁山峦间[①]的众多城堡中的一座，实际上毫不逊于拉德克利夫夫人[②]想象的那种城堡。很明显，城堡的主人在不久前临时外出了。我们在一套最小而且陈设最不奢华的房间里安顿下来。这套房间位于城堡内一个僻静的塔楼里，屋内装饰富丽，但却破败陈旧。室内墙壁上挂着壁毯，装饰着有许多式样各异纹章的战利纪念品。此外，墙上还悬挂有众多生机勃勃的现代绘画，镶嵌在图案精美的金色画框中。这些绘画不仅悬挂在几面主要的墙壁上，还挂在由于城堡建筑奇特而必然会形成的许多墙隅凹面上——也许是我一开始的兴奋使我对这些画产生了浓厚的兴趣；我因而吩咐佩德罗将房间内厚厚的百叶窗关上——因为天色已晚——点燃我床头那座高烛台上的所有蜡烛——并将罩在床上的那镶有流苏的黑丝绒帷帐全都拉开。我希望这一切安排妥当后，即使不能入睡，至少也可以思忖那些画作，或是再细细品读在枕边发现的那卷小书，该书声称对这些画作进行了评价和描述。

久久地——我久久地阅读那卷书——虔诚地、聚精会神地凝视

① 亚平宁山脉，是意大利亚平宁半岛（又称意大利半岛）的主干山脉，是阿尔卑斯山脉主干南伸部分。它呈巨弧形，从西北部靠近滨海阿尔卑斯山脉的卡迪波纳山口 (Cadibona Pass) 起，一直延伸至西西里岛西边埃加迪群岛 (Egadi Islands)，总长约 1 400 千米，宽度为 40—200 千米。

② 安 · 拉德克利夫 (Ann Radcliffe，1764—1823)，英国女作家，尤以写浪漫主义的哥特小说见长，作品多描写发生在亚平宁山脉、阿尔卑斯山脉的城堡中的神秘传奇故事，被司各特称为“第一位写虚构浪漫主义小说的女诗人”。作品融恐怖、焦虑、悬疑的情节和浪漫主义情调于一体，代表作有《林中艳史》(1791)、《奥多芙的神秘》(1794) 和《意大利人》(1797) 等。

and gloriously the hours flew by, and the deep midnight came. The position of the candelabrum displeased me, and outreaching my hand with difficulty, rather than disturb my slumbering valet, I placed it so as to throw its rays more fully upon the book.

But the action produced an effect altogether unanticipated. The rays of the numerous candles (for there were many) now fell within a niche of the room which had hitherto been thrown into deep shade by one of the bed-posts. I thus saw in vivid light a picture all unnoticed before. It was the portrait of a young girl just ripening into womanhood. I glanced at the painting hurriedly, and then closed my eyes. Why I did this was not at first apparent even to my own perception. But while my lids remained thus shut, I ran over in my mind my reason for so shutting them. It was an impulsive movement to gain time for thought — to make sure that my vision had not deceived me — to calm and subdue my fancy for a more sober and more certain gaze. In a very few moments I again looked fixedly at the painting.

That I now saw aright I could not and would not doubt; for the first flashing of the candles upon that canvas had seemed to dissipate the dreamy stupor which was stealing over my senses, and to startle me at once into waking life.

The portrait, I have already said, was that of a young girl. It was a mere head and shoulders, done in what is technically termed a *vignette* manner; much in the style of the favorite heads of Sully. The arms, the bosom and even the ends of the radiant hair, melted imperceptibly into the vague yet deep shadow which formed the background of the whole. The frame was oval, richly gilded and filagreed in *Moresque*. As a thing of art nothing could be more admirable than the painting itself. But

着那些画。几个小时在愉悦中一晃就过去了，不觉已到午夜时分。烛台的位置不合我意，而我又不愿唤醒熟睡的男仆，只得费劲地伸手去挪动烛台，好让烛光更好地照亮书本。

然而这一挪动却产生了出乎意料的效果。许多蜡烛的光线(因为有很多蜡烛)这会儿落到了房间里的一个壁龛上。这壁龛原先一直被一根床柱遮在阴影中。于是我在明亮的灯光中看到了一幅先前未曾注意到的画。这是一幅刚刚成熟为女人的年轻姑娘的画像。我匆匆瞥了它一眼，便闭上了眼睛。一开始连我自己都不明白我为什么要这样做，可是就在我双目紧闭时，脑海中掠过我这样紧闭双眼的缘由。那是一时冲动的举动，为的是有更多时间思索——确定我的眼睛没有欺骗我——去让胡思乱想的头脑平静安定下来，以便更冷静更确切地看个分明。片刻后，我又目不转睛地凝视起这幅画。

此刻我完全看清楚了，不会怀疑，也不容怀疑；因为照在画布上的第一抹烛光看来已将刚才还悄悄向我的意识袭来的梦一般的恍惚给驱散了，而且顿时把我惊醒。

我刚才已经说过，这幅画像画的是一个年轻姑娘。画像中只有头部和双肩，是以那种术语称之为半身晕映画像法[①]来完成的；颇似萨利[②]最拿手的头像画的风格。画像中的双肩、胸部，甚至光艳照

---

① 半身晕映画像法，指增亮或是调暗图片的边缘。它和选择性聚焦的使用原因相同，将分散视线的背景最小化，突出从观赏者角度观看的物体。
② 托马斯·萨利(Thomas Sully，1783—1872)，是19世纪美国杰出的肖像画家。1837年，他奉命创作了一幅维多利亚女王的肖像画。他创作的女王全身肖像画和作浮雕用的半身复制品，成了维多利亚统治早期众所周知的女王最好的肖像画之一。它展示出女王的年轻和美貌，完全不同于今天我们所见到的年迈的女王形象。

it could have been neither the execution of the work, nor the immortal beauty of the countenance, which had so suddenly and so vehemently moved me. Least of all, could it have been that my fancy, shaken from its half slumber, had mistaken the head for that of a living person. I saw at once that the peculiarities of the design, of the *vignetting,* and of the frame, must have instantly dispelled such idea — must have prevented even its momentary entertainment. Thinking earnestly upon these points, I remained, for an hour perhaps, half sitting, half reclining, with my vision riveted upon the portrait. At length, satisfied with the true secret of its effect, I fell back within the bed. I had found the spell of the picture in an absolute *life-likeliness* of expression, which, at first startling, finally confounded, subdued and appalled me. With deep and reverent awe I replaced the candelabrum in its former position. The cause of my deep agitation being thus shut from view, I sought eagerly the volume which discussed the paintings and their histories. Turning to the number which designated the oval portrait, I there read the vague and quaint words which follow:

"She was a maiden of rarest beauty, and not more lovely than full of glee. And evil was the hour when she saw, and loved, and wedded the painter. He, passionate, studious, austere, and having already a bride in his Art; she a maiden of rarest beauty, and not more lovely than full of glee; all light and smiles, and frolicksome as the young fawn; loving and cherishing all things; hating only the Art which was her rival; dreading only the pallet and brushes and other untoward instruments which deprived her of the countenance of her lover. It was thus a terrible thing for this lady to hear the painter speak of his desire to portray even his young bride. But she was humble and obedient, and sat

人的发丝，都不易察觉地与那种朦胧而深沉的阴影融为一体，共同构成了整个画面的背景。画框呈椭圆形，镀着厚厚的一层金，以摩尔式[①]风格装帧得极其精致。作为一件艺术品，最令人叹为观止的还是画像本身。然而，刚才突然强烈打动我的既不是作者精湛的画技，也不是画中人物的绝色容貌。而最为不可能的是，我那从半睡眠状态惊醒的幻觉竟将画像中的头像误认为一个活生生的人。我旋即明白，这幅画采用的半身晕映画像法的构思，加上独具匠心的画框，已经立刻将我的这种想法打消——必定不容我再抱有哪怕片刻的疑惑。约莫一个小时的时间，我一直半倚半坐，目不转睛地盯着那幅画像，认认真真地思忖着画像的这些特点。终于，在领会到这幅画的效果的真正奥秘之后，我才心满意足地躺回床上。我发现，这幅画的魔力在于其表现之绝对逼真。这一开始让我震惊，最后使我困惑，它征服了我，使我大惊失色。怀着诚笃的敬畏之情，我把烛台又挪回到原处。当这促使我极度不安的画像被遮蔽在视线之外后，我便急切地找寻那卷描述这些绘画及其来历的书。翻到描述这幅椭圆形画像的那一页，我读到了下面这段含糊而古怪的文字：

“她是一个绝世美人儿，欢快时最为可爱。但从她与画家一见钟情，并结为伉俪的那刻起，不幸便随之而来。画家激情、勤勉、严厉，并且早已在他的艺术世界中拥有一位新娘；她是一位绝世美人儿，欢快时最为可爱；所有的容光和微笑；嬉戏时犹如幼鹿；热爱并珍视一切；只憎恨成为她情敌的艺术；只害怕那些夺取她爱人笑脸的调色板、画笔和其他画具。因而，听到画家想要为他年轻的新娘作一幅画像时，姑娘认为那真是件可怕的事。可是她生性温良恭

① （建筑或装饰）摩尔式的。摩尔人，北非的阿拉伯人，跨海而来的异乡民族，自公元8世纪起，统治了安达卢西亚地区达近800年。摩尔式建筑特色包含不加装饰的拱顶、简单的圆拱马蹄型，或是拥有繁复装饰的拱形、有亮丽釉彩的青花瓷砖以及阿拉伯文或者几何图形的装饰。开放空间中，水是重点，通常情况下花园中会有喷泉或水道，而建筑物前的水池则有创造倒影并制造光线效果的作用。

meekly for many weeks in the dark high turret-chamber where the light dripped upon the pale canvas only from overhead. But he, the painter, took glory in his work, which went on from hour to hour, and from day to day. And he was a passionate, and wild, and moody man, who became lost in reveries; so that he *would* not see that the light which fell so ghastly in that lone turret withered the health and the spirits of his bride, who pined visibly to all but him. Yet she smiled on and still on, uncomplainingly, because she saw that the painter (who had high renown), took a fervid and burning pleasure in his task, and wrought day and night to depict her who so loved him, yet who grew daily more dispirited and weak. And in sooth some who beheld the portrait spoke of its resemblance in low words, as of a mighty marvel, and a proof not less of the power of the painter than of his deep love for her whom he depicted so surpassingly well. But at length, as the labor drew nearer to its conclusion, there were admitted none into the turret; for the painter had grown wild with the ardor of his work, and turned his eyes from the canvas rarely, even to regard the countenance of his wife. And he *would* not see that the tints which he spread upon the canvas were drawn from the cheeks of her who sat beside him. And when many weeks had passed, and but little remained to do, save one brush upon the mouth and one tint upon the eye, the spirit of the lady again flickered up as the flame within the socket of the lamp. And then the brush was given, and then the tint was placed; and, for one moment, the painter stood entranced before the work which he had wrought; but in the next, while he yet gazed, he grew tremulous and very pallid, and aghast, and crying with a loud voice, 'This is indeed *Life* itself!' turned suddenly to regard his beloved: — *She was dead!*"

顺，就温顺地坐在这高高的阴暗塔楼里好几个星期，这里只有从头顶上方照进来的一点点光亮洒在苍白的画布上。然而他——那个画家——却以自己的工作为荣，日日夜夜，时时刻刻沉湎于绘画中。他本就感情炽热，放荡不羁，喜怒无常，现在又深陷冥想之中，因而他不可能会觉察到那洒在孤寂的塔楼的惨白的光亮正摧残着他的新娘的肉体和灵魂。而除了他谁都能看得出她越来越憔悴。可她始终带着微笑，毫无怨言，因为她看到画家(他很出名)在他的工作中获得了一种炽热的、燃烧着的乐趣。他夜以继日地精心绘制着深爱着他的人的画像，而她却日渐萎靡消瘦。事实上，看到这幅画像的人都悄声惊叹它的传神，称它为非凡的奇迹，认为这不仅证明了画家的功力，而且更证明了他对这位被描绘得如此传神的画中人的爱意。然而到了最后，这项工程即将完成之际，任何人都不许进入塔楼；因为画家已近于疯狂，他的目光很少从画布上移开，甚至不瞧一眼妻子的容貌。他根本不可能会看出那些他涂抹在画布上的色彩就来自坐在他身边的妻子的脸庞。好几个星期已经过去了，眼看着整幅画就要完成，只差嘴角的一笔修饰和眼睛色彩的点缀。这时这位女士的神采闪烁不定，犹如烛光在烛孔中的最后摇曳。于是最后的一笔补上了，眼睛也点上了色彩。有好一会儿，画家出神地站在自己的作品前，但紧接着，就在他继续凝视之时，他开始浑身颤抖，继而脸色苍白，目瞪口呆，最后大喊一声：‘这就是生命！’可当他蓦然回首看他心爱的妻子时——*她已死去！*”

The Man of the Crowd
人群中的人

《人群中的人》(*The Man of the Crowd,* 1840) 描写了一位逃避孤独的老人在冷漠而又喧哗的人群中寻找慰藉。爱伦·坡一生都"在商业经济的洪流中颠簸沉浮，在出版行业的竞争中奋力打拼，在理想与现实中挣扎取舍，在多重身份间游走穿梭"。故事中的老人似乎就是爱伦·坡忙碌而又孤独的人生写照。

故事的题记"不能承受孤独是最大的不幸"，为该篇小说表现人类精神困境的主题埋下了伏笔。故事中的老人为了反抗孤独的折磨，走到熙熙攘攘的大街上寻找川流不息的人群。他没有姓名，没有职业，身上最显著的特征就是孤独。人群中各个社会阶层的人也同样是孤独的，他们在人群中无时不感到孤独和寂寞，他们都想从人群中找到慰藉，但是每个人都拒绝被了解，因此他们永远是孤独的。故事的叙述者"我"也是孤独的。当"我"独自一人欣赏摩肩接踵的人群时，注意到一位异样的老人，"我"对他产生了强烈的好奇心。然而尽管"我"很想了解老人，甚至跟在他后面观察他，但"我"却不愿意与他进行语言交流，而是通过暗中跟踪来满足自己的好奇心。跟踪老人一夜后，"我"产生了和老人交流的想法，然而，"我"并没有和老人寒暄，而是"径直站在那位闲逛者面前，紧盯着他的脸"。老人对"我"的行为没有做出任何反应，继续追逐着人群。因此，"我"和老人只会变得更加孤独。

爱伦·坡对人类生存状态的关注，在当时的社会并没有得到足够的关注，因为他所处的年代正是美国经济和社会蒸蒸日上的鼎盛时期。然而正如卢梭所言，文明的进步导致了人性的堕落，随着工业化、现代化这些所谓的人类文明的程度提高，人们的精神似乎越来越空虚。爱伦·坡的作品提供给人们一种寻找自我的途径，因此他的作品能够与读者产生强烈的共鸣，逐渐受到现当代读者的重视。

Ce grand malheur, de ne pouvoir être seul.

La Bruyère

It was well said of a certain German book that "*er lasst sich nicht lesen*"[①] — it does not permit itself to be read. There are some secrets which do not permit themselves to be told. Men die nightly in their beds, wringing the hands of ghostly confessors, and looking them piteously in the eyes — die with despair of heart and convulsion of throat, on account of the hideousness of mysteries which will not *suffer themselves* to be revealed. Now and then, alas, the conscience of man takes up a burthen so heavy in horror that it can be thrown down only into the grave. And thus the essence of all crime is undivulged.

Not long ago, about the closing in of an evening in autumn, I sat at the large bow window of the D — Coffee-House in London. For some months I had been ill in health, but was now convalescent, and, with returning strength, found myself in one of those happy moods which are so precisely the converse of *ennui* — moods of the keenest appetency, when the film from the mental vision departs — αχλυς υς πριν επηεν[②] — and the intellect, electrified, surpasses as greatly its everyday condition, as does the vivid yet candid reason of Leibnitz, the mad and flimsy rhetoric of Gorgias. Merely to breathe was enjoyment; and I derived positive pleasure even from many of the legitimate sources of pain. I felt a calm but inquisitive interest in everything. With a cigar in my mouth and a newspaper in my lap, I

① 可翻译为 "It cannot be read"，意为"不能被阅读"。
② 希腊语，意为"眼前的阴霾"。

不能承受孤独是最大的不幸。

——拉布吕耶尔[①]

传说有那么一本不能被人阅读的德语书——它不容许人们阅读。有些秘密是不能说出的。人们夜里死在床榻上，紧握着忏悔牧师苍白可怖的手，哀怜地望着牧师的眼睛——死去时心灵绝望，喉咙痉挛，这都是因为他们藏有不堪泄露的可怕秘密。唉！人们的良心时常在担惊受怕中承担着如此重负，以至于只能带进坟墓。所有罪恶的本质才因而未能大白于天下。

不久前，一个秋日的黄昏时分，我坐在伦敦 D 咖啡馆的大凸窗旁。几个月以来，我的健康状况一直欠佳，但是现在已经康复，而且由于精力恢复，我发现自己处于一种与倦怠截然相反的幸福情绪——一种欲望最强烈的情绪中，每当那层薄雾——“眼前阴霾”——从心头消逝，兴奋起来的思维能力超越了其平日状态，会像莱布尼茨[②]一样生动而公正地推理，像高尔吉亚[③]一样疯癫而浮夸地雄辩。单是呼吸空气已是享受；我甚至从许多合理的痛苦之源中获得了纯粹的乐趣。我感到一种平静，但却对一切事物都有想要探究的兴趣。嘴里叼着雪茄，膝上摊份报纸，大半个下午我就这样自得其乐，一会儿专心阅读广告，一会儿观察咖啡馆里杂乱的人群，一会儿又透过被烟雾熏黑的玻璃凝视窗外的大街。

---

① 拉布吕耶尔 (Jean de La Bruyère, 1645—1696), 法国随笔作家、道德家， 该句出自其著作《品格论》(*Les Caractères*, 1688)。
② 莱布尼茨 (1646—1716), 德国自然科学家、哲学家， 微积分、数理逻辑的先驱。
③ 高尔吉亚 (483 B.C.—376 B.C.), 古希腊哲学家、修辞学家。

had been amusing myself for the greater part of the afternoon, now in poring over advertisements, now in observing the promiscuous company in the room, and now in peering through the smoky panes into the street.

This latter is one of the principal thoroughfares of the city, and had been very much crowded during the whole day. But, as the darkness came on, the throng momently increased; and, by the time the lamps were well lighted, two dense and continuous tides of population were rushing past the door. At this particular period of the evening I had never before been in a similar situation, and the tumultuous sea of human heads filled me, therefore, with a delicious novelty of emotion. I gave up, at length, all care of things within the hotel, and became absorbed in contemplation of the scene without.

At first my observations took an abstract and generalizing turn. I looked at the passengers in masses, and thought of them in their aggregate relations. Soon, however, I descended to details, and regarded with minute interest the innumerable varieties of figure, dress, air, gait, visage, and expression of countenance.

By far the greater number of those who went by had a satisfied business-like demeanor, and seemed to be thinking only of making their way through the press. Their brows were knit, and their eyes rolled quickly; when pushed against by fellow-wayfarers they evinced no symptom of impatience, but adjusted their clothes and hurried on. Others, still a numerous class, were restless in their movements, had flushed faces, and talked and gesticulated to themselves, as if feeling in solitude on account of the very denseness of the company around. When impeded in their progress, these people suddenly ceased

那条大街是伦敦的主要街道，一整天都人群熙攘。但是，随着黄昏的临近，人群刹那间聚了起来；而且，到了灯都亮起来的时候，两股摩肩接踵的人潮川流不息地从咖啡馆门前匆匆经过。我从来没有在黄昏的这个时刻待在这样一个位置，所以窗外人头攒动的人海使我心中充满了有趣的新奇感。最后，我完全不再理会咖啡馆里的事物，而是沉浸在对咖啡馆外情景的沉思之中。

起初有一会儿，我对人群的观察抽象且空泛。我看着过往行人，思索着他们的群体关系。然而不久，我开始注意细节，饶有兴趣地观察他们在身材、服装、神态、步法、面容和脸部表情上的千差万别。

到目前为止，来往行人中的大部分都显露出一种心满意足的、有条不紊的神态，而且似乎一心所想的只是穿过蜂拥的人群。他们眉头紧锁，双眼飞快地转动；当被人推搡碰撞时，他们没有表露出丝毫不耐烦，而是整理一下衣服，继续匆忙前行。此外还有为数不少的人，他们焦躁不安地走着，红着脸，边走边自言自语，比比画画，仿佛因为周围人群的密集而感到孤独。当行路遇到阻碍时，这些人会突然停止嘀咕，但会比画得更加厉害，嘴角露出心不在焉而又过分夸张的微笑，等待着前面挡路的人让开道。如果被人碰撞到，他们会毫不吝啬地向碰撞者鞠躬，显得局促不安——除了我所说的这

muttering, but redoubled their gesticulations, and awaited, with an absent and overdone smile upon the lips, the course of the persons impeding them. If jostled, they bowed profusely to the jostlers, and appeared overwhelmed with confusion. — There was nothing very distinctive about these two large classes beyond what I have noted. Their habiliments belonged to that order which is pointedly termed the decent. They were undoubtedly noblemen, merchants, attorneys, tradesmen, stock-jobbers — the Eupatrids and the common-places of society — men of leisure and men actively engaged in affairs of their own — conducting business upon their own responsibility. They did not greatly excite my attention.

The tribe of clerks was an obvious one and here I discerned two remarkable divisions. There were the junior clerks of flash houses — young gentlemen with tight coats, bright boots, well-oiled hair, and supercilious lips. Setting aside a certain dapperness of carriage, which may be termed *deskism* for want of a better word, the manner of these persons seemed to me an exact fac-simile of what had been the perfection of *bon ton*① about twelve or eighteen months before. They wore the cast-off graces of the gentry; — and this, I believe, involves the best definition of the class.

The division of the upper clerks of staunch firms, or of the "steady old fellows," it was not possible to mistake. These were known by their coats and pantaloons of black or brown, made to sit comfortably, with white cravats and waistcoats, broad solid-looking shoes, and thick hose or gaiters. — They had all slightly bald heads, from which the right ears, long used to pen-holding, had an odd habit

① 法语，意为"时髦、优雅"。

些特征之外，这两大人群没有别的不同之处了。他们的着装属于那种明显可称之为庄重的类别。他们毫无疑问都是绅士、商人、代理人、手艺人和股票经纪人——世袭贵族或平民百姓——悠闲自在或忙于自身事务的人——自行负责经营生意。他们没有引起我太多的注意。

职员一族是人群中抢眼的一类人，在此我将其区分为两大显著的类别。一类是住在寄宿房的低级职员——一群年轻绅士，西装紧身，皮靴铿亮，油头粉面并且自命不凡。抛开那种由于没有更恰当的字眼来形容而只能称之为办公室风度的衣冠楚楚的举止，这些人的风度在我看来完全是在模仿十二或十八个月之前的时髦作派。他们拾取绅士阶层的牙慧——我认为这一点是对这一类人做出的最好阐释。

这些低级职员与那些精明强干或老成持重的高级职员的区别是不可能分辨不出的。后者的标志是他们那身剪裁得坐下来也很舒适的黑色或棕色外套与裤子，白色的领带和西装背心，看上去很结实的宽松鞋子和厚厚的长筒袜或鞋罩——他们都微微秃顶，右耳由于长期夹笔而古怪地向外翘着。我注意到，他们总是用双手脱帽或戴帽，总是戴着手表，表带是短短的金链子，结实牢固，式样复古。他们的举止是一种体面人的矫揉造作——如果确实存在一种

of standing off on end. I observed that they always removed or settled their hats with both hands, and wore watches, with short gold chains of a substantial and ancient pattern. Theirs was the affectation of respectability; — if indeed there be an affectation so honorable.

There were many individuals of dashing appearance, whom I easily understood as belonging to the race of swell pick-pockets, with which all great cities are infested. I watched these gentry with much inquisitiveness, and found it difficult to imagine how they should ever be mistaken for gentlemen by gentlemen themselves. Their voluminousness of wristband, with an air of excessive frankness, should betray them at once.

The gamblers, of whom I described not a few, were still more easily recognisable. They wore every variety of dress, from that of the desperate thimble-rig① bully, with velvet waistcoat, fancy neckerchief, gilt chains, and filagreed buttons, to that of the scrupulously inornate clergyman, than which nothing could be less liable to suspicion. Still all were distinguished by a certain sodden swarthiness of complexion, a filmy dimness of eye, and pallor and compression of lip. There were two other traits, moreover, by which I could always detect them; — a guarded lowness of tone in conversation, and a more than ordinary extension of the thumb in a direction at right angles with the fingers. — Very often, in company with these sharpers, I observed an order of men somewhat different in habits, but still birds of a kindred feather. They may be defined as the gentlemen who live by their wits. They seem to prey upon the public in two battalions — that of the dandies

① 藏豆赌博游戏，用三只小杯覆于桌上，其中之一下藏一粒豆，然后快速变化其位置，叫旁观者打赌哪只小杯下藏豆。

矫揉造作如此体面的话。

人群中还有许多闯劲十足的家伙，我一看就知道他们属于每个大城市都少不了的一流的扒手一族。我怀着极大的好奇心观察这些家伙，发现很难想象他们居然被真正的绅士误认为绅士。他们的袖口宽松肥大，显出一种十足的坦率，即刻便暴露出他们的身份。

我曾不止一次地刻画过赌徒，他们更加易于辨认。他们穿着各式各样的服装，从无法无天的恶棍骗子穿戴的丝绒背心、花哨围巾、镀金表链和金丝细工纽扣，到朴素得不打折扣的牧师所穿的教服，然而没有比这种装扮更易引起人们怀疑的了。因酗酒而显得迟钝的黝黑脸庞、朦胧而浑浊的双眼以及苍白而干瘪的嘴唇是辨认他们的依据。此外他们还有两个特征，据此我总是可以辨认出他们：说话时充满戒备地压低嗓音，大拇指总是非同寻常地伸向与其他手指成直角的方向——我注意到，经常与这些赌棍在一起的还有这样一类人，尽管他们的习性与上述人稍有不同，但依然是同林之鸟。他们可以被称作一群靠耍小聪明过活的绅士。他们似乎分为两大类——纨绔子弟和当兵的。前者的主要特征是蓄着长发，满脸堆笑；后者的特征是身着华丽军装，眉头紧锁。

and that of the military men. Of the first grade the leading features are long locks and smiles; of the second frogged coats and frowns.

Descending in the scale of what is termed gentility, I found darker and deeper themes for speculation. I saw Jew pedlars, with hawk eyes flashing from countenances whose every other feature wore only an expression of abject humility; sturdy professional street beggars scowling upon mendicants of a better stamp, whom despair alone had driven forth into the night for charity; feeble and ghastly invalids, upon whom death had placed a sure hand, and who sidled and tottered through the mob, looking everyone beseechingly in the face, as if in search of some chance consolation, some lost hope; modest young girls returning from long and late labor to a cheerless home, and shrinking more tearfully than indignantly from the glances of ruffians, whose direct contact, even, could not be avoided; women of the town of all kinds and of all ages — the unequivocal beauty in the prime of her womanhood, putting one in mind of the statue in Lucian, with the surface of Parian marble, and the interior filled with filth — the loathsome and utterly lost leper in rags — the wrinkled, bejewelled and paint-begrimed beldame, making a last effort at youth — the mere child of immature form, yet, from long association, an adept in the dreadful coquetries of her trade, and burning with a rabid ambition to be ranked the equal of her elders in vice; drunkards innumerable and indescribable — some in shreds and patches, reeling, inarticulate, with bruised visage and lack-lustre eyes — some in whole although filthy garments, with a slightly unsteady swagger, thick sensual lips, and hearty-looking rubicund faces — others clothed in materials which had once been good, and which even now were scrupulously

看完上流社会的人我又去观察下流社会的人，我发现了一些值得思考的更阴暗更深刻的主题。我看见犹太商贩的脸上除了双眼闪着敏锐目光外，其他体貌特征都只呈现一种卑躬屈膝的谦恭相；我看见健壮的职业乞丐怒视那些比他们更名副其实的同类，而只有绝望才会驱使这些同类深夜祈求救济；我看到一些身体虚弱、面如死灰的病人，死神已对他们发出最后通牒，他们侧身蹒跚在人群中，恳求地巴望着每一张脸，似乎在寻找一种不经意间的慰藉，一种失落的希望；我看见一些端庄羞怯的年轻姑娘，在漫长而又拖延的工作之后正赶回她们索然无味的家，她们与其说是愤怒地，不如说是满含泪水地躲避着恶棍们的盯视，甚至无法躲开恶棍对她们的动手动脚；我看到不同类型、不同年龄的街头妓女——她们那种袒胸露背的成熟女性之美，使人想起卢奇安[1]笔下的那尊雕像，表面是帕罗斯岛[2]白大理石，里面却是污秽泥淖——有衣衫褴褛、令人生厌的堕落的麻风病患者——有满脸皱纹、珠光宝气、因浓妆艳抹而脸色晦暗的老太婆，正在为留住青春而做最后一番挣扎——还有一些身体尚未发育成熟的女孩子，但是她们已在长期的卖俏生涯中成了卖弄风情的行业老手，正雄心勃勃地要在这份伤风败俗的行当中与她的老大姐一比高下；我还看见无数难以形容的酒鬼——有些衣衫褴褛，走路踉跄，口齿不清，满脸青肿，两眼无光——有些衣冠肮脏但还完整，步履蹒跚却依然昂首阔步，长着厚厚的耽于酒色的双唇，脸庞红润，容光焕发——还有些人身着曾一度质地优良、现在仍用心刷过的衣服，他们走起路来稳健轻快得不太自然，但他们的面容苍白得可怕，双眼通红得可怖，而且当他们大步穿过人群时，他们发抖

① 卢奇安(一译琉善，120—180)，古罗马作家，无神论者。在其作品《梦》(*Somnium*)中称希腊雕像外表美丽，内部却掩藏着污秽。

② 爱琴海帕罗斯岛，以产白色大理石著称。

well brushed — men who walked with a more than naturally firm and springy step, but whose countenances were fearfully pale, whose eyes hideously wild and red, and who clutched with quivering fingers, as they strode through the crowd, at every object which came within their reach; beside these, pie-men, porters, coal-heavers, sweeps; organ-grinders, monkey-exhibiters and ballad mongers, those who vended with those who sang; ragged artizans and exhausted laborers of every description, and all full of a noisy and inordinate vivacity which jarred discordantly upon the ear, and gave an aching sensation to the eye.

As the night deepened, so deepened to me the interest of the scene; for not only did the general character of the crowd materially alter (its gentler features retiring in the gradual withdrawal of the more orderly portion of the people, and its harsher ones coming out into bolder relief, as the late hour brought forth every species of infamy from its den), but the rays of the gas-lamps, feeble at first in their struggle with the dying day, had now at length gained ascendancy, and threw over everything a fitful and garish lustre. All was dark yet splendid — as that ebony to which has been likened the style of Tertullian.

The wild effects of the light enchained me to an examination of individual faces; and although the rapidity with which the world of light flitted before the window, prevented me from casting more than a glance upon each visage, still it seemed that, in my then peculiar mental state, I could frequently read, even in that brief interval of a glance, the history of long years.

With my brow to the glass, I was thus occupied in scrutinizing the mob, when suddenly there came into view a countenance (that of a decrepid old man, some sixty-five or seventy years of age,) — a

的手指会抓住任何够得着的东西；除了这些人，我还看到卖馅饼的，搬行李的，运煤球的，扫烟囱的，摇风琴的，耍猴戏的，沿街卖唱者以及蓬头垢面的工匠和精疲力竭的各色劳工。这所有的人都充满了喧嚣而放纵的生命力，嘈杂刺耳，让人眼花缭乱。

夜越来越深，我对这一景象的兴趣也越来越浓，这不仅因为人群的基本特征发生了实质上的变化（由于循规蹈矩的那部分人纷纷回家，街头优雅的身影渐渐稀少，而当黑夜从各个阴暗角落将各种丑恶引出，人群中那些不和谐的风景便昭然显露），而且还因为刚才还在与残阳暮色相争的煤气灯光此刻终于占了上风，并在所有物体上投下不规则的眩目光亮。所有的一切漆黑一团却又灿烂夺目——就像一直被比喻为德尔图良[①] 风格的乌木。

灯光的强烈效果使我的目光只能局限于关注每个人的脸。尽管窗前灯光闪烁急促，使我只能对每张脸瞥上一眼，但在当时特殊的精神状态下，甚至在那短暂的一瞥中，我也似乎常常能够读出此人多年的经历。

我将额头靠在窗玻璃上，凝神细看人群。突然，一张面孔映入眼帘（这是一张年纪大约在65岁或70岁的龙钟老翁的脸）——由于这张脸孔具有独一无二的神情，我一下子就被完全吸引住了。我以

① 德尔图良(160—220)，迦太基基督教神学家。他的作品充满睿智、激情，雄辩而精辟，文风以正直著称，如乌木般漆黑华丽。

countenance which at once arrested and absorbed my whole attention, on account of the absolute idiosyncracy of its expression. Anything even remotely resembling that expression I had never seen before. I well remember that my first thought, upon beholding it, was that Retzch, had he viewed it, would have greatly preferred it to his own pictural incarnations of the fiend. As I endeavored, during the brief minute of my original survey, to form some analysis of the meaning conveyed, there arose confusedly and paradoxically within my mind, the ideas of vast mental power, of caution, of penuriousness, of avarice, of coolness, of malice, of blood-thirstiness, of triumph, of merriment, of excessive terror, of intense — of supreme despair. I felt singularly aroused, startled, fascinated. "How wild a history," I said to myself, "is written within that bosom!" Then came a craving desire to keep the man in view — to know more of him. Hurriedly putting on an overcoat, and seizing my hat and cane, I made my way into the street, and pushed through the crowd in the direction which I had seen him take; for he had already disappeared. With some little difficulty I at length came within sight of him, approached, and followed him closely, yet cautiously, so as not to attract his attention.

I had now a good opportunity of examining his person. He was short in stature, very thin, and apparently very feeble. His clothes, generally, were filthy and ragged; but as he came, now and then, within the strong glare of a lamp, I perceived that his linen, although dirty, was of beautiful texture; and my vision deceived me, or, through a rent in a closely-buttoned and evidently second-handed *roquelaire*① which enveloped him, I caught a glimpse both of a diamond and of a

① roquelaire 是 roquelaure 的废弃拼写形式，意为“男用齐膝外套”。

前从不曾见过哪怕与这种神情有丝毫相像的任何表情。我清楚地记得第一眼看见这张脸时脑海中闪过的那个念头：倘若雷茨希[①]见过这张脸，他一定会非常乐意将它作为他所描绘的那个魔鬼的原型。当我试图从那短暂的一瞥之间分析出其所蕴含的意义时，我的脑海里涌出一大堆混乱而又矛盾的概念：巨大的精神力量、谨慎、拮据、贪婪、冷酷、怨恨、凶残、得意、快乐、过分的恐惧、强烈的——极端的绝望。我感到异常的激动、震撼和迷惑。我自言自语道："那胸膛里写着一部多么狂乱的历史！"之后我产生了想要观察他——更多地了解他的强烈欲望。我匆匆穿上外套，抓起帽子和手杖，走向大街，拨开人群，朝刚才我看到老人消失的方向挤去。经过一番周折，我终于看见了他。我向他靠拢，并紧紧跟着他，但我十分小心谨慎，以免引起他的注意。

我现在有机会仔细打量这个人。他个头矮小，身体瘦削，而且看上去非常虚弱。他的衣服基本上是又脏又破的，但借着不时强烈闪烁的灯光，我发现他的亚麻布衬衣裤虽说脏了些，但质地精良；要么是我的眼睛欺骗了我，要么就是我确实从他那件紧扣着的显然是二手货的外套缝中瞥见了一颗钻石和一把匕首。这一发现增强了我的好奇心，于是我决定无论他去哪儿都紧紧跟着他。

---

① 雷茨希(1799—1857)，德国画家，为歌德的《浮士德》、莎士比亚、席勒的部分作品画插图而闻名，作品刻画有魔鬼撒旦的形象。

dagger. These observations heightened my curiosity, and I resolved to follow the stranger whithersoever he should go.

It was now fully night-fall, and a thick humid fog hung over the city, soon ending in a settled and heavy rain. This change of weather had an odd effect upon the crowd, the whole of which was at once put into new commotion, and overshadowed by a world of umbrellas. The waver, the jostle, and the hum increased in a tenfold degree. For my own part I did not much regard the rain — the lurking of an old fever in my system rendering the moisture somewhat too dangerously pleasant. Tying a handkerchief about my mouth, I kept on. For half an hour the old man held his way with difficulty along the great thoroughfare; and I here walked close at his elbow through fear of losing sight of him. Never once turning his head to look back, he did not observe me. By and by he passed into a cross street, which, although densely filled with people, was not quite so much thronged as the main one he had quitted. Here a change in his demeanor became evident. He walked more slowly and with less object than before — more hesitatingly. He crossed and recrossed the way repeatedly without apparent aim; and the press was still so thick, that, at every such movement, I was obliged to follow him closely. The street was a narrow and long one, and his course lay within it for nearly an hour, during which the passengers had gradually diminished to about that number which is ordinarily seen at noon in Broadway near the Park — so vast a difference is there between a London populace and that of the most frequented American city. A second turn brought us into a square, brilliantly lighted, and overflowing with life. The old manner of the stranger reappeared. His chin fell upon his breast, while his eyes

此时天已完全黑下来。浓云密雾笼罩着这个城市，不久就化作了一场连绵不绝的大雨。天气的这一变化在人群中产生了奇妙的效果，整个人群顿时陷入一场新的骚动，全部躲到一把把伞下。人群的晃动、推搡和嘈杂比刚才增加了十倍。我并未怎么在意这场雨——长期潜伏在我体内的热病使得浇在我身上的雨水虽然非常危险但却十分惬意。我用手帕蒙住嘴，继续跟踪前行。老人沿着那条大街艰难地行走了半个小时，我紧跟在他的胳膊肘后，唯恐跟丢。他从不曾回过头来，因而也就没发现我。过了一会儿，他拐进了一条岔路，这条路虽然人来人往，但却不如刚才那条街拥挤。此时他的举动发生了明显的变化。与之前相比，他放慢了脚步，也愈加没有目的性——愈加迟疑。他穿过马路，又穿回来，反反复复，而且没有什么明显意图。街上的人依然很多，他每次穿过街道我都不得不紧紧跟随。这条街又窄又长，他差不多走了一个多小时，其间路上行人慢慢减少，最后剩下的人数与人们在中午时分常看到的百老汇大街靠近公园那一段路上的行人数目相差无几——伦敦人口与美国最繁华城市的人口之间的差别是如此之大。又转了一个弯后，我们来到了一个广场上，这里灯火辉煌，人声鼎沸。老人又恢复旧态，下巴垂到胸前，双眼在紧皱的眉头下乱转，扫视着围在他四周的人群。他坚定不移地挤开前行的路。可我吃惊地发现，当他绕着广场走完一圈后，又转身开始走第二圈。更令我诧异的是，他反反复复走了好几圈——有一次他突然转身，差点儿发现我。

rolled wildly from under his knit brows, in every direction, upon those who hemmed him in. He urged his way steadily and perseveringly. I was surprised, however, to find, upon his having made the circuit of the square, that he turned and retraced his steps. Still more was I astonished to see him repeat the same walk several times — once nearly detecting me as he came round with a sudden movement.

In this exercise he spent another hour, at the end of which we met with far less interruption from passengers than at first. The rain fell fast; the air grew cool; and the people were retiring to their homes. With a gesture of impatience, the wanderer passed into a by-street comparatively deserted. Down this, some quarter of a mile long, he rushed with an activity I could not have dreamed of seeing in one so aged, and which put me to much trouble in pursuit. A few minutes brought us to a large and busy bazaar, with the localities of which the stranger appeared well acquainted, and where his original demeanor again became apparent, as he forced his way to and fro, without aim, among the host of buyers and sellers.

During the hour and a half, or thereabouts, which we passed in this place, it required much caution on my part to keep him within reach without attracting his observation. Luckily I wore a pair of caoutchouc over-shoes, and could move about in perfect silence. At no moment did he see that I watched him. He entered shop after shop, priced nothing, spoke no word, and looked at all objects with a wild and vacant stare. I was now utterly amazed at his behaviour, and firmly resolved that we should not part until I had satisfied myself in some measure respecting him.

A loud-toned clock struck eleven, and the company were fast

他就这样转了一个小时，到最后，我们碰到的人比一开始少了很多。雨下得很急，天气越来越凉，人们正纷纷回家。这个闲荡者以一种不耐烦的姿态，拐进了广场旁边一条比较偏僻的胡同。他顺着胡同大约走了四分之一英里远，便撒腿跑起来，我做梦也想不到如此年迈的人竟有此举，这给我的跟踪造成了很大的麻烦。几分钟后我们来到了一个繁忙的大集市，老人似乎对那个地方很熟悉，又开始故伎重演，在买卖者的人群中漫无目的地挤来挤去。

在我们穿行于这个地方的大约一个半小时里，我必须十分小心，既要跟上他又不能被他察觉。幸运的是，我穿着一双橡胶套鞋，走起路来没有一丝声响。他从未觉察到我在观察他。他从一家家商店进进出出，不询价，也不说一句话，只是急切而茫然地把所有的物品看一遍。现在我对他的行为极为惊异，下定决心跟踪到底，直到多少满足我的好奇心为止。

一座洪钟敲了11下，人们纷纷离开集市。一家商店老板在关

deserting the bazaar. A shop-keeper, in putting up a shutter, jostled the old man, and at the instant I saw a strong shudder come over his frame. He hurried into the street, looked anxiously around him for an instant, and then ran with incredible swiftness through many crooked and peopleless lanes, until we emerged once more upon the great thoroughfare whence we had started — the street of the D — Hotel. It no longer wore, however, the same aspect. It was still brilliant with gas; but the rain fell fiercely, and there were few persons to be seen. The stranger grew pale. He walked moodily some paces up the once populous avenue, then, with a heavy sigh, turned in the direction of the river, and, plunging through a great variety of devious ways, came out, at length, in view of one of the principal theatres. It was about being closed, and the audience were thronging from the doors. I saw the old man gasp as if for breath while he threw himself amid the crowd; but I thought that the intense agony of his countenance had, in some measure, abated. His head again fell upon his breast; he appeared as I had seen him at first. I observed that he now took the course in which had gone the greater number of the audience — but, upon the whole, I was at a loss to comprehend the waywardness of his actions.

As he proceeded, the company grew more scattered, and his old uneasiness and vacillation were resumed. For some time he followed closely a party of some ten or twelve roisterers; but from this number one by one dropped off, until three only remained together, in a narrow and gloomy lane little frequented. The stranger paused, and, for a moment, seemed lost in thought; then, with every mark of agitation, pursued rapidly a route which brought us to the verge of the city, amid regions very different from those we had hitherto traversed. It was the

店门时碰到了那个老人，就在那一刹那我看到老人浑身猛然一阵战栗。他仓促地冲到街上，焦虑不安地环视了一下四周，然后以惊人的敏捷飞快地穿过许多弯弯曲曲、无人行走的小巷，直到我们再次回到那条我们最初出发的大街——D 咖啡馆所在的那条街。但是这条街已不再是原来那番光景。煤气灯依然辉煌，但大雨如注，行人稀少。那个怪人脸色变得苍白起来。他闷闷不乐地在曾经人群熙攘的大街上走了几步，然后深深地叹了口气，转身朝河的方向走去。经过许多偏僻的小巷，我们最后来到了一座大剧院。适逢散场，观众正从剧院门口蜂拥而出。我看见老人大口喘息，好像投入人群使他喘不过气来，但我觉得他脸上的极度苦闷已大为减轻。他的头又垂到了胸前，看上去就像我第一次见到他时那样。我注意到他走上了观众最拥挤的那条路——但是，总体来说，我还是无法参悟他那古怪的行为。

走着走着，人群逐渐散去，于是他又恢复了先前的不安和游移。有一阵子，他紧跟着由十一二个喧闹狂欢的人组成的人群，但是那群人逐一离去，到了一个狭窄阴暗的僻静小巷时，只剩下三个人了。陌生人停下脚步，有一会儿工夫，他似乎陷入了沉思，接着，他异常激动不安地迅速抄起一条路，来到了城市的边缘，这里与我们走过的任何地方都截然不同。这是全伦敦最令人厌恶的地区，一切都打上了最肮脏的贫穷和最严重的犯罪的深刻烙印。借助于偶尔闪烁的微弱灯光，我看到高大古旧的被虫蛀的木制房屋摇摇欲坠。这些

most noisome quarter of London, where everything wore the worst impress of the most deplorable poverty, and of the most desperate crime. By the dim light of an accidental lamp, tall, antique, worm-eaten, wooden tenements were seen tottering to their fall, in directions so many and capricious, that scarce the semblance of a passage was discernible between them. The paving-stones lay at random, displaced from their beds by the rankly-growing grass. Horrible filth festered in the dammed-up gutters. The whole atmosphere teemed with desolation. Yet, as we proceeded, the sounds of human life revived by sure degrees, and at length large bands of the most abandoned of a London populace were seen reeling to and fro. The spirits of the old man again flickered up, as a lamp which is near its death-hour. Once more he strode onward with elastic tread. Suddenly a corner was turned, a blaze of light burst upon our sight, and we stood before one of the huge suburban temples of Intemperance — one of the palaces of the fiend, Gin.

It was now nearly daybreak; but a number of wretched inebriates still pressed in and out of the flaunting entrance. With a half shriek of joy the old man forced a passage within, resumed at once his original bearing, and stalked backward and forward, without apparent object, among the throng. He had not been thus long occupied, however, before a rush to the doors gave token that the host was closing them for the night. It was something even more intense than despair that I then observed upon the countenance of the singular being whom I had watched so pertinaciously. Yet he did not hesitate in his career, but, with a mad energy, retraced his steps at once, to the heart of the mighty London. Long and swiftly he fled, while I followed him in

横七竖八的房屋之间的通道是如此迂回曲折，以至于几乎分辨不出任何像是通道的东西。随意放置的铺路石被茂密蔓生的杂草挤下了路基。堵塞的排水沟淤积着污秽。整个环境充满颓败凄凉。然而，当我们往前走时，人声渐渐鼎沸起来，最后，我看到全伦敦最寡廉鲜耻的一大群人在那里摇来晃去。老人的精神又为之一振，如同一盏将要耗尽的油灯。他的步伐又一次轻快起来。他突然转过一个拐角，一阵炫目的灯光映入眼帘，我们站在一座巨大的郊外纵酒殿堂——一座酒鬼的宫殿。

此时已是破晓时分，可一群酒鬼依然从那扇招摇的门进进出出。老人惊喜地尖叫，挤进人群，顿时恢复不久前的举止，在人群中大踏步走来走去，没有任何明显的目的。但是，他这样没走上几个来回，酒鬼们便从门口涌了出来，原来老板要关门打烊了。这时，在这个被我锲而不舍跟踪的怪老头脸上，我看到了一种比绝望还要强烈的神情。然而，他并没有为他的行程踟蹰，而是立刻以一种疯狂的劲头折回巨大的伦敦中心。他长久而敏捷地飞奔，而我则抱着诧异尾随其后，横下决心决不放弃我目前已倾注全部兴趣的调查。我们赶路时太阳已升起，而当我们再次来到最繁华的市中心、D 咖啡馆所在的那条大街时，街上人们的喧闹拥挤绝不亚于前一天晚上我所看到的景象。在这儿，在骤然增加的混乱人群中，我坚持不懈地

the wildest amazement, resolute not to abandon a scrutiny in which I now felt an interest all-absorbing. The sun arose while we proceeded, and, when we had once again reached that most thronged mart of the populous town, the street of the D — Hotel, it presented an appearance of human bustle and activity scarcely inferior to what I had seen on the evening before. And here, long, amid the momently increasing confusion, did I persist in my pursuit of the stranger. But, as usual, he walked to and fro, and during the day did not pass from out the turmoil of that street. And, as the shades of the second evening came on, I grew wearied unto death, and, stopping fully in front of the wanderer, gazed at him steadfastly in the face. He noticed me not, but resumed his solemn walk, while I, ceasing to follow, remained absorbed in contemplation. "This old man," I said at length, "is the type and the genius of deep crime. He refuses to be alone. *He is the man of the crowd.* It will be in vain to follow; for I shall learn no more of him, nor of his deeds. The worst heart of the world is a grosser book than the '*Hortulus Animae*,'[①] and perhaps it is but one of the great mercies of God that '*er lasst sich nicht lesen.*'"

① 格吕宁格尔所著的《幽灵花园》—— 原注。*Hortulus Animae*(Latin: *Little Garden of the Soul*, 1500) 译作《幽灵花园》，曾被英国学者迪斯雷利 (Isaac D'Israeli, 1766—1848) 在其《文坛奇事》(*Curiosities of Literature*) 中指责含有轻薄猥亵的内容。

紧跟在陌生人身后。然而，一如既往，他来来回回地走，而且一整天都没有走出那条喧闹的街道。当夜幕降临时，我已疲惫得要死，于是我径直站在那个闲逛者面前，紧盯着他的脸。他没有注意到我，而是继续他那庄严的行程，而我，则不再跟踪，陷入了沉思。“这个老头儿，”我最后说道，“一定怀着深重的罪孽并且是个高明的罪犯。他拒绝孤独。他是人群中的人。再跟踪下去也是毫无意义，因为我既不会对他了解更多，也无从知晓他的罪行。世上最坏的心肠是比《幽灵花园》还恶劣的书，它拒绝被人读也许是上帝最大的恩惠吧。”

A Descent into the Maelström[①]

大漩涡底余生记

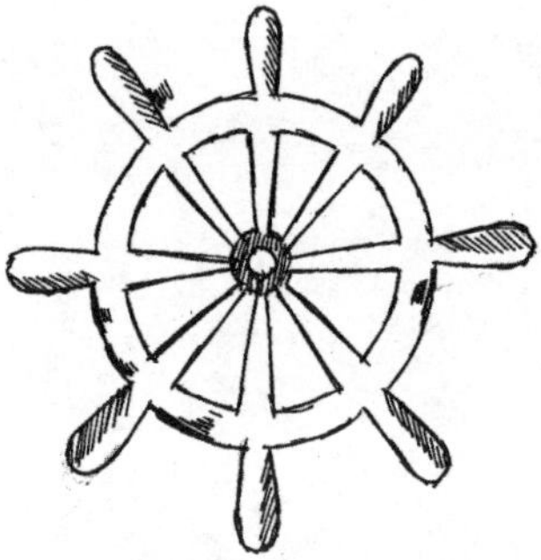

① 在挪威西海岸约北纬68度与罗孚敦较近的地方自然发生的马尔斯特罗姆大漩涡。因为莫斯肯岛位于该现象发生处的海域中间，故又称作莫斯肯漩涡(Moskoeström)。实际上，该漩涡并没有坡笔下的叙述者所说的那般雄伟壮观。但却激发了其他许多故事创作的灵感，如荷马在《奥德赛》中创造了寓言人物卡律布狄斯，儒勒·凡尔纳(Jules Verne)则创作了《海底两万里》(*20 000 Leagues Under the Sea*)。

《大漩涡底余生记》（*A Decent into the Maelström*, 1841）讲述的是一个水手在航海过程中不幸被卷入有名的莫斯肯大漩涡后死里逃生的故事。爱伦·坡的这篇小说满足了当时美国大众的文学趣味和求异心理。当时，美国报刊界处于一种不良的竞争状态，各大报纸为了提高销售量不惜报道各种夸大其词的假新闻，至于那些惊心动魄的冒险故事更是受到广大读者的普遍青睐。正是在这样的情况下，时任《格雷厄姆杂志》编辑的坡写下了《大漩涡底余生记》这篇小说并为该杂志创下了不菲的销售量。不过，即便如此，我们仍不得不佩服坡在这篇小说中所体现出的非凡想象力和卓越的文字表达能力。同时，透过他那张弛有度的语言和丝丝入扣的情节，我们也跟随着他进行了一次探求真理的精神之旅。

首先，爱伦·坡在情节的安排上独具匠心，将人们对同一事物的不同视角巧妙地贯穿一气，却又不给人以造作之感。这一点主要表现在坡对“我”的巧妙安排上。和往常一样，坡以第一人称开始故事的叙述，然而这一次“我”并非故事的主角，而是作为一个旁观者和倾听者，引领读者分别从不同的角度对大漩涡进行全面的观察和切身的感受。故事开始时，“我”以一个旁观者的身份目睹了大漩涡的磅礴气势，增强了故事的真实性，也彰显了“我”的天才表现力。在“我”的描述下，大漩涡的雄伟壮观和摄人心魄都仿佛历历在目。对此，“我”自己似乎也有些自鸣得意，于是，“我”接下来引用大段前人对于大漩涡的描述并插入自己和老头对它们的不屑评论，从而进一步反衬出大漩涡的恢宏气势，同时也显示出“我”对于大漩涡的独到观察和文字表现力。紧接着，作者将笔锋一转，故事交由另一个“我”，即那位亲身经历了大漩涡底劫后余生的挪威老者来叙述。至此，作者完成了多个不同视角的转换，并且让它们衔接自然，从而让读者从三个不同的侧面对大漩涡进行了近距离的接触。

其次，爱伦·坡通过不同叙述者对大漩涡的描述，在空间上营造了一种由远及近、由表及里的透视感，在内涵上也传达了一种探索真理的渐进过程。试想一下，我们可以将作者眼中所见的大漩涡、前人书中记载的大漩涡以及老头亲身经历的大漩涡看作是人们认识真理的三个不同阶段。起先是对真理的一种好奇与向往，这种向往来源于前人史料的记载以及一些道听途说的传闻。然而，作者对所谓的权威提出了质疑，对真理的好奇转变成了一种强烈的探究欲。于是，从耳闻到目睹，再到亲身经历，镜头一点点地拉近，作者凭借想象的翅膀，一步一步深入真理的内核。当故事的主人翁最终被卷进大漩涡以后，其内心的恐惧转变成了好奇，甚至是一种狂热的冲动，使得他“越接近可怕的死亡，这种好奇心似乎越是强烈”。最后，当他开始发现漩涡里的一些奥秘时，他已无法按捺内心的激动，以至于“四肢又开始发抖，心也开始砰砰乱跳起来”。这种对未知事物的蠢蠢欲动以及发现未知事物后的狂喜正印证了作者对真理（美）的不懈追求。

此外，小说中多处出现的关于月光的描写不但给故事蒙上了一层神秘的色彩，同时也起到象征和隐喻的作用。首先，在“我”即将被卷入大漩涡的时候，“我”发现天际起了种种异样的变化，“四面八方依然是漆黑一片，但是几乎在头顶的地方突然一下子裂开，露出一小块圆状的晴朗的天空——就像平日所见的一样晴朗——呈现出一种明亮的深蓝色——就在那儿出现一轮圆月，光彩夺目，闪耀着一种我从不知月亮有过的光华。”在这之前，作者描写的始终是风浪的肆虐，渲染的是一种恐怖的气氛。可以说整个小说都沉浸在一种昏天黑地的氛围中，而此刻突然出现的一轮明月无疑给这种恐怖气氛注入了一道希望之光、真理之光。应该说，月光在这里象征着一种境界，而这种境界正是坡一向追求的美的最高境界——恐怖之美。接下来，当“我”真正进入了大漩涡，眼前又呈现出另一番景象，“月光似乎一直照进了那深渊的最底部，但我依然什么都看不清楚，这是因为一层浓雾将一切都裹住了，而且浓雾之上还悬挂着一道瑰丽的彩虹，犹如那条狭窄而又晃悠悠的小桥：穆斯林所说的连接时间和永生的唯一一条小路。”这段描写充满了诡异的色彩，使得原本就神秘莫测的大漩涡显得更加若即若离，同时还具有了某种超自然的灵气。这从一方面进一步实现了坡所倡导的灵异之美，从另一方面也隐喻了人类在探索真理过程中所产生的如梦似幻的感觉以及横贯在世俗与真理之间的那道瑰丽的彩虹。最后，当“我”历尽艰险最终得以重生的时候，“我”发现“天已转晴，风已减弱，那轮圆月正光灿灿地从天空落下”，多么一派祥和的景象，不曾经历过生死洗礼的人又如何能体会得到这种劫后余生的安详与宁静？

当然，前面所提到的这一切终究还要归功于作者天才的想象力。我们知道，爱伦·坡并不曾目睹过大漩涡的真实面貌，也不曾亲身经历过惊涛骇浪的严峻考验，然而，他却能将大漩涡的神奇威力与瑰丽景象描绘得入木三分，将人们深入大漩涡的惊险之旅与奇妙感受表达得如此淋漓尽致，这不得不令人佩服。

The ways of God in Nature, as in Providence, are not as our ways; nor are the models that we frame any way commensurate to the vastness, profundity, and unsearchableness of His works, which have a depth in them greater than the well of Democritus.

—Joseph Glanville

We had now reached the summit of the loftiest crag. For some minutes the old man seemed too much exhausted to speak.

"Not long ago," said he at length, "and I could have guided you on this route as well as the youngest of my sons; but, about three years past, there happened to me an event such as never happened before to mortal man — or at least such as no man ever survived to tell of — and the six hours of deadly terror which I then endured have broken me up body and soul. You suppose me a very old man — but I am not. It took less than a single day to change these hairs from a jetty black to white, to weaken my limbs, and to unstring my nerves, so that I tremble at the least exertion, and am frightened at a shadow. Do you know I can scarcely look over this little cliff without getting giddy?"

The "little cliff," upon whose edge he had so carelessly thrown himself down to rest that the weightier portion of his body hung over it, while he was only kept from falling by the tenure of his elbow on its extreme and slippery edge — this "little cliff" arose, a sheer unobstructed precipice of black shining rock, some fifteen or sixteen hundred feet from the world of crags beneath us. Nothing would have tempted me to within half a dozen yards of its brink. In truth so deeply was I excited by the perilous position of my companion, that I fell at full length upon the ground, clung to the shrubs around me, and

神之造化万物犹如天意，非同人力之道；自然之浩瀚、奥秘、玄妙亦绝非吾辈构造之物所能比拟，自然之奥妙，比德谟克利特之井[①]更为深邃。

——约瑟夫·格兰威尔[②]

我们现在登上了最高的巉崖顶峰。那位老人一时间似乎累得说不出话来。

“不久前，”他终于开口说道，“我还能像我的小儿子一样利索地带你走这条路。可是，大约三年前，我碰到了一桩事，这事一般人可没有经历过——或者说至少没有幸存者讲述过这种经历——我当时历经的胆战心惊的六个小时将我的身心彻底击垮了。你大概以为我年纪很大吧——其实不然。不到一天的工夫，我乌黑发亮的头发就变成了白发，四肢无力，神经衰弱，以至于现在我一使劲就发抖，看到影子就害怕。你可知道，我从这小小的悬崖往下看都会觉得头晕眼花？”

老人漫不经心地在他所谓的“小小悬崖”边上躺下休息，身体的重心倚在悬崖壁上，一只胳膊肘撑在又陡又滑的岩边才没有摔下来——这“小小悬崖”是一道由乌黑发亮的岩石构成的绝壁，陡峭而无遮拦，从脚底下的巉崖丛石中突兀而起，有1 500~1 600英尺高。我怎么都不敢到离悬崖边五六码的地方去。事实上，看到同伴如此

① 古希腊哲学家德谟克利特曾说：“我们对真理一无所知，因为真理在深渊中。”因此名句，后人将储藏秘密、隐埋真理之深处称为“德谟克利特之井”。爱伦·坡引用此句意指真理之源在深渊处。

② 约瑟夫·格兰维尔(1636—1680)是17世纪晚期查尔斯二世(Charles Ⅱ)时代的一位牧师，他喜欢调查异常现象，尤其是英伦三岛的鬼怪事件。“泰德沃斯(Tedworth)的鼓手”是他调查过的最著名案例。

dared not even glance upward at the sky — while I struggled in vain to divest myself of the idea that the very foundations of the mountain were in danger from the fury of the winds. It was long before I could reason myself into sufficient courage to sit up and look out into the distance.

"You must get over these fancies," said the guide, "for I have brought you here that you might have the best possible view of the scene of that event I mentioned — and to tell you the whole story with the spot just under your eye."

"We are now," he continued, in that particularizing manner which distinguished him — "we are now close upon the Norwegian coast — in the sixty-eighth degree of latitude — in the great province of Nordland — and in the dreary district of Lofoden. The mountain upon whose top we sit is Helseggen, the Cloudy. Now raise yourself up a little higher — hold on to the grass if you feel giddy — so — and look out, beyond the belt of vapor beneath us, into the sea."

I looked dizzily, and beheld a wide expanse of ocean, whose waters wore so inky a hue as to bring at once to my mind the Nubian geographer's account of the Mare Tenebrarum. A panorama more deplorably desolate no human imagination can conceive. To the right and left, as far as the eye could reach, there lay outstretched, like ramparts of the world, lines of horridly black and beetling cliff, whose character of gloom was but the more forcibly illustrated by the surf which reared high up against it its white and ghastly crest, howling and shrieking for ever. Just opposite the promontory upon whose apex we were placed, and at a distance of some five or six miles out at sea, there was visible a small, bleak-looking island; or, more properly, its

危险的姿势，我真为他捏了一把汗。因此我直挺挺地趴在地上，紧紧抓住身旁的灌木丛，甚至不敢抬头看天空——与此同时，我心中有一个念头挥之不去：如果狂风肆虐，这山崖将会崩塌。良久，我才说服自己鼓起勇气坐起来，眺望远处。

“你必须克服这些幻觉，”这位向导说，“因为我带你来这儿就是想让你尽可能地看清那件我所提到的事情的发生地——我给你讲述整个故事时，那个地方就在你的眼皮底下。”

“我们现在，”他以其独特详尽的方式继续讲道，“我们现在在挪威海边——位于北纬68度——在地域辽阔的诺兰德省内——荒凉的罗弗敦区。我们脚下这座山叫赫尔辛根山[1]，也叫云山。把身子坐直一点儿——如果头晕就抓住草茎——就这样——朝远处看，穿过我们身下的那条雾带，一直看到大海。”

我看得头昏眼花，但见汪洋一片，海水呈黑色，这使我一下子想起那位努比亚地理学家[2] 所记述过的黑暗的海洋。眼前是人们没法想象的荒凉凄惨的景象。在目力所及的左右两边延伸着黑森森的悬崖，宛如世界的两道壁垒。不断怒吼咆哮着的海浪高卷起恐怖的白色浪峰，高高拍击着悬崖，使阴森的黑崖更显幽暗。就在我们置身于其巅峰的岬角的对面，在海上五六英里远的地方，有一个看上去很荒凉的小岛；更确切地说，透过小岛周围的万顷波涛，才可依

① 根据相关研究，赫尔辛根山（Helseggen）目前并不存在，或许在坡的时代之后被重新命名过。

② 这里的努比亚地理学家指阿拉伯地理学家阿尔·伊德里斯（Al Idrisi，1100—1165或1166）。他著有《努比亚地理》（*Geographia Nubiensis*），爱伦·坡可能因此将其误认为努比亚人。Mare Tenebrarum 为拉丁文，意为黑暗的海（Sea of Darkness），指大西洋未被地中海居民勘探的一部分。

position was discernible through the wilderness of surge in which it was enveloped. About two miles nearer the land, arose another of smaller size, hideously craggy and barren, and encompassed at various intervals by a cluster of dark rocks.

The appearance of the ocean, in the space between the more distant island and the shore, had something very unusual about it. Although, at the time, so strong a gale was blowing landward that a brig in the remote offing lay to under a double-reefed trysail, and constantly plunged her whole hull out of sight, still there was here nothing like a regular swell, but only a short, quick, angry cross dashing of water in every direction — as well in the teeth of the wind as otherwise. Of foam there was little except in the immediate vicinity of the rocks.

"The island in the distance," resumed the old man, "is called by the Norwegians Vurrgh. The one midway is Moskoe. That a mile to the northward is Ambaaren. Yonder are Islesen, Hotholm, Keildhelm, Suarven, and Buckholm. Farther off — between Moskoe and Vurrgh — are Otterholm, Flimen, Sandflesen, and Stockholm. These are the true names of the places — but why it has been thought necessary to name them at all, is more than either you or I can understand. Do you hear anything? Do you see any change in the water?"

We had now been about ten minutes upon the top of Helseggen, to which we had ascended from the interior of Lofoden, so that we had caught no glimpse of the sea until it had burst upon us from the summit. As the old man spoke, I became aware of a loud and gradually increasing sound, like the moaning of a vast herd of buffaloes upon an American prairie; and at the same moment I perceived that what

稀辨认小岛的位置。靠近陆地两英里处还矗立着一个稍小一点的岛屿，巉岩密布，荒瘠阴森，周围环绕着犬牙交错的黑礁。

远处那座岛屿与海岸之间的那片海域显现出非同寻常的景象。当时正有一股劲风从大海吹向陆地，吹得远处海面上的一条双桅横帆船即使收进双折斜桁纵帆①也停不住颠簸，整个船身不时被巨浪吞噬。海面上根本看不到通常的波浪，只有从四面八方冲击而来的一股气势汹汹、迅疾而短促的海水而已——迎面吹来，或从其他方向吹来。除了贴近岩石的地方，海面上几乎没有泡沫。

“远处的岛屿，”老人接着说，“挪威人称之为浮格岛。中间那个叫莫斯肯岛。往北一英里处是阿姆巴伦岛。再过去依次是伊弗力森岛、霍伊赫尔摩岛、基尔德尔摩岛、苏尔文岛和巴克哥尔摩岛。更远处——在莫斯肯岛和浮格岛之间——是奥特赫尔摩岛、弗里门岛、桑德弗利森岛和斯卡赫尔摩岛。这就是这些地方的确切叫法——至于为什么人们认为有必要全部起个名字就不是你我能弄懂的了。你听见什么了吗？你看到海水有什么变化吗？”

我们在赫尔辛根岛山顶已经待了十分钟光景，我们是从罗弗敦内地爬上来的，所以直到攀爬到绝顶处，大海才豁然出现在眼前。老人说话之际，我听到了一阵巨大的并且越来越大的声响，就像是美洲草原一大群野牛的哀嚎。也就在那时，我在正下方看到水手们称之为汹涌的海水，海水瞬间变成一股潮流，滚滚东去。甚至在我

① 斜桁纵帆：升在前桅和主桅后面的小纵帆，在风暴中用来保持船头顶风。

seamen term the chopping character of the ocean beneath us, was rapidly changing into a current which set to the eastward. Even while I gazed, this current acquired a monstrous velocity. Each moment added to its speed — to its headlong impetuosity. In five minutes the whole sea, as far as Vurrgh, was lashed into ungovernable fury; but it was between Moskoe and the coast that the main uproar held its sway. Here the vast bed of the waters, seamed and scarred into a thousand conflicting channels, burst suddenly into phrensied convulsion — heaving, boiling, hissing — gyrating in gigantic and innumerable vortices, and all whirling and plunging on to the eastward with a rapidity which water never elsewhere assumes except in precipitous descents.

In a few minutes more, there came over the scene another radical alteration. The general surface grew somewhat more smooth, and the whirlpools, one by one, disappeared, while prodigious streaks of foam became apparent where none had been seen before. These streaks, at length, spreading out to a great distance, and entering into combination, took unto themselves the gyratory motion of the subsided vortices, and seemed to form the germ of another more vast. Suddenly — very suddenly — this assumed a distinct and definite existence, in a circle of more than a mile in diameter. The edge of the whirl was represented by a broad belt of gleaming spray; but no particle of this slipped into the mouth of the terrific funnel, whose interior, as far as the eye could fathom it, was a smooth, shining, and jet-black wall of water, inclined to the horizon at an angle of some forty-five degrees, speeding dizzily round and round with a swaying and sweltering motion, and sending forth to the winds an appalling

凝望的时刻，这股潮流就获得了一种可怕的速度。水速时刻在加快——水势时刻都在猛增。不出五分钟，远至浮格岛的整个海面都掀起了势不可挡的滔天怒浪，但在莫斯肯岛和海岸之间，海水最为汹涌狂嚣。巨大的海面分裂成上千股相互碰撞的水流，突然间陷入疯狂的骚动——汹涌翻滚，沸腾呼啸——回旋成无数巨大的漩涡，气势湍急地冲向东面，一般只有在水流急转直下的地方才会像这样湍急。

又过了几分钟，场景又发生了急剧的变化。整个海平面多少平静了些，漩涡也渐渐地消失了，而原来不见白沫的海面上此刻出现了一股股滔天巨浪。这股股泡沫逐渐向远处蔓延，最后汇聚在一起，呈现出下沉漩涡状的旋转运动，仿佛要形成一个更大的漩涡。突然——只一下子——那个大漩涡已清清楚楚地成形，直径超过了一英里，漩涡的周围环绕着宽宽一道闪闪发亮的浪花，但是却没有浪花滑进那可怕的漏斗口里。极目望去，漏斗的内壁是一道光滑、闪亮、乌黑的水墙，与水平线构成大约四十五度角，水壁摇摇晃晃、翻来滚去地旋转，转得人头昏眼花，同时向空中发出可怕的声音，半是吼叫，半是咆哮，连气势磅礴的尼亚加拉大瀑布[①]也从未向苍天这样哀嚎过。

① 尼亚加拉大瀑布，位于加拿大和美国交界的尼亚加拉河中段，号称世界七大奇景之一，与南美的伊瓜苏瀑布及非洲的维多利亚瀑布合称世界三大瀑布。它以宏伟的气势以及丰沛而浩瀚的水汽震撼了所有的游人。从伊利湖滚滚而来的尼亚加拉河水流经此地，突然垂直跌落51米，巨大的水流以银河倾倒之势冲下断崖，声及数里之外，场面震人心魄，形成了气势磅礴的大瀑布。

voice, half shriek, half roar, such as not even the mighty cataract of Niagara ever lifts up in its agony to Heaven.

The mountain trembled to its very base, and the rock rocked. I threw myself upon my face, and clung to the scant herbage in an excess of nervous agitation.

"This," said I at length, to the old man — "this can be nothing else than the great whirlpool of the Maelström."

"So it is sometimes termed," said he. "We Norwegians call it the Moskoe-ström, from the island of Moskoe in the midway."

The ordinary accounts of this vortex had by no means prepared me for what I saw. That of Jonas Ramus, which is perhaps the most circumstantial of any, cannot impart the faintest conception either of the magnificence, or of the horror of the scene — or of the wild bewildering sense of the novel which confounds the beholder. I am not sure from what point of view the writer in question surveyed it, nor at what time; but it could neither have been from the summit of Helseggen, nor during a storm. There are some passages of his description, nevertheless, which may be quoted for their details, although their effect is exceedingly feeble in conveying an impression of the spectacle.

"Between Lofoden and Moskoe," he says, "the depth of the water is between thirty-six and forty fathoms; but on the other side, toward Ver (Vurrgh) this depth decreases so as not to afford a convenient passage for a vessel, without the risk of splitting on the rocks, which happens even in the calmest weather. When it is flood, the stream runs up the country between Lofoden and Moskoe with a boisterous rapidity; but the roar of its impetuous ebb to the sea is

大山连根都在震颤，岩石也在晃动。我紧张害怕极了，俯伏在地，紧抓住身边的几根荒草。

“这，”我终于对老人说，“这一定是著名的马尔斯特罗姆大漩涡。”

“有时候人们也这么叫它，”他说，“但是我们挪威人称之为莫斯肯漩涡。这名字来自海岸和浮格岛之间的那个莫斯肯岛。”

关于大漩涡的一般性记述根本没能使我对眼前景象有任何准备。乔纳斯·雷玛斯[1]的记述也许是最为详尽的，但完全不会给人们足够的印象，让他们意识到这番景象是何等壮丽，或这场面是何等恐怖——更不会想象到人们目睹这种新奇景象时所强烈感受到的不知所措和惶惑不安。我不清楚这位作者是从什么角度观察大漩涡的，也不清楚他是在什么时间进行的观察，但是他既不可能是从赫尔辛根山顶，也不可能是在一次暴风雨期间观察到的。尽管如此，他的描述中有几段特别详细，我们不妨将其抄录于此，虽然在传达对那种奇观异景的感受上，这些文字还是太过苍白无力。

他写道：“在莫斯肯岛和罗弗敦海岸之间，水深在36至40英寻之间，但在该岛与浮岛（即浮格岛）之间，水却浅到船只都无法顺利通过，即便在风平浪静的日子，船只也有触礁的危险。涨潮时，潮流狂暴地冲过罗弗敦和莫斯肯岛之间，而它急遽退潮时所发出的吼声简直连最震耳欲聋、最可怕恐怖的大瀑布也难以相提并论。那种吼

① 乔纳斯·雷玛斯（1649—1718），挪威牧师和历史学家，著有《挪威历代帝王史》《挪威志》等，曾对莫斯肯漩涡有过描述。

scarce equalled by the loudest and most dreadful cataracts; the noise being heard several leagues off, and the vortices or pits are of such an extent and depth, that if a ship comes within its attraction, it is inevitably absorbed and carried down to the bottom, and there beat to pieces against the rocks; and when the water relaxes, the fragments thereof are thrown up again. But these intervals of tranquility are only at the turn of the ebb and flood, and in calm weather, and last but a quarter of an hour, its violence gradually returning. When the stream is most boisterous, and its fury heightened by a storm, it is dangerous to come within a Norway mile[①] of it. Boats, yachts, and ships have been carried away by not guarding against it before they were within its reach. It likewise happens frequently, that whales come too near the stream, and are overpowered by its violence; and then it is impossible to describe their howlings and bellowings in their fruitless struggles to disengage themselves. A bear once, attempting to swim from Lofoden to Moskoe, was caught by the stream and borne down, while he roared terribly, so as to be heard on shore. Large stocks of firs and pine trees, after being absorbed by the current, rise again broken and torn to such a degree as if bristles grew upon them. This plainly shows the bottom to consist of craggy rocks, among which they are whirled to and fro. This stream is regulated by the flux and reflux of the sea—it being constantly high and low water every six hours. In the year 1645, early in the morning of Sexagesima Sunday, it raged with such noise and impetuosity that the very stones of the houses on the coast fell to the ground."

In regard to the depth of the water, I could not see how this could

① Norway mile, 挪里，一挪里相当于4.68英里。

声几海里之外都能听到；那些漩涡或陷阱极宽，极深，如果船只进入其引力圈，就不可避免地被吸进去，卷入海底，在暗礁上撞得粉碎；而当海面平静时，残骸碎片才重新浮出水面。然而，只有在涨潮与退潮之间的间歇，在无风的日子里，这种短暂的平静才会出现，而且最多只能持续十五分钟，随即狂暴又会渐渐卷土重来。当那股海流最为强烈，而且又有暴风雨助威时，离它四五英里之内都危机重重。小船、快艇、帆船等若不小心谨慎，不等靠近海流就会被卷走。同样，鲸鱼太靠近漩涡时，也经常被水力制服；它们徒然地挣扎，以求脱身，并发出怒号吼叫，这种情形绝非笔墨所能形容。有一次，一头熊想要从罗弗敦游到莫斯肯去，却被卷入洪流。它拼命嘶叫，岸上的人都能听得到。枞树和松树的巨大树干被卷进激流中，之后又浮上来，遍体鳞伤，仿佛浑身长满了鬃毛。这清楚地表明，海底礁石林立，卷下去的树干就在这礁石间来回打转。这股水流随着海潮涨落或急或缓——通常每隔六个小时水位高低就会变换。1645年，六旬斋[①] 的周日清晨，潮水狂暴喧嚣，声势汹汹，沿海一带房屋上的石头都被震落在地。”

说到水深，我可看不出在大漩涡附近一带如何确定海水的深

① 六旬斋，大斋节前的第二个星期日。

have been ascertained at all in the immediate vicinity of the vortex. The "forty fathoms" must have reference only to portions of the channel close upon the shore either of Moskoe or Lofoden. The depth in the centre of the Moskoe-ström must be immeasurably greater; and no better proof of this fact is necessary than can be obtained from even the sidelong glance into the abyss of the whirl which may be had from the highest crag of Helseggen. Looking down from this pinnacle upon the howling Phlegethon below, I could not help smiling at the simplicity with which the honest Jonas Ramus records, as a matter difficult of belief, the anecdotes of the whales and the bears; for it appeared to me, in fact, a self-evident thing, that the largest ship of the line in existence, coming within the influence of that deadly attraction, could resist it as little as a feather the hurricane, and must disappear bodily and at once.

The attempts to account for the phenomenon — some of which, I remember, seemed to me sufficiently plausible in perusal — now wore a very different and unsatisfactory aspect. The idea generally received is that this, as well as three smaller vortices among the Ferroe islands, "have no other cause than the collision of waves rising and falling, at flux and reflux, against a ridge of rocks and shelves, which confines the water so that it precipitates itself like a cataract; and thus the higher the flood rises, the deeper must the fall be, and the natural result of all is a whirlpool or vortex, the prodigious suction of which is sufficiently known by lesser experiments." — These are the words of the Encyclop aedia Britannica and others imagine that in the centre of the channel of the Maelström is an abyss penetrating the globe, and issuing in some very remote part — the Gulf of Bothnia being

度。“40英寻”的说法肯定是指靠近莫斯肯海岸或罗弗敦海岸的那一部分的深度。莫斯肯漩涡中心一定深不可测，站在赫尔辛根最高的巉崖之顶峰朝那旋转着的深渊看上一眼，哪怕仅仅是斜眼一瞥，就足以证实这一点。从山顶俯瞰下面那条咆哮的冥河[①]，我忍不住嘲笑老实的乔纳斯·雷玛斯的天真，居然把鲸鱼和熊的传说当作难以置信的事件来记载，因为事实上在我看来，这是件不证自明的事。这世上最大的战舰，一旦开进那个致命的吸力圈，也会像鸿毛无法抵抗飓风一样，必定顷刻间连人带船整个儿消失。

那些解释这一现象的尝试——其中一些，我记得，对我来说似乎言之有理——现在看来却完全不同了，难以令人满意。一般认为，同费罗群岛间的三个较小的漩涡一样，“其原因不外乎是潮涨潮落，水流起伏时，波浪与一列岩石和暗礁形成的分水岭相撞击，海水被分水岭挡住，从而产生了瀑布一般的推动力，因而，潮水涨得越高，退落就越深，结果就形成了涡流或漩涡。稍做实验，就会尽知漩涡的强大吸力。”——以上摘自《大英百科全书》[②]。珂雷等人曾

① 又作 flaming，一般称作“火河”，又名所罗河，是希腊神话中冥府四大河之一。其他三条河流为守誓河、苦恼河和悲叹河。其中火河最长最大，上游在第五狱，在尤拉部落外的海勒悬崖断开，形成飞鹰瀑布；中游在第六狱，流经龙怒之谷；下游在第七狱，环绕而形，成为帝都罗德欧加的护城河。

② 《不列颠百科全书》，又称《大英百科全书》，诞生于1768年，历经两百多年修订和再版，发展成当今享有盛誉的32册鸿篇巨制。《不列颠百科全书》由世界各国、各学术领域的著名专家学者（包括众多诺贝尔奖得主）为其撰写条目。该书囊括了对人类知识各重要学科的详尽介绍，和对历史及当代重要人物、事件的翔实叙述，其学术性和权威性为世人所公认。阿塔纳斯·珂雷（Athanasius Kircher，1601或1602—1680），17世纪德国考古学家、数学家、医学家等，喜欢研究各种科学。《大英百科全书》上的“漩涡”一段即摘自珂雷的作品。

somewhat decidedly named in one instance. This opinion, idle in itself, was the one to which, as I gazed, my imagination most readily assented; and, mentioning it to the guide, I was rather surprised to hear him say that, although it was the view almost universally entertained of the subject by the Norwegians, it nevertheless was not his own. As to the former notion he confessed his inability to comprehend it; and here I agreed with him — for, however conclusive on paper, it becomes altogether unintelligible, and even absurd, amid the thunder of the abyss.

"You have had a good look at the whirl now," said the old man, "and if you will creep round this crag, so as to get in its lee, and deaden the roar of the water, I will tell you a story that will convince you I ought to know something of the Moskoe-ström."

I placed myself as desired, and he proceeded.

"Myself and my two brothers once owned a schooner-rigged smack of about seventy tons burthen, with which we were in the habit of fishing among the islands beyond Moskoe, nearly to Vurrgh. In all violent eddies at sea there is good fishing, at proper opportunities, if one has only the courage to attempt it; but among the whole of the Lofoden coastmen, we three were the only ones who made a regular business of going out to the islands, as I tell you. The usual grounds are a great way lower down to the southward. There fish can be got at all hours, without much risk, and therefore these places are preferred. The choice spots over here among the rocks, however, not only yield the finest variety, but in far greater abundance; so that we often got in a single day, what the more timid of the craft could not scrape together in a week. In fact, we made it a matter of desperate speculation —

推测，莫斯肯漩涡的涡流中心有个无底深渊直穿地球，在地球另一端一个非常遥远的地方穿出——波斯尼亚湾或多或少被人们断然认作出口处。这种观点本身并无根据，但当我凝视眼前的漩涡时，心中却不由得表示赞同；当我对向导提出这个话题，他认为虽然这是挪威人几乎一致公认的说法，但却不是他的见解，我对此非常吃惊。至于前一种见解，他承认自己无法理解；在这一点上我与他相同——因为，不管书上写得多么头头是道，人们一旦置身于这无底深渊的雷鸣般的咆哮声中，就会觉得书上所言完全莫名其妙，甚至荒唐可笑。

“你已经仔细看过了漩涡，”老人说，“如果你愿意绕过这巉崖，爬到背风的地方，避开海水震耳欲聋的咆哮，我就讲个故事给你听，让你相信我对莫斯肯漩涡确实有几分了解。”

我爬到他所说的地方，他便开始讲故事。

“从前，我和我那两位兄弟曾有一条载重70吨的纵帆渔船，我们常常驾驶这条渔船驶过莫斯肯岛，在靠近浮格岛的岛屿间捕鱼。只要有胆量到湍急的漩涡处试一试，碰到运气好的时候，就能捕到不少鱼。然而，罗弗敦一带所有的渔民中，只有我们三个常去我告诉你的那些岛屿间捕鱼。通常的渔场在南边下游很远的地方。那儿随时都能捕到鱼，而且没有风险，因此人们都愿意去那儿。然而，这礁石丛中的好去处不仅有许多名贵鱼种，捕捞量也很大，所以我们一天捕到的鱼往往比那些胆小的同行一星期捕的鱼还要多。事实上，我们将这营生当作玩命的投机生意——不必辛勤劳作却冒生命之险，以勇气博取资本。

the risk of life standing instead of labor, and courage answering for capital.

"We kept the smack in a cove about five miles higher up the coast than this; and it was our practice, in fine weather, to take advantage of the fifteen minutes' slack to push across the main channel of the Moskoe-ström, far above the pool, and then drop down upon anchorage somewhere near Otterholm, or Sandflesen, where the eddies are not so violent as elsewhere. Here we used to remain until nearly time for slack-water again, when we weighed and made for home. We never set out upon this expedition without a steady side wind for going and coming — one that we felt sure would not fail us before our return — and we seldom made a mis-calculation upon this point. Twice, during six years, we were forced to stay all night at anchor on account of a dead calm, which is a rare thing indeed just about here; and once we had to remain on the grounds nearly a week, starving to death, owing to a gale which blew up shortly after our arrival, and made the channel too boisterous to be thought of. Upon this occasion we should have been driven out to sea in spite of everything, (for the whirlpools threw us round and round so violently, that, at length, we fouled our anchor and dragged it) if it had not been that we drifted into one of the innumerable cross currents — here today and gone tomorrow — which drove us under the lee of Flimen, where, by good luck, we brought up.

"I could not tell you the twentieth part of the difficulties we encountered 'on the grounds' — it is a bad spot to be in, even in good weather — but we made shift always to run the gauntlet of the Moskoe-ström itself without accident; although at times my heart has

“我们将船停泊在这海岸上游大约五英里的一个海湾里，趁着好天气，利用十五分钟的平潮期[①]迅速驶过莫斯肯漩涡的主水道，远远开在深渊上头，然后顺风漂下，在涡流相对缓和的奥特赫尔摩或桑德弗利森岛附近停泊下来。在那儿我们一般停留到第二次平潮期，然后起锚返航。来回航程中一直刮着侧风——对于这阵风我们有把握在返航之前不会变向——否则我们绝不会扬帆出海，而且我们对此的预测几乎没有出过错。六年里，我们只有两次被迫在那儿抛锚过夜，因为一丝风都没有，这在当地确实是件少有的事；还有一次我们不得不在那边的渔场上停留了近一个星期，饿得要死，那是因为我们刚到渔场就刮起了狂风，水道怒浪滔天，返航的事想都别想。不管怎么说，那一次我们本该被冲进深海（因为那些漩涡使我们的船直打转，到最后我们缠住锚并拖住它）。那一次我们漂进那些无数横流中的一条——今天漂到这儿，明天漂到那儿——最后漂到弗里门的背风一面，在那儿我们侥幸地抛了锚，要不是这样，我们无论如何都会被冲进深海。

“在‘渔场那儿’遭遇的困难我根本无法向你讲明——那是个险恶的地方，即使是在好天气中——但我们总是能设法平安无事地逃出莫斯肯漩涡的魔掌；即便如此，每当碰巧与平潮期相差一分钟

① 平潮期。水面相对平静，适合航行。由于月亮及太阳引力的作用，海洋存在着潮汐现象。海水由低位升到高位的过程谓之涨潮，由高位回到低位的过程谓之落潮，海水处于最高位时的暂时平静期谓之平潮，处于最低位时的暂时平静期谓之停潮。

been in my mouth when we happened to be a minute or so behind or before the slack. The wind sometimes was not as strong as we thought it at starting, and then we made rather less way than we could wish, while the current rendered the smack unmanageable. My eldest brother had a son eighteen years old, and I had two stout boys of my own. These would have been of great assistance at such times, in using the sweeps, as well as afterward in fishing — but, somehow, although we ran the risk ourselves, we had not the heart to let the young ones get into the danger — for, after all is said and done, it was a horrible danger, and that is the truth.

"It is now within a few days of three years since what I am going to tell you occurred. It was on the tenth day of July, 18 — , a day which the people of this part of the world will never forget — for it was one in which blew the most terrible hurricane that ever came out of the heavens. And yet all the morning, and indeed until late in the afternoon, there was a gentle and steady breeze from the south-west, while the sun shone brightly, so that the oldest seaman among us could not have foreseen what was to follow.

"The three of us — my two brothers and myself — had crossed over to the islands about two o'clock P. M., and had soon nearly loaded the smack with fine fish, which, we all remarked, were more plenty that day than we had ever known them. It was just seven, by my watch, when we weighed and started for home, so as to make the worst of the Ström at slack water, which we knew would be at eight.

"We set out with a fresh wind on our starboard quarter, and for some time spanked along at a great rate, never dreaming of danger, for indeed we saw not the slightest reason to apprehend it. All at once

左右时，我的心还是会提到嗓子眼儿上。有时，起航时的风并不像我们预想的那样强劲，到后来潮流冲得渔船没法操控，我们的航程比预想的大大缩短。我的哥哥有个十八岁的儿子，我也有两个健壮的儿子，每逢使用长桨划船或出海捕鱼时，孩子们理应是得力助手——但是，不知为什么，我们自己玩命，却不忍心让孩子们去冒险——因为，那毕竟是一种可怕的危险，而且这话千真万确。

"再过几天，我要讲给你听的故事就发生整整三年了。那是18×× 年7月10日，这一带的人们永远也忘不了这个日子——因为这天刮过一场空前可怕的飓风。然而那天上午，实际上一直到黄昏时分，天上一直都吹着柔和而稳定的西南风，艳阳高照，因而即使我们当中最年老的水手也未曾料到接下来会骤然变天。

"我们三人——我的两个兄弟和我自己——大约在下午两点钟的时候到达了那边的岛屿，并很快装满了一船好鱼。我们都认为，那天捕的鱼比以往任何时候都多。我们知道平潮期将会是八点钟，为了利用平潮期，我的表七点整时，我们就起锚返航了。

"起航时，右舷后部吹送来一股清风，船飞快地行驶了好一阵。此时我们压根儿没有想到危险，因为我们的确看不出有任何值得担忧的迹象。突然之间，赫尔辛根山那边吹来一阵风，令我们大吃一

we were taken aback by a breeze from over Helseggen. This was most unusual — something that had never happened to us before — and I began to feel a little uneasy, without exactly knowing why. We put the boat on the wind[①], but could make no headway at all for the eddies, and I was upon the point of proposing to return to the anchorage, when, looking astern, we saw the whole horizon covered with a singular copper-colored cloud that rose with the most amazing velocity.

"In the meantime the breeze that had headed us off fell away, and we were dead becalmed, drifting about in every direction. This state of things, however, did not last long enough to give us time to think about it. In less than a minute the storm was upon us — in less than two the sky was entirely overcast — and what with this and the driving spray, it became suddenly so dark that we could not see each other in the smack.

"Such a hurricane as then blew it is folly to attempt describing. The oldest seaman in Norway never experienced any thing like it. We had let our sails go by the run before it cleverly took us; but, at the first puff, both our masts went by the board as if they had been sawed off — the mainmast taking with it my youngest brother, who had lashed himself to it for safety.

"Our boat was the lightest feather of a thing that ever sat upon water. It had a complete flush deck, with only a small hatch near the bow, and this hatch it had always been our custom to batten down when about to cross the Ström, by way of precaution against the chopping seas. But for this circumstance we should have foundered

① put the boat on the wind，航海用语，意为调转为逆风向行驶，船首向风。

惊。这种情况非同寻常——我们以前从未经历过——虽然说不出其中缘由，但我开始感到有些不安。我们调转船头，顺着风向，可是船根本不朝漩涡的方向开。我正要提议返回原来停船的地方时，我们往后一望，只见整个天际被一种正急速涌起的黄铜色怪云笼罩。

“与此同时，刚才阻挠我们前进的那阵风也消失了，我们完全无法行驶，只能顺着水势漂流。但这种情况没有持续多久，甚至连给我们思考的工夫都没有。不出一分钟，风暴就来了——不到两分钟，天空布满了乌云——在这种情势下，再加上浪花涌起，我们周围顿时漆黑一片，在同一条船上都看不清彼此。

“要想描述那场飓风可真是痴心妄想。连年纪最长的挪威水手都不曾有过类似的经历。我们趁飓风还没有吞噬我们之前，赶紧放下了风帆。但是，第一阵风就把我们的两根桅杆刮断，掉到海里，就像是被锯断了似的——我的弟弟原先为了安全，把自己绑在了主桅上，现在被主桅带到海里去了。

“我们的船是海上航行船只中最轻巧的那一种。它的甲板十分光滑，在靠近船头的地方有一个小小的舱口，我们一直习惯于在驶越大漩涡之前将舱口密封，防止汹涌的海水灌入。要不是这样，恐怕我们早就沉入大海了——因为有一阵子我们完全被淹没在水里。我说不出哥哥是如何逃过那场浩劫的，因为我根本没有机会去弄明白。至于我，一放下前帆我就趴在甲板上，两脚紧紧抵住船头狭窄

at once — for we lay entirely buried for some moments. How my elder brother escaped destruction I cannot say, for I never had an opportunity of ascertaining. For my part, as soon as I had let the foresail run, I threw myself flat on deck, with my feet against the narrow gunwale[①] of the bow, and with my hands grasping a ring-bolt near the foot of the fore-mast. It was mere instinct that prompted me to do this — which was undoubtedly the very best thing I could have done — for I was too much flurried to think.

"For some moments we were completely deluged, as I say, and all this time I held my breath, and clung to the bolt. When I could stand it no longer I raised myself upon my knees, still keeping hold with my hands, and thus got my head clear. Presently our little boat gave herself a shake, just as a dog does in coming out of the water, and thus rid herself, in some measure, of the seas. I was now trying to get the better of the stupor that had come over me, and to collect my senses so as to see what was to be done, when I felt somebody grasp my arm. It was my elder brother, and my heart leaped for joy, for I had made sure that he was overboard — but the next moment all this joy was turned into horror — for he put his mouth close to my ear, and screamed out the word 'Moskoe-ström! '

"No one ever will know what my feelings were at that moment. I shook from head to foot as if I had had the most violent fit of the ague. I knew what he meant by that one word well enough — I knew what he wished to make me understand. With the wind that now drove us on, we were bound for the whirl of the Ström, and nothing could save us!

"You perceive that in crossing the Ström channel, we always

① gunwale，名词，舷缘，小船船舷的上缘。又作 gunnel。

的舷边，双手则死死地抓住前桅杆下的一个带环螺栓。我这样做仅仅是出于本能——那毫无疑问是我能做出的最好选择——因为我紧张得无法细想。

“正如我刚才所说的，有一阵子我们完全被淹没在水下，其间我一直屏住呼吸，并紧紧抓住那个带环螺栓。当我实在坚持不住时，我才跪起身来，但双手依然紧抓不放，以保持头脑清醒。这时船身抖了一抖，就像是狗从水中钻出来时抖动身子一样，这样它多少甩掉了一些海水。我正试图驱散刚才向我袭来的一阵恍惚，定下神来考虑该怎么办时，突然感觉到有人抓住我的胳膊。原来是我的哥哥。我高兴得心怦怦跳，因为我还以为刚才他一定掉下船去了——但是这种快乐转眼间变成了恐惧——因为他将嘴凑到我的耳边，惊惧地喊出了那几个字，‘莫斯肯漩涡！’

“没有人知道那一刻我的感受。我浑身上下直打哆嗦，就像是发了一场极为严重的疟疾。我很清楚他喊出的那几个字意味着什么——我很清楚他想让我明白什么。我们被那阵风驱赶着，正驶向莫斯肯漩涡，而且任凭什么都无法拯救我们。

“你知道，我们每次穿过这漩涡的主水道时，总是绕开一大段

went a long way up above the whirl, even in the calmest weather, and then had to wait and watch carefully for the slack — but now we were driving right upon the pool itself, and in such a hurricane as this! 'To be sure,' I thought, we shall get there just about the slack — there is some little hope in that' — but in the next moment I cursed myself for being so great a fool as to dream of hope at all. I knew very well that we were doomed, had we been ten times a ninety-gun ship.

"By this time the first fury of the tempest had spent itself, or perhaps we did not feel it so much, as we scudded before it, but at all events the seas, which at first had been kept down by the wind, and lay flat and frothing, now got up into absolute mountains. A singular change, too, had come over the heavens. Around in every direction it was still as black as pitch, but nearly overhead there burst out, all at once, a circular rift of clear sky — as clear as I ever saw — and of a deep bright blue — and through it there blazed forth the full moon with a lustre that I never before knew her to wear. She lit up every thing about us with the greatest distinctness — but, oh God, what a scene it was to light up!

"I now made one or two attempts to speak to my brother — but, in some manner which I could not understand, the din had so increased that I could not make him hear a single word, although I screamed at the top of my voice in his ear. Presently he shook his head, looking as pale as death, and held up one of his finger, as if to say 'listen!'

"At first I could not make out what he meant — but soon a hideous thought flashed upon me. I dragged my watch from its fob. It was not going. I glanced at its face by the moonlight, and then burst into tears as I flung it far away into the ocean. It had run down at

路，驶到漩涡的上头。即便是在最平静的天气中也是如此，然后我们还得小心翼翼地等待平潮期——可是现在我们却径直驶向大漩涡，而且是在这样的一场飓风中！‘可以肯定的是，’我心想，‘我们抵达那儿刚好是平潮期——这样我们还有一线生机’——但是紧接着我就咒骂自己如此蠢笨，竟然还幻想生还。我心里非常清楚，就算我们这条船比一条有九十门大炮的战舰还要大十倍，我们也注定要完蛋。

“此刻，风暴的头一阵狂怒已经减弱，也许是因为我们顺风而行，不大能觉察出来。但是无论如何，刚才被狂风镇服的、平息了的，且冒着泡沫的大海现在卷起了排山倒海的巨浪。天空也起了奇异的变化。四面八方依然是漆黑一片，但是几乎在头顶的地方突然一下子裂开，露出一小块圆状的晴朗天空——就像平日所见的一样晴朗——呈现出一种明亮的深蓝色——就在那儿出现一轮圆月，光彩夺目，闪耀着一种我从不知月亮有过的光华。它将一切都照得清清楚楚——但是，天哪，它照亮的是一番怎样的景象！

“我有一两次试图与哥哥说话——可是我不明白是怎么回事，嘈杂声越来越大，即使我对着他的耳朵扯开喉咙喊也无法让他听见一个字。不久，他摇了摇头，面如死灰，并竖起一根手指，仿佛在说，‘听！’

“起初我没弄懂他的意思——但旋即脑海里掠过一个可怕的念头。我从表袋里拉出表。表已经不走了。我借着月光瞥了一眼表盘，一下子哭了出来，随即把表扔进了大海。表停在了七点钟。我们错过了平潮期，而大漩涡的涡圈正在狂怒之中！

seven o'clock! We were behind the time of the slack, and the whirl of the Ström was in full fury!

"When a boat is well built, properly trimmed, and not deep laden, the waves in a strong gale, when she is going large, seem always to slip from beneath her — which appears very strange to a landsman — and this is what is called riding[①], in sea phrase. Well, so far we had ridden the swells very cleverly; but presently a gigantic sea happened to take us right under the counter, and bore us with it as it rose — up — up — as if into the sky. I would not have believed that any wave could rise so high. And then down we came with a sweep, a slide, and a plunge, that made me feel sick and dizzy, as if I was falling from some lofty mountain-top in a dream. But while we were up I had thrown a quick glance around — and that one glance was all sufficient. I saw our exact position in an instant. The Moskoe-ström whirlpool was about a quarter of a mile dead ahead—but no more like the everyday Moskoe-ström, than the whirl as you now see it is like a mill-race. If I had not known where we were, and what we had to expect, I should not have recognised the place at all. As it was, I involuntarily closed my eyes in horror. The lids clenched themselves together as if in a spasm.

"It could not have been more than two minutes afterward until we suddenly felt the waves subside, and were enveloped in foam. The boat made a sharp half turn to larboard[②], and then shot off in its new direction like a thunderbolt. At the same moment the roaring noise of the water was completely drowned in a kind of shrill shriek

① riding 本意为骑，乘骑，搭乘，这里翻译成"骑浪"，即船掠着浪尖飞过。
② larboard, 旧时的左舷名称，后来为了避免与 starboard（右舷）相混淆，于1844年被官方改称为 port。

“一条船若是建造精良，结构匀称，且载货不多，开船时又碰上顺风，那么被强风掀起的海浪看起来总是从船底一滑而过——这对不谙航海的人来说显得非常奇怪——而用海上行话来说，这叫骑浪。好吧，我们一直都在骑浪而行。但不久，一个巨大的海浪就在船底将我们托住，并将我们越举越高——向上——仿佛要将我们举到云霄中去。我真不敢相信浪能涌起那么高。接着船身掠浪飞出，滑落，并骤然前倾跌落水中，这让我头晕眼花，直犯恶心，就像是梦中从高山山巅跌落。但当我们被托起时，我朝四下匆匆瞥了一眼——这一瞥就足够了。我立刻就看清了我们的准确位置，莫斯肯漩涡就在我们正前方大约四分之一英里处——但它已不像是平日里的莫斯肯大漩涡，而像你现在所看到的涡流一样，宛如水车用的水流。如果我们不知道我们在哪儿，不清楚我们将遭遇的事情，那我根本不会认出那个地方。像先前一样，我惊惧得不禁闭上了双眼——上下眼皮就像抽筋似的，紧紧地贴在一起。

“之后可能还不到两分钟，我们突然感觉到波涛平息了，周围白浪一片。渔船猛地朝左舷方向直转九十度，接着闪电般朝新的方向飞驶而去。与此同时，大海的咆哮完全被一种尖利的呼啸声吞没——想象一下几千艘汽艇同时排汽的声音，你就知道这种声音了。当时我们正在那条总是环绕着大漩涡的浪带上。我以为下一分钟我们必然会跌入那个深渊——由于船以惊人的速度行驶，我无法看清深渊下面。但是船不像是要沉入海中的样子，而是像气泡一

— such a sound as you might imagine given out by the waste-pipes of many thousand steam-vessels, letting off their steam all together. We were now in the belt of surf that always surrounds the whirl; and I thought, of course, that another moment would plunge us into the abyss — down which we could only see indistinctly on account of the amazing velocity with which we were borne along. The boat did not seem to sink into the water at all, but to skim like an air-bubble upon the surface of the surge. Her starboard side was next the whirl, and on the larboard arose the world of ocean we had left. It stood like a huge writhing wall between us and the horizon.

"It may appear strange, but now, when we were in the very jaws of the gulf, I felt more composed than when we were only approaching it. Having made up my mind to hope no more, I got rid of a great deal of that terror which unmanned me at first. I suppose it was despair that strung my nerves.

"It may look like boasting — but what I tell you is truth — I began to reflect how magnificent a thing it was to die in such a manner, and how foolish it was in me to think of so paltry a consideration as my own individual life, in view of so wonderful a manifestation of God's power. I do believe that I blushed with shame when this idea crossed my mind. After a little while I became possessed with the keenest curiosity about the whirl itself. I positively felt a wish to explore its depths, even at the sacrifice I was going to make; and my principal grief was that I should never be able to tell my old companions on shore about the mysteries I should see. These, no doubt, were singular fancies to occupy a man's mind in such extremity — and I have often thought since, that the revolutions of the

样擦过汹涌的波涛表面。船的右舷靠近漩涡，左舷边就是我们刚才离开的那片汪洋。那片汪洋像是一堵巨大的扭动着的墙，横亘在我们与地平线之间。

“听起来有些奇怪，当我们处在漩涡的边缘时，我却比刚才驶向漩涡时更平静了——一旦我下定决心不再怀抱希望，先前那使我失魂落魄的恐惧便消逝了大半。我想先前使我神经紧张的大概是绝望。

“这听起来像是吹牛——可我告诉你这是事实——我开始觉得以这种方式死去是何等壮观，想到在目睹上帝如此令人叹为观止的力量时，我竟然愚蠢地去考虑自己微不足道的生命。我确信，当这种想法闪过我的脑海之际，我羞愧难当。过了不一会儿，我开始对漩涡本身产生强烈的好奇心。我十分明确地感受到一种想去探测那漩涡深度的欲望，就算牺牲生命也在所不惜；而我最大的遗憾是永远不能够将我所看见的神秘事物告诉岸上那些老朋友。这无疑是一个身陷绝境的人头脑中的胡思乱想——后来我常常想，也许是小船绕着漩涡急速旋转使我有些神志恍惚了。

boat around the pool might have rendered me a little light-headed.

"There was another circumstance which tended to restore my self-possession; and this was the cessation of the wind, which could not reach us in our present situation — for, as you saw yourself, the belt of surf is considerably lower than the general bed of the ocean, and this latter now towered above us, a high, black, mountainous ridge. If you have never been at sea in a heavy gale, you can form no idea of the confusion of mind occasioned by the wind and spray together. They blind, deafen, and strangle you, and take away all power of action or reflection. But we were now, in a great measure, rid of these annoyances — just us death-condemned felons in prison are allowed petty indulgences, forbidden them while their doom is yet uncertain.

"How often we made the circuit of the belt it is impossible to say. We careered round and round for perhaps an hour, flying rather than floating, getting gradually more and more into the middle of the surge, and then nearer and nearer to its horrible inner edge. All this time I had never let go of the ring-bolt. My brother was at the stern, holding on to a small empty water-cask which had been securely lashed under the coop of the counter, and was the only thing on deck that had not been swept overboard when the gale first took us. As we approached the brink of the pit he let go his hold upon this, and made for the ring, from which, in the agony of his terror, he endeavored to force my hands, as it was not large enough to afford us both a secure grasp. I never felt deeper grief than when I saw him attempt this act — although I knew he was a madman when he did it — a raving maniac through sheer fright. I did not care, however, to contest the point with

“使我恢复镇静的还有另外一个原因，那就是风停了。在当时的情形之下，风吹不到我们——因为，正如你自己看到的那样，那圈浪带比大海的一般水位要低得多，当时海面正高居在我们头顶，如一排又高又黑的山岭。如若从未在海上经历过飓风，你就无法联想风浪交加下人们的那种慌乱。风浪吹打使你看不清，听不见，透不过气来，让你没有力气行动，没有精力思考。然而当时我们却基本上摆脱了这些烦扰——就像是牢狱中被宣判死刑的囚徒被允许稍微放纵一下，而在没有被宣判死刑前，这是不允许的。

“我说不上那圈浪带转了多少圈。我们就这样急速地转圈，转了约莫一小时之久。我们与其说是在漂流，不如说是在狂飞，并逐渐移到浪带中间，然后一点点向浪带可怕的内缘靠近。这期间我一直没有松开带环螺栓。我的哥哥则在船尾抓住一只空的小水桶，那水桶一直牢固地拴在船尾的捕鱼网下面，是甲板上唯一没有被头一阵飓风刮下船的东西。当我们向深渊边缘贴近时，他突然丢下那只水桶，来抓带环螺栓。他在极度恐惧中力图使我松开双手，因为带环螺栓不大，容不下我们两个同时抓牢。当我看出他的这种企图时，我感到前所未有的悲哀——尽管心里清楚他做这事儿时已经疯了——极度的恐惧已使他成为一个狂野的疯子。尽管如此，我不屑与他争夺这个地方。我知道谁抓住带环螺栓结果都不会有什么不同；于是我让他抓住带环螺栓，自己则去船尾抓那只水桶。这样做并不太难，因为我们这只渔船旋转得非常平稳，船头船尾就在同一水平面上——只是随着漩涡强烈的翻滚而来回摆动。我还没在新

him. I knew it could make no difference whether either of us held on at all; so I let him have the bolt, and went astern to the cask. This there was no great difficulty in doing; for the smack flew round steadily enough, and upon an even keel — only swaying to and fro, with the immense sweeps and swelters of the whirl. Scarcely had I secured myself in my new position, when we gave a wild lurch to starboard, and rushed headlong into the abyss. I muttered a hurried prayer to God, and thought all was over.

"As I felt the sickening sweep of the descent, I had instinctively tightened my hold upon the barrel, and closed my eyes. For some seconds I dared not open them — while I expected instant destruction, and wondered that I was not already in my death-struggles with the water. But moment after moment elapsed. I still lived. The sense of falling had ceased; and the motion of the vessel seemed much as it had been before, while in the belt of foam, with the exception that she now lay more along. I took courage, and looked once again upon the scene.

"Never shall I forget the sensations of awe, horror, and admiration with which I gazed about me. The boat appeared to be hanging, as if by magic, midway down, upon the interior surface of a funnel vast in circumference, prodigious in depth, and whose perfectly smooth sides might have been mistaken for ebony, but for the bewildering rapidity with which they spun around, and for the gleaming and ghastly radiance they shot forth, as the rays of the full moon, from that circular rift amid the clouds which I have already described, streamed in a flood of golden glory along the black walls, and far away down into the inmost recesses of the abyss.

"At first I was too much confused to observe anything accurately.

位置站稳脚，船就向右侧一歪，头朝下一头栽进了深渊。我匆匆向上帝小声做祷告，心想，这下全完了。

“当我感觉到下坠的那种恶心时，我早已本能地抓紧了水桶，并且闭上双眼。有好几秒钟，我都不敢睁开眼睛——我在等待那瞬息间的毁灭，甚至不解自己为什么还没有沉入海水，做垂死挣扎。然而时间一分钟一分钟地过去了。我依然活着。下降的感觉也消失了，小船的运动似乎又与刚才在浪带上时一样了，只是现在船身更为倾斜。我鼓起勇气，再一次看了看那场景。

“我永远也忘不了我凝视周围一切时那交织着敬畏、恐惧和赞美的心情。小船仿佛被施了魔法，看起来像是处于半空，悬挂在一只硕大而深邃惊人的漏斗内壁表面上。若不是那光滑的内壁正以令人眩晕的速度旋转，若不是它正反射出闪闪的幽光，那光滑的表面或许会被误认作乌木，此时那轮圆月正从我刚才描述过的云层罅隙中沿着乌黑的涡壁倾泻下一大片金辉，远远地照进漩涡最幽深处。

“起初，我心慌意乱，根本无法清楚地观察一切。我所看到的就

The general burst of terrific grandeur was all that I beheld. When I recovered myself a little, however, my gaze fell instinctively downward. In this direction I was able to obtain an unobstructed view, from the manner in which the smack hung on the inclined surface of the pool. She was quite upon an even keel — that is to say, her deck lay in a plane parallel with that of the water — but this latter sloped at an angle of more than forty-five degrees, so that we seemed to be lying upon our beam-ends. I could not help observing, nevertheless, that I had scarcely more difficulty in maintaining my hold and footing in this situation, than if we had been upon a dead level; and this, I suppose, was owing to the speed at which we revolved.

"The rays of the moon seemed to search the very bottom of the profound gulf; but still I could make out nothing distinctly, on account of a thick mist in which everything there was enveloped, and over which there hung a magnificent rainbow, like that narrow and tottering bridge which Mussulmen say is the only pathway between Time and Eternity. This mist, or spray, was no doubt occasioned by the clashing of the great walls of the funnel, as they all met together at the bottom — but the yell that went up to the Heavens from out of that mist, I dare not attempt to describe.

"Our first slide into the abyss itself, from the belt of foam above, had carried us a great distance down the slope; but our farther descent was by no means proportionate. Round and round we swept — not with any uniform movement — but in dizzying swings and jerks, that sent us sometimes only a few hundred yards — sometimes nearly the complete circuit of the whirl. Our progress downward, at each revolution, was slow, but very perceptible.

是这瞬间出现的无比壮观的景象。然而，等我稍稍回过神来后，我便本能地朝下凝视。小船悬挂在漩涡倾斜的表面上，正是以这样的视角我得以一览无余地看到下面的景象。小船现在非常平稳——也就是说，它的甲板与水面完全平行——但由于水面倾斜的角度大于四十五度，我们看起来几乎要倾覆。尽管如此，我仍忍不住观察到，在这种情况下抓住水桶并且站稳脚跟并不比在绝对水平面上困难。我想，这或许可以归因于我们旋转时的速度。

“月光似乎一直照进了那深渊的最底部，但我依然什么都看不清楚，这是因为一层浓雾将一切都裹住了，而且浓雾之上还悬挂着一道瑰丽的彩虹，犹如那条狭窄而又晃悠悠的小桥：穆斯林所说的连接时间和永生的唯一通道。这层浓雾，或者说是水沫，无疑是漩涡巨大的水壁在漩涡底汇聚、相撞形成的——可是从那层浓雾冲出的响彻云霄的呼啸，我可不敢形容。

“我们第一次从那条涌着泡沫的浪带上滑向深渊已经使我们沿着倾泻的水壁向下滑了一大段距离，可是其后的下降与刚才完全不成比例。我们一圈一圈地随着漩涡壁旋转——但并不规则——而是一种令人头晕目眩的摇摆，有时一摆之间只滑行几英里——有时却几乎绕漩涡转了一圈。我们每转一圈就会下降一段，虽然下降不快，但却显而易见。

"Looking about me upon the wide waste of liquid ebony on which we were thus borne, I perceived that our boat was not the only object in the embrace of the whirl. Both above and below us were visible fragments of vessels, large masses of building timber and trunks of trees, with many smaller articles, such as pieces of house furniture, broken boxes, barrels and staves. I have already described the unnatural curiosity which had taken the place of my original terrors. It appeared to grow upon me as I drew nearer and nearer to my dreadful doom. I now began to watch, with a strange interest, the numerous things that floated in our company. I must have been delirious — for I even sought amusement in speculating upon the relative velocities of their several descents toward the foam below. 'This fir tree,' I found myself at one time saying, 'will certainly be the next thing that takes the awful plunge and disappears,' — and then I was disappointed to find that the wreck of a Dutch merchant ship overtook it and went down before. At length, after making several guesses of this nature, and being deceived in all — this fact — the fact of my invariable miscalculation — set me upon a train of reflection that made my limbs again tremble, and my heart beat heavily once more.

"It was not a new terror that thus affected me, but the dawn of a more exciting hope. This hope arose partly from memory, and partly from present observation. I called to mind the great variety of buoyant matter that strewed the coast of Lofoden, having been absorbed and then thrown forth by the Moskoe-ström. By far the greater number of the articles were shattered in the most extraordinary way — so chafed and roughened as to have the appearance of being stuck full of splinters — but then I distinctly recollected that there were some

“环顾那道承载着我们的乌木似的巨大水壁，我发现漩涡里不止我们这条船。我们的上面和下面都可看得见船只的残骸、房屋梁柱和树干，还有不少小的物件，如家具、破箱子、木桶和木板等。我已经跟你讲过我那种驱散了先前恐怖感的反常好奇心，当我越来越接近可怕的死亡时，这种好奇心似乎越是强烈，现在又开始饶有兴趣地观看那些随我们一起漂流的数不尽的物体。我一定是神经错乱了——因为我居然从推测这些物体坠入漩涡底部水沫时的相对速度中寻找乐趣。有一次我发现自己竟然说出声来：‘这下该轮到那棵枞树一头栽进深渊，无影无踪了’——可随后我就失望地发现，一条荷兰商船的残骸超过了那棵枞树，抢先跌进去了。之后我又猜测了好几次，但每次都无一例外地猜错——这个事实——这个我每次都猜错的事实——终于引起我一连串的思索，以致我的四肢又开始发抖，心也开始砰砰乱跳起来。

“使我发抖的并非一种新的恐惧，而是一种更激动人心的希望的曙光。这种希望一半来自记忆，一半出自当时的观察。我想起了那些曾被莫斯肯漩涡卷入又抛出，最后飘散在罗弗敦海岸的各种各样的东西，其中的大部分都破败得不成样子——被波浪冲刷撞击得零碎和粗糙，就像是沾满了碎片一样——可接着我清楚地回忆起也有一些没有变形走样的。当时我无法理解这种差异，除非假定只有那些破碎得完全不成样子的东西才被完全卷入了漩涡底部——其他的或者是涨潮末期才被卷入漩涡，或者是被卷入后由于某种原因

of them which were not disfigured at all. Now I could not account for this difference except by supposing that the roughened fragments were the only ones which had been completely absorbed — that the others had entered the whirl at so late a period of the tide, or, for some reason, had descended so slowly after entering, that they did not reach the bottom before the turn of the flood came, or of the ebb, as the case might be. I conceived it possible, in either instance, that they might thus be whirled up again to the level of the ocean, without undergoing the fate of those which had been drawn in more early, or absorbed more rapidly. I made, also, three important observations. The first was, that, as a general rule, the larger the bodies were, the more rapid their descent — the second, that, between two masses of equal extent, the one spherical, and the other of any other shape, the superiority in speed of descent was with the sphere — the third, that, between two masses of equal size, the one cylindrical, and the other of any other shape, the cylinder was absorbed the more slowly. Since my escape, I have had several conversations on this subject with an old school-master of the district; and it was from him that I learned the use of the words 'cylinder' and 'sphere.' He explained to me — although I have forgotten the explanation — how what I observed was, in fact, the natural consequence of the forms of the floating fragments — and showed me how it happened that a cylinder, swimming in a vortex, offered more resistance to its suction, and was drawn in with greater difficulty than an equally bulky body, of any form whatever.①

① 见阿基米德著《论浮体》卷二——原注。阿基米德(Archimedes, 287 B.C.—212 B.C.),古希腊著名的数学家、物理学家,静力学和流体静力学的奠基人。其《论浮体》,是流体静力学的第一部专著,阿基米德把数学推理成功地运用于分析浮体的平衡上,并用数学公式表示浮体平衡的规律。书中他研究了旋转抛物体在流体中的稳定性。

下降非常慢，结果在潮势转变之前或者说退潮之前没有沉落到漩涡底部。无论是哪种情况，我认为这些东西都有可能重新浮回水面，而不遭受那些早些被卷入或沉得快的东西所遭受的厄运。我还得出三个重要的观察结论：一、一般来说，物体越大，沉降越快；二、两个体积相等的物体，一个是球形，一个是球形以外的其他任何形状，球形物体下降速度较快；三、两个大小相等的物体，一个是圆柱形，一个是任何其他形状，圆柱形物体下降较慢。自从死里逃生以来，我曾多次同这个地区的一名老教师谈论这个话题；就是从他那儿，我学会了'圆柱形''球形'这些词儿。他跟我解释——尽管我也忘记了解释的内容——我看到的其实就是各种形状漂浮碎片的必然结果——而且他还示范给我看，圆柱形浮体在漩涡中如何较之其他形状的同体积浮体更能抵消漩涡的吸力，因而也就更加难以被吸入漩涡底部。

"There was one startling circumstance which went a great way in enforcing these observations, and rendering me anxious to turn them to account, and this was that, at every revolution, we passed something like a barrel, or else the yard or the mast of a vessel, while many of these things, which had been on our level when I first opened my eyes upon the wonders of the whirlpool, were now high up above us, and seemed to have moved but little from their original station.

"I no longer hesitated what to do. I resolved to lash myself securely to the water cask upon which I now held, to cut it loose from the counter, and to throw myself with it into the water. I attracted my brother's attention by signs, pointed to the floating barrels that came near us, and did everything in my power to make him understand what I was about to do. I thought at length that he comprehended my design — but, whether this was the case or not, he shook his head despairingly, and refused to move from his station by the ring-bolt. It was impossible to reach him; the emergency admitted of no delay; and so, with a bitter struggle, I resigned him to his fate, fastened myself to the cask by means of the lashings which secured it to the counter, and precipitated myself with it into the sea, without another moment's hesitation.

"The result was precisely what I had hoped it might be. As it is myself who now tell you this tale — as you see that I did escape — and as you are already in possession of the mode in which this escape was effected, and must therefore anticipate all that I have farther to say — I will bring my story quickly to conclusion. It might have been an hour, or thereabout, after my quitting the smack, when, having descended to a vast distance beneath me, it made three or four wild gyrations in rapid succession, and, bearing my loved brother with it,

“还有一个惊人的事实可以证明我的那些结论，并使我跃跃欲试，那就是，当我们一圈一圈旋转时，我们超过了不少诸如大木桶或残枞断桅之类的东西，而许多那样的东西在我最开始睁开双眼观看漩涡奇观时与我们在同一水平线上，可后来却留在我们上面，似乎比原来的位置并没有下降多少。

“我不再犹豫。我下定决心把自己牢牢绑在我正抓住的那只水桶上，然后脱开船尾，与它一起跳入水中。我通过手势引起大哥的注意，指着那些漂浮在我们周围的水桶，用尽一切办法让他明白我打算做的事情。最后，我想他明白了我的意图——可是，不管他明白与否，只是绝望地向我摇头，不肯离开带环螺栓。我无法靠近他；事情紧急，刻不容缓；于是我非常痛苦地狠下心来，随他听天由命，径自用船尾拴水桶的绳子将自己绑在水桶上，猛然地与水桶一起跳入大海，没有一丝犹豫。

“结果与我所期望的完全一样。因为现在是我在给你讲这个故事——因为你看到了，我确实劫后余生——因为你已经知道了我逃命的方法，也一定料得到我接下去要讲什么——因此我会尽快讲完这个故事。大约在我弃船后一个小时，渔船已经降到我下面很远的位置，它飞速地一连转了三四个圈，然后带着我心爱的哥哥，头朝下永远地栽进了涡底那水沫喧腾的深渊中。绑着我的那只水桶下沉得很慢，只从我跳入水中的位置朝涡底下降了一半多一点点的距离。此时漩涡的性质发生了巨大的变化。倾泻的涡壁越来越不陡

plunged headlong, at once and forever, into the chaos of foam below. The barrel to which I was attached sunk very little farther than half the distance between the bottom of the gulf and the spot at which I leaped overboard, before a great change took place in the character of the whirlpool. The slope of the sides of the vast funnel became momently less and less steep. The gyrations of the whirl grew, gradually, less and less violent. By degrees, the froth and the rainbow disappeared, and the bottom of the gulf seemed slowly to uprise. The sky was clear, the winds had gone down, and the full moon was setting radiantly in the west, when I found myself on the surface of the ocean, in full view of the shores of Lofoden, and above the spot where the pool of the Moskoe-ström had been. It was the hour of the slack — but the sea still heaved in mountainous waves from the effects of the hurricane. I was borne violently into the channel of the Ström, and in a few minutes was hurried down the coast into the 'grounds' of the fishermen. A boat picked me up — exhausted from fatigue — and (now that the danger was removed) speechless from the memory of its horror. Those who drew me on board were my old mates and daily companions — but they knew me no more than they would have known a traveller from the spirit-land. My hair which had been raven-black the day before, was as white as you see it now. They say too that the whole expression of my countenance had changed. I told them my story — they did not believe it. I now tell it to you — and I can scarcely expect you to put more faith in it than did the merry fishermen of Lofoden."

峭了。漩涡的旋转摇摆慢慢变得不再强烈。水沫和彩虹逐渐消失，漩涡的底端似乎也在徐徐上升。天已转晴，风已减弱，那轮圆月正光灿灿地从西边的天空落下，我发现自己已浮回到海面上，罗弗敦海岸清楚地呈现在眼前，而我所在的地方正是莫斯肯大漩涡的涡洞之上。当时是平潮期，但是飓风的余威依然使得海面卷起了小山般的波浪。我被猛力推到了大漩涡的水道上，不消几分钟就顺着海岸被冲到了渔民们捕鱼的'渔场'——一条渔船将我打捞起——我已累得精疲力竭——而且（危险已过去）恐怖的记忆使我说不出一句话来。那些救我上船的人是我的老伙计和经常见面的老朋友——可他们仅仅把我当成一个从冥界来的旅行者。我那头一天还乌黑发亮的头发那时已变成了你现在所看到的苍苍白发。他们还说我脸上的神情也变了。我告诉他们我的经历——可他们并不相信。我现在告诉你——可我并不指望你比那些快活无忧的罗弗敦渔民更相信我的故事。"

Silence — A Fable
静——寓言一则

静谧中的死亡构成了《静——寓言一则》（*Silence — A Fable*, 1837）这篇小说的框架。这是爱伦·坡的短篇小说中既传承又突破的一部作品，传承了他笔下经常出现的死亡主题，同时又闪现着强烈的现代感——文章所传达的落寞、无助正是当今人们无法逃避的问题。小说中有一个被强化的“死亡”意象：一开始，喧哗和骚动是那么奇异扭曲，最后一切终于安静下来，以寂静——死一般的寂静作为结尾，那块石头上的“静”字也蕴含着死亡的主题，只有死亡才能让一切的喧哗骚动平息下来，也只有死亡才能告别生的浮华，真正让一切停下来。这种叙述方式正印证了爱伦·坡的美学理念，即美有奇异感。他对死亡主题感兴趣的一个现实原因就是当时的社会因素。在一个科技开始迅猛发展，宗教信仰渐趋衰落的时代，探寻真正的自我及人的潜意识是爱伦·坡作品的主旨。爱伦·坡及西方现代主义作家笔下人物的变态行为隐喻了社会的没落，揭示出了企图隐身于自我选定的荒僻精神境地的人无法摆脱社会现实折磨的真实状况。作为社会造成的病态个体，他们几乎被推到了地狱的边缘。对他们来说，“他人的存在就是自己的地狱”（萨特语），在现实的社会中他们找不到出路，只好在社会之外寻找自我，实现自我。爱伦·坡用自己的悲剧和作品中人物的悲剧预示并诠释了 20 世纪“现代人”的精神病综合征。

The mountain pinnacles slumber; valleys, crags and caves are silent.

Alcman

"Listen to *me*," said the Demon, as he placed his hand upon my head. "The region of which I speak is a dreary region in Libya, by the borders of the river Zäire. And there is no quiet there, nor silence."

"The waters of the river have a saffron and sickly hue; and they flow not onward to the sea, but palpitate forever and forever beneath the red eye of the sun with a tumultuous and convulsive motion. For many miles on either side of the river's oozy bed is a pale desert of gigantic water-lilies. They sigh one unto the other in that solitude, and stretch towards the heaven their long and ghastly necks, and nod to and fro their everlasting heads. And there is an indistinct murmur which cometh out from among them like the rushing of subterrene water. And they sigh one unto the other."

"But there is a boundary to their realm—the boundary of the dark, horrible, lofty forest. There, like the waves about the Hebrides, the low underwood is agitated continually. But there is no wind throughout the heaven. And the tall primeval trees rock eternally hither and thither with a crashing and mighty sound. And from their high summits, one by one, drop everlasting dews. And at the roots strange poisonous flowers lie writhing in perturbed slumber. And overhead, with a rustling and loud noise, the gray clouds rush westwardly forever, until they roll, a cataract, over the fiery wall of the horizon. But there is no wind throughout the heaven. And by the shores of the river Zäire there is neither quiet nor silence."

山峰在休眠，山谷、险崖和洞穴一片寂静。

——阿尔克曼

“听我说，”魔鬼说着，将手放在我的头上，“我讲的这个地方是利比亚一个荒僻的地方，位于扎伊尔河畔。那里既无安宁，也无寂静。”

“扎伊尔河的河水泛着一种橘黄色的病态色泽。河水不是流向大海，而是在火红的太阳下永不停息地奔腾翻滚。两岸延绵数英里的软泥河床是一片苍白的荒原，上面长满了硕大的睡莲。在这荒凉之地，睡莲相互悲泣，朝天伸着它们颀长而可怖的颈，左右摇摆着它们的头，无休无止。一种模糊不清的低语从它们中间传来，像是奔涌的熔岩。它们相互悲泣。”

“然而，睡莲的王国有一道疆界——以那片阴森、恐怖、高高耸立的森林为界。在那儿，低矮的灌木丛犹如赫布里底斯群岛[①]的波浪，骚动不止。然而天空没有一丝风。参天古树永不止息地左右摇摆，发出一阵阵巨大的声响。从高高的树冠上，一滴滴露珠长年滴落不止。树根处，奇异的毒花在不安的睡眠中扭动。头顶上，灰色的云亘古不变地奔向西方，发出阵阵喧闹的声响，直至在天边燃烧着的火墙上方翻卷成一场暴雨。然而，整个天空没有一丝风。扎伊尔河畔既无安宁，也无寂静。”

① 赫布里底群岛，位于苏格兰沿海。岛上最突出的莫过于翻腾急涌的海浪、空旷的沙滩、危立的悬崖。曾经众多作家和画家被吸引到这个世界末日感沉重的地方汲取灵感。

"It was night, and the rain fell; and, falling, it was rain, but, having fallen, it was blood. And I stood in the morass among the tall lilies, and the rain fell upon my head — and the lilies sighed one unto the other in the solemnity of their desolation."

"And, all at once, the moon arose through the thin ghastly mist, and was crimson in color. And mine eyes fell upon a huge gray rock which stood by the shore of the river, and was lighted by the light of the moon. And the rock was gray, and ghastly, and tall, — and the rock was gray. Upon its front were characters engraven in the stone; and I walked through the morass of water-lilies, until I came close unto the shore, that I might read the characters upon the stone. But I could not decypher them. And I was going back into the morass, when the moon shone with a fuller red, and I turned and looked again upon the rock, and upon the characters; — and the characters were DESOLATION."

"And I looked upwards, and there stood a man upon the summit of the rock; and I hid myself among the water-lilies that I might discover the actions of the man. And the man was tall and stately in form, and was wrapped up from his shoulders to his feet in the toga of old Rome. And the outlines of his figure were indistinct — but his features were the features of a deity; for the mantle of the night, and of the mist, and of the moon, and of the dew, had left uncovered the features of his face. And his brow was lofty with thought, and his eye wild with care; and, in the few furrows upon his cheek I read the fables of sorrow, and weariness, and disgust with mankind, and a longing after solitude.

"And the man sat upon the rock, and leaned his head upon his hand, and looked out upon the desolation. He looked down into the

“适值夜间，下雨了；下的时候，是雨；落下的时候，是血。我立在泥淖里，周围是硕大的睡莲，雨水浇在我头上——在荒凉与庄重中，睡莲相互悲泣。”

“骤然，月亮从死灰色的薄雾中升起，一片血红。我的目光落在一块巨大的灰色岩石上。它耸立在河岸，被月光照亮。这块岩石苍白阴郁，岿然独立——这岩石苍白阴郁。岩石的正面镌刻着字，我穿过满是睡莲的泥淖，一直走到岩石近旁，以便能看清那些镌刻在岩石上的字。可我无法解密这些字。我正要返回泥淖中时，月光变得更红。我转身再次看那块岩石，看那个字——一个“荒”字。”

“我朝上看，一个人立于岩顶；我藏在睡莲之中，以便能够观察那人的举动。他身材魁梧，神情威严，从头到脚裹着一件古罗马人穿的宽袍。他身影的轮廓模糊不清——但他的相貌却是神的模样；因为黑夜、薄雾、月光和露珠都没能遮住他那张面孔。他表情高傲，一副沉思的样子，眼神失魂落魄，充满忧虑；从他脸上的几道皱纹，我读出了他对人类的惋惜、厌倦和憎恶，看出了他对孤独的向往。

“那人坐在了岩石上，用一只手撑着头，远眺这片荒凉之地。他低头看那些不安的低矮灌木，抬头看那些参天古树，接着向上望窸

low unquiet shrubbery, and up into the tall primeval trees, and up higher at the rustling heaven, and into the crimson moon. And I lay close within shelter of the lilies, and observed the actions of the man. And the man trembled in the solitude; — but the night waned, and he sat upon the rock."

"And the man turned his attention from the heaven, and looked out upon the dreary river Zäire, and upon the yellow ghastly waters, and upon the pale legions of the water-lilies. And the man listened to the sighs of the water-lilies, and to the murmur that came up from among them. And I lay close within my covert and observed the actions of the man. And the man trembled in the solitude; — but the night waned and he sat upon the rock."

"Then I went down into the recesses of the morass, and waded afar in among the wilderness of the lilies, and called unto the hippopotami which dwelt among the fens in the recesses of the morass. And the hippopotami heard my call, and came, with the behemoth, unto the foot of the rock, and roared loudly and fearfully beneath the moon. And I lay close within my covert and observed the actions of the man. And the man trembled in the solitude; — but the night waned and he sat upon the rock."

"Then I cursed the elements with the curse of tumult; and a frightful tempest gathered in the heaven where, before, there had been no wind. And the heaven became livid with the violence of the tempest — and the rain beat upon the head of the man — and the floods of the river came down — and the river was tormented into foam — and the water-lilies shrieked within their beds — and the forest crumbled before the wind — and the thunder rolled — and the

窣作响的天空，然后凝望那轮血红的月亮。我藏在睡莲丛下，观察那人的一举一动。那人在孤独中颤抖——但夜色将尽，而他坐在岩石上。”

“那人将目光从天空收回，远眺令人沮丧的扎伊尔河，远望它那昏黄可怖的河水，远看那茫茫一片的睡莲。他倾听睡莲的叹息，聆听它们发出的低语。我藏在隐蔽之处，观察那人的一举一动。那人在孤独中颤抖——但夜色将尽，而他坐在岩石上。”

“于是我退到泥淖深处，在睡莲的荒芜之地，我向远处艰难跋涉，呼唤那些住在泥淖深处沼泽地中的河马。河马听到了我的呼唤，与巨兽们一起来到那块岩石脚下，它们在月光下怒吼，声音响亮而可怖。我藏在隐蔽之处，观察那人的一举一动。那人在孤独中颤抖——但夜色将尽，而他坐在岩石上。”

“于是我用骚动之咒诅咒天气；一场可怕的暴风雨积聚在从未有过风的天空。天空因暴风雨而变成死灰色——雨打在那人的头上——扎伊尔河水水位上涨——河水翻腾着泡沫浊浪——睡莲在水中发出声声尖叫——森林在风中摇摇欲坠——雷声隆隆——电光闪闪——那块岩石连根基都在摇晃。我藏在隐蔽之处，观察那人的一举一动。那人在孤独中颤抖——但夜色将尽，而他坐在岩石上。”

lightning fell — and the rock rocked to its foundation. And I lay close within my covert and observed the actions of the man. And the man trembled in the solitude; — but the night waned and he sat upon the rock."

"Then I grew angry and cursed, with the curse of *silence*, the river, and the lilies, and the wind, and the forest, and the heaven, and the thunder, and the sighs of the water-lilies. And they became accursed, and *were still*. And the moon ceased to totter up its pathway to heaven — and the thunder died away — and the lightning did not flash — and the clouds hung motionless — and the waters sunk to their level and remained — and the trees ceased to rock — and the water-lilies sighed no more-and the murmur was heard no longer from among them, nor any shadow of sound throughout the vast illimitable desert. And I looked upon the characters of the rock, and they were changed; — and the characters were SILENCE."

"And mine eyes fell upon the countenance of the man, and his countenance was wan with terror. And, hurriedly, he raised his head from his hand, and stood forth upon the rock and listened. But there was no voice throughout the vast illimitable desert, and the characters upon the rock were SILENCE. And the man shuddered, and turned his face away, and fled afar off, in haste, so that I beheld him no more."

Now there are fine tales in the volumes of the Magi [1] —in the iron-bound, melancholy volumes of the Magi. Therein, I say, are glorious histories of the Heaven, and of the Earth, and of the mighty sea—and of the Genii that overruled the sea, and the earth, and the

① Magi 是 Magus 复数的拉丁形式，指东方三博士，即《圣经》中由东方来朝见初生耶稣的三贤人。

“于是我愈发愤怒，用‘静’的咒语诅咒扎伊尔河，诅咒那些睡莲，诅咒风，诅咒森林，诅咒苍天，诅咒雷电，诅咒那些睡莲的叹息。它们受到诅咒，全都静止下来。月亮不再在天空摇摇晃晃——雷声骤然消失——电光不再闪亮——云块一动不动地在天空漂浮——河水退回到原来的水位——树林不再摇晃——睡莲不再叹息——也听不到它们发出的低语，茫无边际的荒原听不到任何声音。我抬眼看了看岩石上的字，发现已经改变了——成了‘静’字。”

“我的目光落在那人的脸上，他的脸因受到恐吓而毫无血色。他猛然抬起头，起立，倾身聆听。但是茫无边际的荒原毫无声响，而岩石上的字是‘静’。那人突然颤抖着将脸扭过去，匆匆逃去，结果我再也没有见过他。”

如今，在东方三博士的卷帙中有许多好故事——在东方三博士那些用铁皮装帧的令人忧郁的卷帙中。这些卷帙中，有天空、大地和浩瀚大海的辉煌历史——有关于魔鬼统治海洋、大地和天空的神怪故事。有许多传说是关于西彼尔斯[1]所做出的预言，有一些非常神

① 希腊或罗马女预言家。

lofty heaven. There was much lore too in the sayings which were said by the Sybils; and holy, holy things were heard of old by the dim leaves that trembled around Dodona — but, as Allah liveth, that fable which the Demon told me as he sat by my side in the shadow of the tomb, I hold to be the most wonderful of all! And as the Demon made an end of his story, he fell back within the cavity of the tomb and laughed. And I could not laugh with the Demon, and he cursed me because I could not laugh. And the lynx which dwelleth forever in the tomb, came out therefrom, and lay down at the feet of the Demon, and looked at him steadily in the face.

圣的事情在很久以前被多多纳神庙[①]周围颤抖的隐约不见的树叶听到——然而，尽管真主活着，我依然认为，在坟墓的阴影中，魔鬼坐在我身边对我讲的这则寓言是最奇妙的故事。魔鬼讲完故事，哈哈大笑着退回墓穴。我不能与魔鬼一起大笑，他因此诅咒我。永远居住在坟墓中的猞猁这时蹿了出来，依偎在魔鬼的脚下，一动不动地盯着他的脸。

① 多多纳神庙坐落于伊庇鲁斯(Epirus)地区，在约阿尼纳城(Ioannina)的西北方向，与约阿尼纳城相距大约22千米，被认为是古希腊最古老的神谕所。

The Balloon-Hoax
气球骗局

发表于1844年的科幻小说《气球骗局》(*The Balloon-Hoax*, 1844)采用新闻报道的形式，“科学”地报道了梅森先生乘坐最新研制的热气球飞越大西洋的事件，可以说这是爱伦·坡关注科学发展、尊崇科学的典型例子。小说的标题“气球骗局”已经指出本文纯属虚构，但高明的爱伦·坡却在其中注入了某些真实色彩，于是骗局就越发扑朔迷离。其一，它反映了人类征服天空的梦想。可以说，《气球骗局》是顺乎民意而作，是“新瓶装旧酒”，是旧梦在工业革命时代披上缤纷外衣的再次呈现。其二，它基于科学知识和科学发现之上。其三，《气球骗局》是建立在“科学原理”之上。在小说中，坡对飞越大西洋的气球的技术细节做了精确描述，对关键之处的科学原理进行了说明。最后，坡的《气球骗局》采取了新闻报道的形式。种种科学的叙事手段让坡的《气球骗局》显得更加真实。坡的《气球骗局》带有很强的现实色彩，他关注人们的梦想，追踪最新的科技发展，采用“科学”的叙述方式，通过热气球载人飞行的情节结构，介绍了假想的飞行过程。他抓住人们的好奇心，利用夹杂最离奇幻想的物理定律和自己虚构出的一些科学定律来解释一切自然秘密。不管是既定的科学学说还是时兴的科学假说，爱伦·坡都喜欢将其融入自己的小说。这样一来，他就虚构了一个人们不得不信的科学谎言。因为，这样的骗局再一次激起了人们心中潜存的空中飞行的梦想，你说，谁还会忍心去撕破它那美丽无比的柔情面纱呢。本文节选了该短篇的前半部分，详细介绍了用气球制造骗局的经过。

[Astounding News by Express, *via* Norfolk! — The Atlantic crossed in Three Days! Signal Triumph of Mr. Monck Mason's Flying Machine! — Arrival at Sullivan's Island, near Charles town, S.C., of Mr. Mason, Mr. Robert Holland, Mr. Henson, Mr. Harrison Ainsworth, and four others, in the Steering Balloon, "Victoria," after a passage of Seventy-five Hours from Land to Land! Full Particulars of the Voyage!

The subjoined *jeu d'esprit* with the preceding heading in magnificent capitals, well interspersed with notes of admiration, was originally published, as matter of fact, in the "New York Sun," a daily newspaper, and therein fully subserved the purpose of creating indigestible aliment for the *quid-nuncs* during the few hours intervening between a couple of the Charleston mails. The rush for the "sole paper which had the news," was something beyond even the prodigious; and, in fact, if (as some assert) the "Victoria" *did* not absolutely accomplish the voyage recorded, it will be difficult to assign a reason why she *should* not have accomplished it.]

THE great problem is at length solved! The air, as well as the earth and the ocean, has been subdued by science, and will become a common and convenient highway for mankind. *The Atlantic has been actually crossed in a Balloon*! and this too without difficulty — without any great apparent danger — with thorough control of the machine — and in the inconceivably brief period of seventy-five hours from shore to shore! By the energy of an agent at Charleston, S.C., we are enabled to be the first to furnish the public with a detailed account of this most extraordinary voyage, which was performed between Saturday, the 6th instant, at 11, A.M., and 2, P.M., on Tuesday, the 9th instant, by Sir Everard Bringhurst; Mr. Osborne, a nephew of Lord

发自诺福克的特快新闻：三天跨越大西洋！蒙克·梅森先生的飞行器获得巨大成功！梅森先生、罗伯特·霍兰先生、亨森先生、哈里森·埃斯沃斯先生以及另四人乘坐可控气球“维多利亚”号，历经75个小时的越洋飞行后，抵达南卡罗来纳州查尔斯顿市附近的萨利文岛！所有飞行细节为您一一道来！

上述摘要用醒目的大写字母写成，随后的正文妙趣横生，充满溢美之词，其实它最初是发表在《纽约太阳报》这家日报上的。在邮差给查尔斯顿市分别送来快报和日报之间的几个小时内，它为那些热衷于小道消息的人提供了一份食而不化的美食。随后，人们蜂拥而至，购买“刊登独家新闻”的这份报纸，场面十分壮观。说实在的，如果像有的人说的那样，“维多利亚”号根本没有彻底完成报纸刊登的这次航行，那要找一个它竟然没有完成的理由也是颇为困难的。

这个重要的问题终于被解决了！继地球和海洋之后，天空也被科学征服了，并将成为人类一条常见且便捷的通道。千真万确，人类乘坐气球飞越了大西洋！而且这次飞越没有任何困难——没有遇到任何明显的危险——气球也始终在控制之下——且在短短的75个小时之内从大西洋一岸飞抵另一岸，不可思议。由于本报在南卡罗来纳州查尔斯顿市的一名代理人的努力，我们得以第一时间向公众详细报道此次非同寻常的航行。此次航行从本月6日星期六上午11点开始到本月9日星期二下午2点结束。埃弗拉德·布林霍斯特爵士、本廷克勋爵的侄子奥斯本先生、著名的气球驾驶员蒙克·梅森先生和罗伯特·霍兰先生、《杰克·雪柏德》等书的作者哈里森·埃斯沃斯先生、亨森先生（他最近设计的飞行器并未成功）——以及来

Bentinck's; Mr. Monck Mason and Mr. Robert Holland, the well-known ronauts; Mr. Harrison Ainsworth, author of "Jack Sheppard," etc.; and Mr. Henson, the projector of the late unsuccessful flying machine — with two seamen from Woolwich — in all, eight persons. The particulars furnished below may be relied on as authentic and accurate in every respect, as, with a slight exception, they are copied *verbatim* from the joint diaries of Mr. Monck Mason and Mr. Harrison Ainsworth, to whose politeness our agent is also indebted for much verbal information respecting the balloon itself, its construction, and other matters of interest. The only alteration in the MS. received, has been made for the purpose of throwing the hurried account of our agent, Mr. Forsyth, into a connected and intelligible form.

THE BALLOON.

Two very decided failures, of late — those of Mr. Henson and Sir George Cayley — had much weakened the public interest in the subject of aerial navigation. Mr. Henson's scheme (which at first was considered very feasible even by men of science,) was founded upon the principle of an inclined plane, started from an eminence by an extrinsic force, applied and continued by the revolution of impinging vanes, in form and number resembling the vanes of a windmill. But, in all the experiments made with models at the Adelaide Gallery, it was found that the operation of these fans not only did not propel the machine, but actually impeded its flight. The only propelling force it ever exhibited, was the mere *impetus* acquired from the descent of the inclined plane; and this *impetus* carried the machine farther when the vanes were at rest, than when they were in motion — a fact

自英国乌里奇的两名水手——总共八人参加了此次航行。以下提供的细节全都准确可靠，因为除了一点稍稍例外，其余的就像是逐字逐句抄自蒙克·梅森先生和哈里森·埃斯沃斯先生共同记录的日记。他们彬彬有礼，还向我们的代理人口头介绍了许多关于气球本身及其构造的知识，和其他一些有趣的情况。我们对来稿唯一的改动就是把我们的代理人福赛思先生匆匆写就的报道变成前后连贯、通俗易懂的文字。

气　球

最近的两次彻底的失败——亨森先生和乔治·卡利爵士的两次失败——大大降低了人们对于空中航行这个话题的兴趣。亨森先生的方案最初连科学家都认为是切实可行的，它所依据的是斜面原理，通过外力使飞行器从一高地起飞，然后由空气冲击叶片所形成的旋转提供动力保持飞行，叶片的形状和数量都与风车的叶片类似。但是在阿德莱德展馆[①]用模型进行的所有试验中，人们发现这些叶片的转动不但没有推动飞行器，事实上反而阻碍了它的飞行。飞行器显现的唯一动力仅仅是靠斜面下降所获得的推动力，并且这个推动力在叶片静止时比叶片运动时能使飞行器飞行得更远——这一事实充分地证明了这些叶片毫无用处。而失去了同时作为支持力的推动力，飞行器必然会坠落。有鉴于此，乔治·卡利爵士才仅考

① 阿德莱德展馆，1830年雅各布·帕金斯建立的一座博物馆，旨在伦敦展览新发明。或作“皇家阿德莱德展览馆”。

which sufficiently demonstrates their inutility; and in the absence of the propelling, which was also the *sustaining* power, the whole fabric would necessarily descend. This consideration led Sir George Cayley to think only of adapting a propeller to some machine having of itself an independent power of support — in a word, to a balloon; the idea, however, being novel, or original, with Sir George, only so far as regards the mode of its application to practice. He exhibited a model of his invention at the Polytechnic Institution. The propelling principle, or power, was here, also, applied to interrupted surfaces, or vanes, put in revolution. These vanes were four in number, but were found entirely ineffectual in moving the balloon, or in aiding its ascending power. The whole project was thus a complete failure.

It was at this juncture that Mr. Monck Mason (whose voyage from Dover to Weilburg in the balloon, "Nassau," occasioned so much excitement in 1837,) conceived the idea of employing the principle of the Archimedean screw for the purpose of propulsion through the air — rightly attributing the failure of Mr. Henson's scheme, and of Sir George Cayley's, to the interruption of surface in the independent vanes. He made the first public experiment at Willis's Rooms, but afterwards removed his model to the Adelaide Gallery.

Like Sir George Cayley's balloon, his own was an ellipsoid. Its length was thirteen feet six inches — height, six feet eight inches. It contained about three hundred and twenty cubic feet of gas, which, if pure hydrogen, would support twenty-one pounds upon its first inflation, before the gas has time to deteriorate or escape. The weight of the whole machine and apparatus was seventeen pounds — leaving about four pounds to spare. Beneath the centre of the balloon, was a

虑将推进器装进某种自身拥有独立支撑力的飞行器——也就是说，把推进器装在气球上。乔治爵士的这个想法虽然是新颖的，具有独创性的，但只是要运用实践检验的一个方法。他在理工学院展示了他发明的模型，推动原理或者说是推动力展示时也被运用到不断旋转、各自独立的叶面，或者说叶片上。叶片共有四个，但是对于推动气球一点用处也没有，也无法推动它上升。因此这整个方案就是个彻底的失败。

就是在这个时刻，蒙克·梅森[①]先生(他曾在1837年乘坐"拿骚"号[②]从多佛抵达威尔堡，引起巨大轰动)想到了使用阿基米德螺旋[③]原理，以达到空中推进的目的——他不无道理地将亨森先生和乔治·卡利爵士计划的失败归咎于各叶片被分割成多个叶面。他在威利斯实验室进行了第一次公开试验，但随后把模型迁至阿德莱德展馆。

他的气球和乔治·卡利爵士的一样，也是椭圆形的，长13英尺6英寸，高6英尺8英寸。气球能容纳约320立方英尺的气体，如果充

① 作者根据英国气球驾驶员托马斯·蒙克·梅森创造的人物。

② "拿骚"号气球，原名"皇家沃克斯豪尔气球"(The Royal Vauxhall Balloon)，1836年11月7日，该气球由伦敦皇家沃克斯豪尔花园成功飞抵德国拿骚。为纪念降落地点，后来改名为"拿骚"号。托马斯·梅森、罗伯特·霍兰德、查尔斯·格林等四人参加了此次飞行。

③ 阿基米德螺旋，古希腊数学家阿基米德为解决用尼罗河水灌溉土地的难题，发明了圆筒状的螺旋扬水器，后人称它为"阿基米德螺旋"。当把阿基米德螺旋装置浸入水中并旋转摇柄时，它能把水抽上来。这里采用了同样的方法使气球中的汽油上升。

frame of light wood, about nine feet long, and rigged on to the balloon itself with a network in the customary manner. From this framework was suspended a wicker basket or car.

The screw consists of an axis of hollow brass tube, eighteen inches in length, through which, upon a semi-spiral inclined at fifteen degrees, pass a series of steel wire radii, two feet long, and thus projecting a foot on either side. These radii are connected at the outer extremities by two bands of flattened wire — the whole in this manner forming the framework of the screw, which is completed by a covering of oiled silk cut into gores, and tightened so as to present a tolerably uniform surface. At each end of its axis this screw is supported by pillars of hollow brass tube descending from the hoop. In the lower ends of these tubes are holes in which the pivots of the axis revolve. From the end of the axis which is next the car, proceeds a shaft of steel, connecting the screw with the pinion of a piece of spring machinery fixed in the car. By the operation of this spring, the screw is made to revolve with great rapidity, communicating a progressive motion to the whole. By means of the rudder, the machine was readily turned in any direction. The spring was of great power, compared with its dimensions, being capable of raising forty-five pounds upon a barrel of four inches diameter, after the first turn, and gradually increasing as it was wound up. It weighed, altogether, eight pounds six ounces. The rudder was a light frame of cane covered with silk, shaped somewhat like a battledoor, and was about three feet long, and at the widest, one foot. Its weight was about two ounces. It could be

入的是纯氢气的话，那么在刚刚充气之后、气体有所漏掉或者纯度降低之前，它能支撑起21磅的重量。整个飞行器及其装置的重量为17磅——预留了大约4磅的承载能力。气球的正下方是一个轻木料做成的框架，大约9英尺长，以惯常的方式用一个网固定在气球上。此框架悬吊着一个藤编筐，或者可以叫做吊舱。

这个螺旋装置有一根18英寸长的空心铜管轴，一条条两英尺长的钢线辐条倾斜15度，以半螺旋方式穿过中心轴，因此在它两边各伸出一英尺。辐条的外端用两根扁平的金属线相互连接——就此构成了螺旋装置的框架。最后蒙上多块三角形的油绸将其绷紧，表面基本平整。在中心轴的两端，螺旋装置由一根根空心铜管柱子支撑着，这些柱子则是从箍环垂下的，它们底端有孔，中心轴的转轴可旋于其中。中心轴接近吊舱的一端延伸出一根钢柄，将螺旋装置和固定在吊舱上的一个发条装置的齿轮相连。通过这个发条的运作，螺旋装置便能以极快的速度旋转，从而使整个飞行器向前运动。再经由舵的操控，飞行器便能轻易地改变航行方向。与其大小相比，这个发条装置可说功能强大。直径4英寸的圆管拧了第一圈之后，便能提起45磅的重量，然后随着发条越拧越紧，拉力也逐渐增加。发条装置自身重量为8磅6盎司。舵是一个轻巧的木质框架，包着油绸，形状有点类似球拍，大约3英尺长，最宽处有1英尺，重约2盎司。这个舵可以平置，也可以上下左右随意控制，这样气球驾驶员就能把在航行途中由于倾斜而必然产生的空气阻力传送到他想要施加力量的任何一边，从而从相反方向控制气球飞行方向。

turned *flat*, and directed upwards or downwards, as well as to the right or left; and thus enabled the ronaut to transfer the resistance of the air which in an inclined position it must generate in its passage, to any side upon which he might desire to act; thus determining the balloon in the opposite direction.

This model (which, through want of time, we have necessarily described in an imperfect manner,) was put in action at the Adelaide Gallery, where it accomplished a velocity of five miles per hour; although, strange to say, it excited very little interest in comparison with the previous complex machine of Mr. Henson — so resolute is the world to despise anything which carries with it an air of simplicity. To accomplish the great desideratum of rial navigation, it was very generally supposed that some exceedingly complicated application must be made of some unusually profound principle in dynamics.

So well satisfied, however, was Mr. Mason of the ultimate success of his invention, that he determined to construct immediately, if possible, a balloon of sufficient capacity to test the question by a voyage of some extent — the original design being to cross the British Channel, as before, in the Nassau balloon. To carry out his views, he solicited and obtained the patronage of Sir Everard Bringhurst and Mr. Osborne, two gentlemen well known for scientific acquirement, and especially for the interest they have exhibited in the progress of rostation. The project, at the desire of Mr. Osborne, was kept a profound secret from the public — the only persons entrusted with the design being those actually engaged in the construction of the machine, which was built (under the superintendence of Mr. Mason, Mr. Holland, Sir Everard Bringhurst, and Mr. Osborne,) at the seat of the latter gentleman near Penstruthal,

由于时间关系，这个模型我们只能简要介绍。在阿德莱德展馆投入试飞时，它的速度达到了每小时5英里。尽管说来奇怪，但与亨森先生之前那个复杂的飞行器相比，这个飞行器模型并没有引起众人的兴趣——世人是如此决然地藐视任何看似简单的东西。人们普遍认为，要实现伟大的空中航行目标，就必须用一些异常深奥的动力学原理来制造某种极其复杂的飞行器。

然而，梅森先生确信他的发明终将获得成功，因此他决定只要一有可能，就立即制造一个容量足够大的气球，用一次距离适中的航行来检验他的看法——最初他计划像之前驾驶“拿骚”号气球一样，飞越英吉利海峡。为了实现他的想法，他恳求并且得到了埃弗拉德·布林霍斯特爵士和奥斯本先生的资助。这两位绅士在科学方面的学识闻名遐迩，尤其为大家所熟知的是，他们对气球飞行方面所取得的进步饶有兴趣。依照奥斯本先生的愿望，这项方案对公众完全保密——知道这项设计的只有那些真正参与飞行器建造工作的人。该飞行器在梅森先生、霍兰先生、埃弗拉德·布林霍斯特爵士以及奥斯本先生的监督下，建于奥斯本先生位于威尔士彭斯特拉索尔附近的别墅。亨森先生在朋友埃斯沃斯先生的陪同下，于上周六被允许亲眼看到了气球——当时两位绅士签署了参与本次历险活动的最终协议。至于两名水手为何也参与了探险小组，本报不得而

in Wales. Mr. Henson, accompanied by his friend Mr. Ainsworth, was admitted to a private view of the balloon, on Saturday last — when the two gentlemen made final arrangements to be included in the adventure. We are not informed for what reason the two seamen were also included in the party — but, in the course of a day or two, we shall put our readers in possession of the minutest particulars respecting this extraordinary voyage.

The balloon is composed of silk, varnished with the liquid gum caoutchouc. It is of vast dimensions, containing more than 40,000 cubic feet of gas; but as coal gas was employed in place of the more expensive and inconvenient hydrogen, the supporting power of the machine, when fully inflated, and immediately after inflation, is not more than about 2,500 pounds. The coal gas is not only much less costly, but is easily procured and managed.

For its introduction into common use for purposes of aerostation, we are indebted to Mr. Charles Green. Up to his discovery, the process of inflation was not only exceedingly expensive, but uncertain. Two, and even three days, have frequently been wasted in futile attempts to procure a sufficiency of hydrogen to fill a balloon, from which it had great tendency to escape, owing to its extreme subtlety, and its affinity for the surrounding atmosphere. In a balloon sufficiently perfect to retain its contents of coal-gas unaltered, in quantity or amount, for six months, an equal quantity of hydrogen could not be maintained in equal purity for six weeks.

The supporting power being estimated at 2,500 pounds, and the united weights of the party amounting only to about 1,200, there was left a surplus of 1,300, of which again 1,200 was exhausted by ballast,

知——但在这一两天内，我们将让读者获悉本次非凡之旅的所有相关细节。

气球是由涂有液体橡胶的绸布制成的，它庞大的体积可以容纳超过40 000立方英尺的气体，但由于使用了煤气而不是更加昂贵、也不方便的氢气，当气球刚刚充满气之后，飞行器的承受力不会超过2 500英磅。煤气不仅便宜得多，而且容易购买，使用方便。

煤气在气球飞行方面的普遍应用，应当归功于查尔斯·格林[①]先生。在他之前，气球充气不仅极为昂贵，而且不稳定，人们常常徒劳地花上两三天去获取足以充满一个气球的氢气。因为氢极其活泼，对周围大气有很强的亲和性，它非常容易从气球中漏掉。如果一个气球能很好地将充入其内的煤气保持六个月，重量不变，那么同等重量的氢气，想要保持同样的纯度，六个星期都做不到。

飞行器的承受力估计在2 500磅左右，探险小组成员的总重量

① 查尔斯·格林(1785—1870)，19世纪英国最有名的气球驾驶员，1821年首次驾驶煤气气球飞行。下文提及的调节绳也是他发明的。

arranged in bags of different sizes, with their respective weights marked upon them — by cordage, barometers, telescopes, barrels containing provision for a fortnight, water-casks, cloaks, carpet-bags, and various other indispensable matters, including a coffee-warmer, contrived for warming coffee by means of slack-lime, so as to dispense altogether with fire, if it should be judged prudent to do so. All these articles, with the exception of the ballast, and a few trifles, were suspended from the hoop overhead. The car is much smaller and lighter, in proportion, than the one appended to the model. It is formed of a light wicker, and is wonderfully strong, for so frail looking a machine. Its rim is about four feet deep. The rudder is also very much larger, in proportion, than that of the model; and the screw is considerably smaller. The balloon is furnished besides with a grapnel, and a guide-rope; which latter is of the most indispensable importance. A few words, in explanation, will here be necessary for such of our readers as are not conversant with the details of aerostation.

As soon as the balloon quits the earth, it is subjected to the influence of many circumstances tending to create a difference in its weight; augmenting or diminishing its ascending power. For example, there may be a disposition of dew upon the silk, to the extent, even, of several hundred pounds; ballast has then to be thrown out, or the machine may descend. This ballast being discarded, and a clear sunshine evaporating the dew, and at the same time expanding the gas in the silk, the whole will again rapidly ascend. To check this ascent, the only recource [recourse] is, (or rather *was*, until Mr. Green's invention of the guide-rope,) the permission of the escape of gas from the valve; but, in the loss of gas, is a proportionate general loss of

只有大约1 200磅，剩余的1 300磅中有1 200磅被压舱物所消耗了。压舱物装在大小不等的袋子里，各自标有自身的重量——其余物品有绳索、气压计、望远镜、装有两周食物的几个桶、水桶、斗篷、旅行袋以及其他各种各样的必需品，包括为了避免生火而用熟石灰热咖啡的咖啡壶，不知这么做算不算得上谨慎。除了压舱物和几件零零碎碎的东西，其他物品全都悬挂在头顶的箍环上。按比例讲，吊舱比模型上的更小更轻巧。它是用很轻的藤条编织而成的，对于看起来如此不坚固的飞行器来说，它显得非常结实。吊舱的边框大约4英尺高。按其比例来说，方向舵也比原来的模型大得多，而螺旋装置则小很多。此外气球也配置了一个小铁锚和一根导绳，后者必不可少、十分重要。在此有必要作些补充说明，因为我们的一些读者对于气球飞行的细节并不熟悉。

气球一离开地面，就会受到许多因素的影响，重量有可能会改变，从而增加或者减小它的爬升力。比如说，气球上会凝聚许多露水，甚至能够重达几百磅。这样的话必须抛出压舱物，不然飞行器就会下降。在抛掉压舱物以后，如果晴朗的阳光使露水蒸发，同时气囊中的气体膨胀，整个飞行器就会快速上升。为了控制这种上升状态，只能借助于通过阀门放掉气体，或者更准确地说，在格林先生发明调节绳之前，只能这么做；但在放掉气体的同时，爬升力也会相应降低，所以在较为短暂的一段时间内，性能最好的气球必须彻底利用一切资源，返回地面。这在过去极大地妨碍了长途飞行。

ascending power; so that, in a comparatively brief period, the best-constructed balloon must necessarily exhaust all its resources, and come to the earth. This was the great obstacle to voyages of length.

The guide-rope remedies the difficulty in the simplest manner conceivable. It is merely a very long rope which is suffered to trail from the car, and the effect of which is to prevent the balloon from changing its level in any material degree. If, for example, there should be a deposition of moisture upon the silk, and the machine begins to descend in consequence, there will be no necessity for discharging ballast to remedy the increase of weight, for it is remedied, or counteracted, in an exactly just proportion, by the deposit on the ground of just so much of the end of the rope as is necessary. If, on the other hand, any circumstances should cause undue levity, and consequent ascent, this levity is immediately counteracted by the additional weight of rope upraised from the earth. Thus, the balloon can neither ascend or descend, except within very narrow limits, and its resources, either in gas or ballast, remain comparatively unimpaired. When passing over an expanse of water, it becomes necessary to employ small kegs of copper or wood, filled with liquid ballast of a lighter nature than water. These float, and serve all the purposes of a mere rope on land. Another most important office of the guide-rope, is to point out the direction of the balloon. The rope drags, either on land or sea, while the balloon is free; the latter, consequently, is always in advance, when any progress whatever is made: a comparison, therefore, by means of the compass, of the relative positions of the two objects, will always indicate the course. In the same way, the angle formed by the rope with the vertical axis of

调节绳以人们能够想到的最简单的方式克服了这个困难。它只是一根拖在吊舱后面的很长的绳子，其作用是阻止气球的水平飞行产生任何实质性变化。例如，如果气囊上凝结了露水，飞行器因此而下降，此时没有必要抛出压舱物来抵消增加的重量，因为严格按照比例，将所需长度的调节绳拖在地上，就可以抵消了；另一方面，如果任何情况致使气球过轻并且因此上升，从地面上收回调节绳所增加的重量会马上纠正这种过轻的现象。这样，除了在非常有限的范围内，气球既不会上升也不会下降，而它的资源，不管是气体还是压舱物，相对而言没有削减。当飞越辽阔的水域时，就需要使用一些小的铜制或者木制的水桶，其中装满比重比水轻的液体。这些水桶漂浮水面，作用如同陆地上的调节绳。调节绳另一个重要的功能就是指引气球的方向。当气球升在空中时，调节绳无论是在陆地还是海洋上，都会拖在下面，因此气球前进时，都处在调节绳的前方。这样，用指南针比较两者的相对位置，就能测出气球的航向。同样地，调节绳与飞行器纵坐标轴形成的夹角就能表明飞行速度。当角度为零时——也就是说当调节绳垂直悬挂时，整个装置是静止不动的；但是角度越大，也就是说，气球离调节绳末端越远，速度也就会越大。反之则越慢。

the machine, indicates the velocity. When there is no angle — in other words, when the rope hangs perpendicularly, the whole apparatus is stationary; but the larger the angle, that is to say, the farther the balloon precedes the end of the rope, the greater the velocity; and the converse.

As the original design was to cross the British Channel, and alight as near Paris as possible, the voyagers had taken the precaution to prepare themselves with passports directed to all parts of the Continent[①], specifying the nature of the expedition, as in the case of the Nassau voyage, and entitling the adventurers to exemption from the usual formalities of office: unexpected events, however, rendered these passports superfluous.

The inflation was commenced very quietly at daybreak, on Saturday morning, the 6th instant, in the Court-Yard of Weal-Vor House, Mr. Osborne's seat, about a mile from Penstruthal, in North Wales; and at 7 minutes past 11, every thing being ready for departure, the balloon was set free, rising gently but steadily, in a direction nearly South; no use being made, for the first half hour, of either the screw or the rudder. We proceed now with the journal, as transcribed by Mr. Forsyth from the joint MSS. of Mr. Monck Mason, and Mr. Ainsworth. The body of the journal, as given, is in the hand-writing of Mr. Mason, and a P. S. is appended, each day, by Mr. Ainsworth, who has in preparation, and will shortly give the public a more minute, and no doubt, a thrillingly interesting account of the voyage.

① 指欧洲大陆。实际上，英国属于欧洲，但是英国却习惯把英国以外的其他欧洲地区称为欧洲大陆。

因为最初的计划是飞越英吉利海峡[1]，尽可能靠近巴黎降落，所有参与飞行者都事先准备好了出入欧洲各国的护照，就像"拿骚"号飞行那次一样说明了本次探险的性质，这样探险者便能免除办理常规的手续。然而，一些意想不到的事情使这些护照变得多余。

本月6日星期六早上，威尔士北部距离彭斯特拉索尔大约一英里处，在奥斯本先生的别墅，威尔沃庄园[2]的庭院中，充气在破晓时分静静地开始了。11点零7分，飞行的一切事务准备就绪，气球开始飞离地面，一直朝偏南方徐徐上升。在一开始的半小时内，螺旋装置和方向舵均未使用。下面本报将报导福赛思先生抄录的蒙克·梅森先生和埃斯沃斯先生的联合日记，日记正文由梅森先生执笔，每天的附记由埃斯沃斯先生完成。就此次航行，他正在准备一篇更为详细、无疑也更能引人入胜的报道，不久就可以与读者见面。

① 英吉利海峡，是隔离英国与欧洲大陆之间的海峡（西经1度0分，北纬50度20分）。其最狭窄的水域为多佛尔海峡，多佛尔隔海与法国加莱相望。历史上曾在此发生多次军事冲突和海战。

② 是坡小说中人物的虚构庄园，是"维多利亚"号气球飞往萨利文岛之前的装配地。

The Premature Burial
过早埋葬

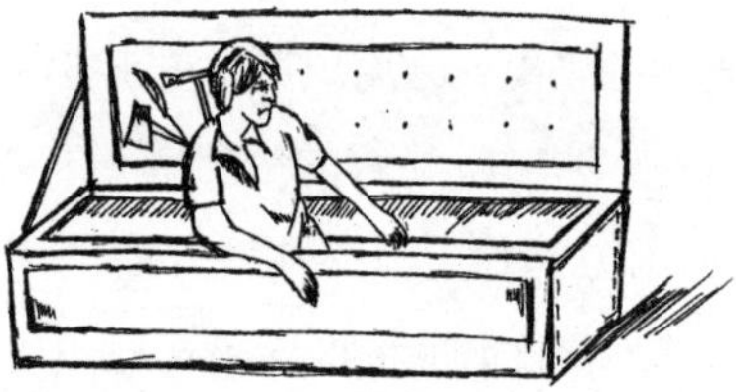

《过早埋葬》(*The Premature Burial*, 1844) 描写了主人公对死亡的恐惧，唤起了众多读者的共鸣。这一恐惧沉积在人们内心深处，是人们在头一秒钟划过脑海，不愿意花费第二秒钟多加考虑的事情。然而坡却洋洋洒洒数千字，通过引用医学上和平常经历中的直接证据来证明活埋一直在上演。被活埋者有男人有女人，有炮兵军官有市民的妻子，对于活埋的时间、地点，主人公均加以详细说明。最令人毛骨悚然的是，主人公通过自己因为失忆令他以为自己被埋在棺材里的真实经历，让读者与其共同经历了一次起死回生的体验。通过这一手法，小说所营造出的恐怖可谓达到了令人发指的地步。据说许多人看了爱伦·坡的小说后对土葬产生了恐惧心理，害怕自己也被“过早埋葬”了。这在一定程度上说明了爱伦·坡营造的恐怖之深。小说展现的是对假死状态的恐惧，突出了由假死走向死亡的痛苦过程的体验。《过早埋葬》并非全然是哥特式的怪异和恐怖，而是建立在科学基础之上，这使得小说具有更真实的恐怖氛围。诚然，我们不能简单地说爱伦·坡只是为了制造恐怖来取悦读者。他借主人公之口表达了他对人生的看法：“有的时候，悲惨的人世也许像地狱一样，即使在理性的冷静眼光里，也是如此。但人类的想象绝不能像卡拉提斯那样，随心所欲地在每一个洞穴探险。唉，源源不断的阴森恐惧不能当作单纯的想象，但是，如同阿弗拉斯布游历奥克苏同时陪伴他左右的群魔一样，这些恐惧必须沉沉睡去，否则它们就会一口吞噬我们——他们必须受点委屈，睡过去，否则我们就是死路一条。”小说结尾这一段话意味深长。坡借主人公的死亡经历阐明了这样一个道理：人要战胜恐惧，不能被恐惧打倒。或者也可以说，人最大的敌人是自我，恐惧是内心深处畏惧前进的表现，要战胜恐惧，唯有战胜自我。由此我们可以看到，隐藏在作品深处的是爱伦·坡对人类内心思维的探索和观察，是对人类生存状况的关注和思考。本文为节选。

My own case differed in no important particular from those mentioned in medical books. Sometimes, without any apparent cause, I sank, little by little, into a condition of semi-syncope, or half swoon; and, in this condition, without pain, without ability to stir, or, strictly speaking, to think, but with a dull lethargic consciousness of life and of the presence of those who surrounded my bed, I remained, until the crisis of the disease restored me, suddenly, to perfect sensation. At other times I was quickly and impetuously smitten. I grew sick, and numb, and chilly, and dizzy, and so fell prostrate at once. Then, for weeks, all was void, and black, and silent, and Nothing became the universe. Total annihilation could be no more. From these latter attacks I awoke, however, with a gradation slow in proportion to the suddenness of the seizure. Just as the day dawns to the friendless and houseless beggar who roams the streets throughout the long desolate winter night — just so tardily — just so wearily — just so cheerily came back the light of the Soul to me.

Apart from the tendency to trance, however, my general health appeared to be good; nor could I perceive that it was at all affected by the one prevalent malady — unless, indeed, an idiosyncrasy in my ordinary *sleep* may be looked upon as superinduced. Upon awaking from slumber, I could never gain, at once, thorough possession of my senses, and always remained, for many minutes, in much bewilderment and perplexity; — the mental faculties in general, but the memory in especial, being in a condition of absolute abeyance.

In all that I endured there was no physical suffering, but of moral distress an infinitude. My fancy grew charnel. I talked "of worms, of tombs and epitaphs." I was lost in reveries of death, and the idea of

我的情况与医学书上说的大同小异。有的时候，虽然没有明显的原因，我也会慢慢地陷入似睡非睡的状态，或者说是半昏迷的状态。此时，我感受不到疼痛，无法动弹，严格地说，也无法思考，但昏昏然还能意识到生命的存在，能意识到病床旁边那些人的存在。我就那么躺着，直到病情突变，冷不防完全恢复了知觉。有的时候，病魔突然猛烈袭击，我就会病倒，失去知觉，浑身冰冷，头昏眼花，一下子倒在地上。然后几个星期，一切都是虚空，一切都是漆黑一团，一切都是寂静无声的，天地万物，一片虚无，彻底的毁灭也不过如此。相比于发病速度，从这样的发作中苏醒，速度很慢。就像漫漫冬夜，萧索无人，流浪街头的乞丐举目无亲，上无片瓦，下无寸土，黎明降临于他，就如同灵魂之光重归我身，如此缓慢，如此慵懒，却又如此让人振奋。

不过，除了容易昏厥，我的健康大体上还是好的，我也看不出来这种不可一世的疾病对我的健康有什么影响，只是平常的睡眠似乎平添了一种异常之处。醒来的时候，我从来都不能一下子完全恢复意识，总是要迷迷糊糊好一会儿，智力，尤其是记忆力，处于完全中止的状态。

我忍受的不是身体上的痛苦，而是心理上无尽的煎熬。我的幻想变得阴森恐怖，我会提到“爬虫、坟墓和墓志铭”，我深陷于死亡的狂想，被活埋的想法时刻占据着我的大脑。我可能遭受的危险令

premature burial held continual possession of my brain. The ghastly Danger to which I was subjected, haunted me day and night. In the former, the torture of meditation was excessive — in the latter, supreme. When the grim Darkness overspread the Earth, then, with very horror of thought, I shook — shook as the quivering plumes upon the hearse. When Nature could endure wakefulness no longer, it was with a struggle that I consented to sleep — for I shuddered to reflect that, upon awaking, I might find myself the tenant of a grave. And when, finally, I sank into slumber, it was only to rush at once into a world of phantasms, above which, with vast, sable, overshadowing wing, hovered, predominant, the one sepulchral Idea.

From the innumerable images of gloom which thus oppressed me in dreams, I select for record but a solitary vision. Methought I was immersed in a cataleptic trance of more than usual duration and profundity. Suddenly there came an icy hand upon my forehead, and an impatient, gibbering voice whispered the word "Arise!" within my ear.

I sat erect. The darkness was total. I could not see the figure of him who had aroused me. I could call to mind neither the period at which I had fallen into the trance, nor the locality in which I then lay. While I remained motionless, and busied in endeavors to collect my thoughts, the cold hand grasped me fiercely by the wrist, shaking it petulantly, while the gibbering voice said again:

"Arise! did I not bid thee arise?"

"And who," I demanded, "art thou?"

"I have no name in the regions which I inhabit," replied the voice, mournfully; "I was mortal, but am fiend. I was merciless, but am pitiful. Thou dost feel that I shudder. My teeth chatter as I speak,

人胆战心寒，不分白天黑夜缠绕着我。胡思乱想的折磨在白天让人不堪忍受，到了晚上，更是登峰造极。狰狞的黑暗笼罩着大地的时候，我心里全是恐怖的念头，浑身发抖，就像灵柩上飘摇的羽毛。出于本能，我实在犯困时，勉强入睡前总要挣扎一番，因为一想到醒来的时候，可能发现自己葬身坟墓，我就瑟瑟发抖。好不容易睡着了，却只是一刻不停地冲进幽灵的世界，那个阴森森的念头张开遮天蔽日、硕大无朋的黑翅膀，盘旋其上，主宰万物。

数不胜数的惨象在梦中压迫着我，从中我挑一个独一无二的幻象记录于此。我觉得自己强直性昏厥发作，时间比平时更长，程度更甚。突然，一只冰冷的手按着我的额头，有人对着我的耳朵极不耐烦、含混不清地小声说道："站起来！"

我坐了起来。四周一片黑暗，我看不到是谁唤醒了我，我既想不起昏厥时的情形，也想不起自己身处何处。我一动不动，竭力集中精神，那只冰冷的手猛地抓住我的手腕，粗暴地晃着，这时，含混不清的声音再次响起：

"站起来！我不是让你站起来吗？"

"你是谁？"我问道。

"在我生活的地方，我没有名字。"那个声音惨兮兮地回答道。"我曾经是人，如今是鬼，曾经冷酷，如今怜悯。你却能感到我在发抖，我说话时，牙齿咯咯作响，但不是因为夜的凄冷，不是因为无边

yet it is not with the chilliness of the night — of the night without end. But this hideousness is insufferable. How canst *thou* tranquilly sleep? I cannot rest for the cry of these great agonies. These sights are more than I can bear. Get thee up! Come with me into the outer Night, and let me unfold to thee the graves. Is not this a spectacle of wo? — Behold!"

I looked; and the unseen figure, which still grasped me by the wrist, had caused to be thrown open the graves of all mankind; and from each issued the faint phosphoric radiance of decay; so that I could see into the innermost recesses, and there view the shrouded bodies in their sad and solemn slumbers with the worm. But, alas! the real sleepers were fewer, by many millions, than those who slumbered not at all; and there was a feeble struggling; and there was a general sad unrest; and from out the depths of the countless pits there came a melancholy rustling from the garments of the buried. And, of those who seemed tranquilly to repose, I saw that a vast number had changed, in a greater or less degree, the rigid and uneasy position in which they had originally been entombed. And the voice again said to me, as I gazed:

"Is it not —oh! is it *not* a pitiful sight?" But, before I could find words to reply, the figure had ceased to grasp my wrist, the phosphoric lights expired, and the graves were closed with a sudden violence, while from out them arose a tumult of despairing cries, saying again, "Is it not — oh, God! is it *not* a very pitiful sight?"

Phantasies such as these, presenting themselves at night, extended their terrific influence far into my waking hours. My nerves became thoroughly unstrung, and I fell a prey to perpetual horror. I

之夜的凄冷。这惨象不堪忍受，你如何能睡得这般平静？这些痛苦的哀号让我不得宁静，这些景象我无法忍受。起来！和我一起走进黑夜之外的黑夜，让我展示万千坟墓给你看。看哪，这难道不是惨象？”

我放眼望去，那个无形之人仍然抓住我的手腕，他把人类所有的坟墓都打开了，每间墓室都因为腐烂而发出了微弱的磷光，我得以看到最隐秘的地方，目睹尸布裹身的尸体哀怨肃穆地与虫蚁共眠。天哪！真正的安息者要比那些根本没有入睡的人少上千万哪！无力的挣扎，到处都是哀怨的骚动，不计其数的坟墓深处，传来被埋者尸布的沙沙声，很是凄惨。那些看起来安然而眠的，我发现有不少或多或少地改变了最初下葬时僵直且不舒服的姿势。我正看着呢，那个声音又对我说道：

“这景象，啊，这景象难道不值得同情？”我还没想好如何回答，那个身影已经松开了我的手腕，磷光熄灭，万千坟墓猛地合上了，墓穴外响起一阵绝望的哀号，再次质问道：“这景象，啊，上帝呀，这景象难道不值得同情？”

诸如此类的幻象在夜里出现，我醒着的时候也深受可怕的影响。我变得极其神经质，时时刻刻都受着恐惧的折磨。无论是骑马，还是步行，还是纵情于任何一种需要我外出的活动，我都犹疑不

hesitated to ride, or to walk, or to indulge in any exercise that would carry me from home. In fact, I no longer dared trust myself out of the immediate presence of those who were aware of my proneness to catalepsy, lest, falling into one of my usual fits, I should be buried before my real condition could be ascertained. I doubted the care, the fidelity of my dearest friends. I dreaded that, in some trance of more than customary duration, they might be prevailed upon to regard me as irrecoverable. I even went so far as to fear that, as I occasioned much trouble, they might be glad to consider any very protracted attack as sufficient excuse for getting rid of me altogether. It was in vain they endeavored to reassure me by the most solemn promises. I exacted the most sacred oaths, that under no circumstances they would bury me until decomposition had so materially advanced as to render farther preservation impossible. And, even then, my mortal terrors would listen to no reason — would accept no consolation. I entered into a series of elaborate precautions. Among other things, I had the family vault so remodelled as to admit of being readily opened from within. The slightest pressure upon a long lever that extended far into the tomb would cause the iron portals to fly back. There were arrangements also for the free admission of air and light, and convenient receptacles for food and water, within immediate reach of the coffin intended for my reception. This coffin was warmly and softly padded, and was provided with a lid, fashioned upon the principle of the vault-door, with the addition of springs so contrived that the feeblest movement of the body would be sufficient to set it at liberty. Besides all this, there was suspended from the roof of the tomb, a large bell, the rope of which, it was designed, should extend

决。说实在的，我已不敢离开那些知道我会犯强直性昏厥症的人，害怕犯病时，还没等到实际情况搞清楚就被埋葬了。我怀疑最亲密的朋友对我的关怀与忠诚，我害怕如果某次昏厥比平时更久，别人会说服他们，视我为无可救药。我甚至害怕，由于我带来这么多麻烦，他们可能乐于把时间较长的发作当作彻底摆脱我的充分理由。他们竭力安慰我，郑重其事地向我保证，但这一切都是徒劳。我逼着他们许下最神圣的誓言，任何情况下，都要等我腐烂到不可能继续保存，才能下葬。但即便如此，我对死亡的恐惧使得我对理智置若罔闻，对别人的劝慰概不理会。我采取了一系列周密的预防措施，改建了家族墓穴，使其从内部可以轻易打开，如此等等。只需轻轻按动深入墓穴的长杆，铁门就会打开。此外，空气和光线可以随意透入墓穴，非常方便的地方放置了食物和水，在我的棺材里伸手就可以拿到。棺材的垫子柔软暖和，盖子是按金库门的原理设计的，另外装上了弹簧，身体的任何动作都足以把它打开。除了这一切，墓穴里还吊着一只大铃铛，按设计，铃铛的绳子应当穿过棺材，系在尸体的一只手上。但是，天啊，命运无常，岂可提防？即便这些设计巧妙的安全措施，也救不了命中注定要受活埋之苦的人，他还是要深受折磨啊！

through a hole in the coffin, and so be fastened to one of the hands of the corpse. But, alas! what avails the vigilance against the Destiny of man? Not even these well contrived securities sufficed to save from the uttermost agonies of living inhumation, a wretch to these agonies foredoomed!

There arrived an epoch — as often before there had arrived — in which I found myself emerging from total unconsciousness into the first feeble and indefinite sense of existence. Slowly — with a tortoise gradation — approached the faint gray dawn of the psychal day. A torpid uneasiness. An apathetic endurance of dull pain. No care — no hope — no effort. Then, after a long interval, a ringing in the ears; then, after a lapse still longer, a pricking or tingling sensation in the extremities; then a seemingly eternal period of pleasurable quiescence, during which the awakening feelings are struggling into thought; then a brief re-sinking into non-entity; then a sudden recovery. At length the slight quivering of an eyelid, and immediately thereupon, an electric shock of a terror, deadly and indefinite, which sends the blood in torrents from the temples to the heart. And now the first positive effort to think. And now the first endeavor to remember. And now a partial and evanescent success. And now the memory has so far regained its dominion, that, in some measure, I am cognizant of my state. I feel that I am not awaking from ordinary sleep. I recollect that I have been subject to catalepsy. And now, at last, as if by the rush of an ocean, my shuddering spirit is overwhelmed by the one grim Danger — by the one spectral and ever-prevalent Idea.

For some minutes after this fancy possessed me, I remained without motion. And why? I could not summon courage to move. I

如同以前时有发生的那样，一个新的纪元开始了，我发现自己走出了完全无意识的状态，第一次有了若有若无、含混不清的生命意识。渐渐地，极其缓慢地，微弱的、鱼肚白的精神黎明来临了，麻木的不安，漠然的忍受隐痛，没有牵挂，没有希望，没有努力。然后，过了很久，耳朵里叮叮作响；然后，过了更久，手尖脚尖有了刺痛感；然后，好似没有尽头，是令人愉悦的静止，其间渐渐苏醒的情感竭力想转变为思考；然后，再一次暂时坠入虚无；然后是蓦然清醒。最后，眼皮轻轻跳动，随即，一阵致命的、模糊不清的恐惧触电一般地袭来，血液从太阳穴涌向心脏。这个时候，有了第一次主动思考；这个时候，有了第一次拼命回忆；这个时候，有了得而复失的局部胜利；这个时候，记忆力光复故土，在一定程度上，我明了了自己的情形。我觉得我不是从惯常的睡眠中清醒过来，我想起来了，自己一直深受强直性昏厥症之苦。最后，仿佛是大海奔涌而来，那个阴森恐怖的危险，那个幽灵般无所不在的念头，淹没了我颤抖的心灵。

我深陷于这种幻想不能自拔，有好一会儿，我一动不动。为什么呢？我没有勇气动弹，我不敢去求证自己的命运，然而我心底

dared not make the effort which was to satisfy me of my fate — and yet there was something at my heart which whispered me *it was sure*. Despair — such as no other species of wretchedness ever calls into being — despair alone urged me, after long irresolution, to uplift the heavy lids of my eyes. I uplifted them. It was dark — all dark. I knew that the fit was over. I knew that the crisis of my disorder had long passed. I knew that I had now fully recovered the use of my visual faculties — and yet it was dark — all dark — the intense and utter raylessness of the Night that endureth for evermore.

I endeavored to shriek; and my lips and my parched tongue moved convulsively together in the attempt — but no voice issued from the cavernous lungs, which, oppressed as if by the weight of some incumbent mountain, gasped and palpitated, with the heart, at every elaborate and struggling inspiration.

The movement of the jaws, in this effort to cry aloud, showed me that they were bound up, as is usual with the dead. I felt, too, that I lay upon some hard substance; and by something similar my sides were, also, closely compressed. So far, I had not ventured to stir any of my limbs — but now I violently threw up my arms, which had been lying at length, with the wrists crossed. They struck a solid wooden substance, which extended above my person at an elevation of not more than six inches from my face. I could no longer doubt that I reposed within a coffin at last.

And now, amid all my infinite miseries, came sweetly the cherub Hope — for I thought of my precautions. I writhed, and made spasmodic exertions to force open the lid: it would not move. I felt my wrists for the bell-rope: it was not to be found. And now the

某种东西对我悄声说它无须求证。在长时间的优柔寡断之后，绝望——其他任何一种不幸都不可能带来的绝望——独自敦促我抬起沉重的眼皮。我睁开眼睛，四周一片黑暗，我知道病情发作结束了，我知道疾病早有了转机，我知道我已经完全恢复了视觉，但四周是黑暗的，一片黑暗，漫漫长夜驱之不去、完完全全的黑暗。

我拼命尖叫，双唇和干燥的舌头一起抽搐，但胸腔并无声音传出，仿佛压着一座大山，每次用力的艰难呼吸，肺部就呼呼喘气，和心脏一起悸动。

我竭力大声喊叫，双唇的运动表明它们动弹不得，如同死人身上常见的那样，我还感到身下硬硬的，腰部两侧也被硬硬的东西紧紧压迫着。直到这个时候，我还没敢活动手脚，我的胳膊一直平伸、双手交叉，这时我猛地举起，撞在了某件结实的木质东西上，它就在我头顶不到六英寸的地方。我不再怀疑自己终于躺进了棺材。

这个时候，在我无限的苦难之中，款款走来了希望天使，因为我想起来了自己所做的预防措施。我扭动着，抽搐着，想要打开棺材盖子，可它一动不动。我在手腕上摸索着寻找铃铛的绳子，可它不见踪影。这个时候，慰藉逃之夭夭，令人更加望而生畏的绝望得

Comforter fled for ever, and a still sterner Despair reigned triumphant; for I could not help perceiving the absence of the paddings which I had so carefully prepared — and then, too, there came suddenly to my nostrils the strong peculiar odor of moist earth. The conclusion was irresistible. I was *not* within the vault. I had fallen into a trance while absent from home — while among strangers — when, or how, I could not remember — and it was they who had buried me as a dog — nailed up in some common coffin — and thrust, deep, deep, and for ever, into some ordinary and nameless *grave*.

As this awful conviction forced itself, thus, into the innermost chambers of my soul, I once again struggled to cry aloud. And in this second endeavor I succeeded. A long, wild, and continuous shriek, or yell, of agony, resounded through the realms of the subterrene Night.

"Hillo! hillo, there!" said a gruff voice, in reply.

"What the devil's the matter now?" said a second.

"Get out o' that!" said a third.

"What do you mean by yowling in that ere kind of style, like a cattymount"? said a fourth; and hereupon I was seized and shaken without ceremony, for several minutes, by a junto of very rough-looking individuals. They did not arouse me from my slumber — for I was wide awake when I screamed — but they restored me to the full possession of my memory.

This adventure occurred near Richmond, in Virginia. Accompanied by a friend, I had proceeded, upon a gunning expedition, some miles down the banks of the James River. Night approached, and we were overtaken by a storm. The cabin of a small sloop lying at anchor in the stream, and laden with garden mould, afforded us the

意洋洋地凌驾了一切，因为我发现自己小心翼翼备下的垫子不见了，而且，一股潮湿泥土强烈的怪味突然钻进我的鼻孔。结论不容置疑，我不在我家的墓穴之中，我昏昏睡去，却远在异乡，周围都是陌生人。这一切发生于何时，又是怎么发生的，我已经记不起来了，但就是这些陌生人，把我像狗一样埋掉了，钉在普普通通的棺材里，深深地、深深地、永永远远地把我扔进了一座普普通通的无名之墓。

正当这种可怕的想法占据了我灵魂最深处，我再一次拼命大叫。这一次成功了，长长的痛苦尖叫，或者说哀号，十分狂乱，连绵不绝，在冥冥长夜回荡。

"喂！喂！怎么了？"有人很不客气地回应道。

"到底怎么回事？"另一个人问道。

"别嚷嚷！"第三个人说道。

"你刚才那样像山猫一样嗥叫，什么意思？"第四个人问道。这时，几个看上去很野的家伙抓住我，肆意摇晃，他们没能把我从沉睡中唤醒——因为我尖叫的时候十分清醒——但他们帮助我彻底恢复了记忆力。

这件奇遇发生在弗吉尼亚州里士满市附近，我和一位朋友一起外出打猎，沿着詹姆士河走了几英里。夜幕降临，我们突遇暴雨，一条装满用于种花的泥土的小船，停在河边，成了我们唯一的栖身之地。我们充分利用这条船，在上面过了夜。我睡的铺位是船上仅有的两个之一——一艘六七十来吨的小船，其铺位就不用多说了吧。

only available shelter. We made the best of it, and passed the night on board. I slept in one of the only two berths in the vessel — and the berths of a sloop of sixty or seventy tons need scarcely be described. That which I occupied had no bedding of any kind. Its extreme width was eighteen inches. The distance of its bottom from the deck overhead, was precisely the same. I found it a matter of exceeding difficulty to squeeze myself in. Nevertheless, I slept soundly; and the whole of my vision — for it was no dream, and no nightmare — arose naturally from the circumstances of my position — from my ordinary bias of thought — and from the difficulty, to which I have alluded, of collecting my senses, and especially of regaining my memory, for a long time after awaking from slumber. The men who shook me were the crew of the sloop, and some laborers engaged to unload it. From the load itself came the earthly smell. The bandage about the jaws was a silk handkerchief in which I had bound up my head, in default of my customary nightcap.

The tortures endured, however, were indubitably quite equal, for the time, to those of actual sepulture. They were fearfully — they were inconceivably hideous; but out of Evil proceeded Good; for their very excess wrought in my spirit an inevitable revulsion. My soul acquired tone — acquired temper. I went abroad. I took vigorous exercise. I breathed the free air of Heaven. I thought upon other subjects than Death. I discarded my medical books. "Buchan[①]" I burned. I read no "Night Thoughts" — no fustian about church-yards — no bugaboo tales[②] — *such as this*. In short I became a new man, and lived a man's

① 指苏格兰医生威廉·巴肯 (William Buchan, 1729—1805) 所著的《家庭医学》一书。
② bugabootales，鬼怪故事，吓唬人的东西，常常夸大了其令人害怕或恐惧的程度。以前拼作 buggybow。

我睡的那个床铺没有被褥，最宽处也只有18英寸，从床到头顶的甲板恰好也是18英寸，我发现要挤上床极其困难。不过，我睡得很沉，我看到的一切——这绝不是梦，绝不是噩梦——自然是因为我所处位置的环境，因为我一贯偏执的想法，因为我上文提及的神志清醒很不容易，特别是因为醒后半天我还不能恢复记忆力。那些摇晃我的人是船员和卸货工人，货物本身有泥土气息，缠住嘴巴的是我缠在头上的一条丝质手绢，用来代替平时用的睡帽。

然而，我当时经受的折磨无疑和真正被活埋时的相差无几，这种折磨极其可怕，可怕得超乎想象。不过，否极泰来，过度的折磨不可避免地在我心里引起突变，我的灵魂获得了健康，获得了安宁。我周游列国，大力锻炼，呼吸着天空自由的空气，思考死亡以外的问题。我扔掉了医学书籍，烧掉了巴肯的书，不再阅读《夜思》[①]，有关墓地的天方夜谭以及鬼怪故事——例如本文。总之，我焕然一新，过上了正常人的生活。自从那个难忘的夜晚，我就永远地扔掉了阴森的恐惧，强直性昏厥症也随之消失。或许，恐惧不是这种病的结果，而是其原因吧。

① 指英国诗人爱德华·杨 (Edward Yong,1681—1765) 所著长诗《夜思》。

life. From that memorable night, I dismissed forever my charnel apprehensions, and with them vanished the cataleptic disorder, of which, perhaps, they had been less the consequence than the cause.

There are moments when, even to the sober eye of Reason, the world of our sad Humanity may assume the semblance of a Hell — but the imagination of man is no Carathis, to explore with impunity its every cavern. Alas! the grim legion of sepulchral terrors cannot be regarded as altogether fanciful — but, like the Demons in whose company Afrasiab made his voyage down the Oxus, they must sleep, or they will devour us — they must be suffered to slumber, or we perish.

有的时候，悲惨的人世也许像地狱一样，即使在理性的冷静眼光里，也是如此。但人类的想象绝不能像卡拉提斯[1]那样，随心所欲地在每一个洞穴探险。唉，源源不断的阴森恐惧不能当作单纯的想象，但是，如同阿弗拉斯布[2]游历奥克苏河时陪侍他左右的群魔一样，这些恐惧必须沉沉睡去，否则它们就会一口吞噬我们——他们必须受点委屈，睡过去，否则我们就是死路一条。

① 英国小说家贝克福德在其作品《瓦特克》(*Vathek*, 1786) 提到过卡拉提斯，将这位波斯历史上的真实人物描写成女巫。美国作家华莱士 (Horace Binney Wallace) 在其作品《斯坦利》中写道："he explored, with the indomitable spirit of Carathis, every chamber and cavern of the earthly hell of bad delights." 此处，爱伦·坡借用这个人物，意在说明我们不应该深究人类思想中黑暗的点点滴滴。

② 波斯诗人菲尔多西 (Ferdows, 940–1020) 史诗《列王纪》中的国王，由于阿弗拉斯布是伊朗的死敌，故诗人说他恶魔陪侍左右。

A Tale of the Ragged Mountains
凹凸山的传说

《凹凸山的传说》(*A Tale of the Ragged Mountains*, 1844) 以恐怖阴郁的笔触描写了奥古斯塔斯·贝德尔奥耶先生的一次山中奇遇，与华盛顿·欧文的《瑞普·凡·温克尔》有异曲同工之妙。在情节设置中，爱伦·坡选用了与华盛顿·欧文使用的相似手法，采用山间漫步继而发生奇遇的情节设置，成功地摧毁时间的藩篱，完成了创作主题的展现。在欧文的作品中，瑞普入睡 20 年，他的家庭和外面的世界发生了翻天覆地的变化，醒来后他已由英国乔治王的臣民变成了美利坚合众国的公民，以往游手好闲的田园式生活已被嘈杂紧张的工业化生活所代替。而在《凹凸山的传说》中，爱伦·坡塑造了一位神秘的奥古斯塔斯·贝德洛先生，是 1780 年切特·辛格叛乱中遇害的娄德贝先生复活变成的一个人。小说通过真实的死亡体验和灵魂出窍后的观感，渲染了小说的恐怖色彩，强调了人物内心的恐惧体验。此外，华盛顿·欧文与爱伦·坡在各自的作品中，展现了相似的时间观。首先，时间是绝对的，不可逆转的。同时，两位作者在文中均展现了时间的相对性与多维性。《瑞普·凡·温克尔》中不同的人对于这逝去的 20 年有着不同的体会与经历。《凹凸山的传说》的主题在于死人复活，相应地，故事中时间的绝对性界限必被打破。时间观的二重性一方面强调了时间变迁下社会的冷漠；另一方面帮助作者突破了时间绝对性的束缚，使主人公得以自由地折回于历史的长河中，进而更深刻地体现文章的主题。然而值得注意的是，虽然两篇小说采取了相似的奇遇情节和两重性时间观，但阐释了迥异的主题。华盛顿·欧文在《瑞普·凡·温克尔》一文中，利用神话故事的成功移植和看似简单、实则幽默深奥的语言，凸显了 20 年中美国社会的巨变。而他对山村的描写则暗示了他对古典式乡村生活的眷恋以及对现代破碎生活的迷茫与怀疑。《凹凸山的传说》的主题是死人复活。“死尸复活”“借尸还魂”是爱伦·坡“死亡”主题中最具有恐怖魅力的。

During the fall of the year 1827, while residing near Charlottesville, Virginia, I casually made the acquaintance of Mr. Augustus Bedloe. This young gentleman was remarkable in every respect, and excited in me a profound interest and curiosity. I found it impossible to comprehend him either in his moral or his physical relations. Of his family I could obtain no satisfactory account. Whence he came, I never ascertained. Even about his age — although I call him a young gentleman — there was something which perplexed me in no little degree. He certainly *seemed* young — and he made a point of speaking about his youth — yet there were moments when I should have had little trouble in imagining him a hundred years of age. But in no regard was he more peculiar than in his personal appearance. He was singularly tall and thin. He stooped much. His limbs were exceedingly long and emaciated. His forehead was broad and low. His complexion was absolutely bloodless. His mouth was large and flexible①, and his teeth were more wildly uneven, although sound, than I had ever before seen teeth in a human head②. The expression of his smile, however, was by no means unpleasing, as might be supposed; but it had no variation whatever. It was one of profound melancholy — of a phaseless and unceasing gloom. His eyes were abnormally large, and round like those of a cat. The pupils, too, upon any accession or diminution of light, underwent contraction or dilation, just such as is observed in the feline tribe. In moments of excitement the orbs grew bright to a degree almost inconceivable; seeming to emit luminous rays, not of a reflected, but

① 用"flexible"形容嘴巴，指的是这个人上下颚动起来很灵活。此处译文根据前文说他相貌奇特，选用了贬义词"变形"。
② 请注意"in a human head"的翻译。再举一例：《达·芬奇密码》第一章有一句是"The face staring back at him was thin and washed out."很显然，这里只能译为"门外盯着他看的那个人脸庞瘦削、满面倦容。"

1827年的秋天，我住在弗吉尼亚州夏洛茨维尔市[①]附近，无意间结识了奥古斯塔斯·贝德洛先生。这位年轻的先生在各个方面都很杰出，这使我对他产生了浓厚的兴趣。我发现从精神和肉体两个方面，我都不可能理解他。关于他的家庭，我找不到令人满意的记载；他来自何处，我从不确定；甚至于他的年龄也令我满腹疑云——虽然我称他为“年轻的先生”。当然啦，他看上去很年轻——他也常常强调自己的年轻——但有的时候，我不知不觉就会认为他已经一百岁了。但最奇特的，莫过于他的外貌。他身材奇高，瘦得吓人，背驼得厉害，四肢极为瘦长，脑门很宽，但额头很低，形容枯槁。嘴巴很大，有些变形，牙齿虽然完好无损，但我见过的人中，没有比他更参差不齐的。然而，出人意料的是，他的笑容绝不难看，只是毫无变化。这是一种深邃的忧郁——无时无刻、永无止境的忧郁。他的眼睛大得出奇，圆溜溜的，就像猫眼一样。瞳孔也随着光线的忽明忽暗而放大或者收缩，如同人们在猫科动物身上看到的那样。他激动的时候，眼球会明亮到不可思议的地步，看上去光芒四射，如同烛光或太阳光，是由自身发出的，并不是靠反射发光的。但在一般情况下，他两眼无光，翳翳然似在发呆，以至于令人想起早已下葬的死人的眼睛。

① 夏洛茨维尔，是位于弗吉尼亚首府里士满西南部的一个城市。坡曾就读于托马斯·杰斐逊1819年成立的维吉尼亚大学，年轻时曾到过夏洛茨维尔。

of an intrinsic lustre, as does a candle or the sun; yet their ordinary condition was so totally vapid, filmy and dull, as to convey the idea of the eyes of a long-interred corpse.

These peculiarities of person appeared to cause him much annoyance, and he was continually alluding to them in a sort of half explanatory, half apologetic strain, which, when I first heard it, impressed me very painfully. I soon, however, grew accustomed to it, and my uneasiness wore off. It seemed to be his design rather to insinuate than directly to assert that, physically, he had not always been what he was — that a long series of neuralgic attacks had reduced him from a condition of more than usual personal beauty, to that which I saw. For many years past he had been attended by a physician, named Templeton — an old gentleman, perhaps seventy years of age — whom he had first encountered at Saratoga. and from whose attention, while there, he either received, or fancied that he received, great benefit. The result was that Bedloe, who was wealthy, had made an arrangement with Dr. Templeton, by which the latter, in consideration of a liberal annual allowance, had consented to devote his time and medical experience exclusively to the care of the invalid.

Doctor Templeton had been a traveller in his younger days, and at Paris, had become a convert, in great measure, to the doctrines of Mesmer. It was altogether by means of magnetic remedies that he had succeeded in alleviating the acute pains of his patient[①]; and this success had very naturally inspired the latter with a certain degree of confidence in the opinions from which the remedies had been educed.

① 此处 patient 为单数，可知不是泛泛地指这位大夫的病人，而是指贝德洛。翻译时，为了避免指代不明，没有翻译成“病人”，而是依据中文表达习惯直接处理为“贝德洛”。本段另一个词 sufferer 处理方法类似，但 mesmerist 并没有按这种方法翻译。

相貌上的这些奇特之处似乎使他非常烦恼，他一再拐弯抹角地提起，半是解释，半是道歉。我第一次听他讲起这些时，感到非常痛苦。然而我很快就习惯了，不再觉得不自在。他的目的似乎就是暗示而不是明说，他的外表以前并非如此，接二连三的神经痛使他从一位美男子变成了现在这个样子。多年以来，一位名叫邓普顿的医生一直在照料他。这位医生年纪很大，可能有70岁了。他们初次见面是在萨拉托加[①]，就在那儿，邓普顿医生的照料使他受益良多，或者说他自以为受益良多。结果阔绰的贝德洛与邓普顿大夫商定：他每年拿出一笔优厚的酬金，作为回报，邓普顿大夫同意专门照顾他。

邓普顿医生年轻时周游四方。在巴黎时，他开始信奉麦斯默[②]的理论，十分虔诚。正是靠着磁力疗法，他才成功地减轻了贝德洛剧烈的疼痛，因而后者很自然地相信这一疗法背后的诸多观点。然而，就像所有的狂热分子一样，邓普顿医生极力要让自己的学生完全皈依于他，最后他终于成功地劝说饱受折磨的贝德洛先生参与了

① 萨拉托加，美国加利福尼亚西部一城市，位于圣何塞西南部，夏洛茨维尔北部，靠近里士满。

② 法兰兹·安东·麦斯默 (Franz Anton Mesmer, 1734–1815)，德国著名医生。他所提出的动物磁性说 (animal magnetism)，成了英国医师布雷德创立现代催眠术的基础。英文动词 mesmerize(催眠) 即来自他的名字。

The Doctor, however, like all enthusiasts, had struggled hard to make a thorough convert of his pupil, and finally so far gained his point as to induce the sufferer to submit to numerous experiments. — By a frequent repetition of these, a result had arisen, which of late days has become so common as to attract little or no attention, but which, at the period of which I write, had very rarely been known in America. I mean to say, that between Doctor Templeton and Bedloe there had grown up, little by little, a very distinct and strongly marked rapport, or magnetic relation. I am not prepared to assert, however, that this rapport extended beyond the limits of the simple sleep-producing power; but this power itself had attained great intensity. At the first attempt to induce the magnetic somnolency, the mesmerist entirely failed. In the fifth or sixth he succeeded very partially, and after long continued effort. Only at the twelfth was the triumph complete. After this the will of the patient succumbed rapidly to that of the physician, so that, when I first became acquainted with the two, sleep was brought about almost instantaneously, by the mere volition of the operator, even when the invalid was unaware of his presence. It is only now, in the year 1845, when similar miracles are witnessed daily by thousands, that I dare venture to record this apparent impossibility as a matter of serious fact.

The temperament of Bedloe was, in the highest degree, sensitive, excitable, enthusiastic. His imagination was singularly vigorous and creative; and no doubt it derived additional force from the habitual use of morphine, which he swallowed in great quantity, and without which he would have found it impossible to exist. It was his practice to take a very large dose of it immediately after breakfast, each morning —

无数次试验。不断的试验之后，终于取得某种成果。这种成果今天十分普遍，引不起多少关注了，但在我所提及的那个时代，美国很少有人知道。我是说，在邓普顿医生和贝德洛之间，已经慢慢滋生出一种独特而明显的融洽，也可以叫做磁铁般的关系吧。不过，我并不是说这种融洽已经超出了简单的催眠术的范围，我只是想说，这种催眠术本身力量变得十分强大。第一次试图磁力催眠时，这位麦斯默的信徒彻底失败了。在第五次还是第六次时，他经过长时间的努力，取得了部分成功。直到第十二次时，才大功告成。从此以后，贝德洛的意志总是很快就受到邓普顿医生的控制。我第一次认识他们俩时，医生一动意念，贝德洛就会立即被催眠，他甚至都不知道医生在场。只有在今天，1845年的今天，每天有成千上万的人见证这样的奇迹，我才敢将这种看似不可能的事当作严肃的事实记录下来。

贝德洛生性极其敏感，容易激动，而且热情奔放。他的想象力丰富而独特，毋庸置疑，习惯性地吞服吗啡使得他又多了几分想象力。他大量服用吗啡[①]，离了它就活不下去。每天早上吃过早饭后——或者更确切地说，喝完一杯浓咖啡后，因为他早上什么都不

① 吗啡，一种精神科药物，主要用于镇痛。因为吗啡具有梦境一般的镇痛效果，所以科学家就以希腊神话当中的梦境与睡眠之神——摩耳甫斯的名称将这种麻醉式镇痛剂命名为“吗啡”。因为病痛的长期折磨，贝德洛使用大剂量的吗啡缓解疼痛。

or rather immediately after a cup of strong coffee, for he ate nothing in the forenoon — and then set forth alone, or attended only by a dog, upon a long ramble among the chain of wild and dreary hills that lie westward and southward of Charlottesville, and are there dignified by the title of the Ragged Mountains.

Upon a dim, warm, misty day, towards the close of November, and during the strange interregnum of the seasons which in America is termed the Indian Summer[①], Mr. Bedloe departed as usual, for the hills. The day passed, and still he did not return.

About eight o'clock at night, having become seriously alarmed at his protracted absence, we were about setting out in search of him, when he unexpectedly made his appearance, in health no worse than usual, and in rather more than ordinary spirits. The account which he gave of his expedition, and of the events which had detained him, was a singular one indeed.

"You will remember," said he[②], "that it was about nine in the morning when I left Charlottesville. I bent my steps immediately to the mountains, and, about ten, entered a gorge which was entirely new to me. I followed the windings of this pass with much interest. — The scenery which presented itself on all sides, although scarcely entitled to be called grand, had about it an indescribable and to me a delicious aspect of dreary desolation. The solitude seemed absolutely virgin. I could not help believing that the green sods and the gray rocks upon

① "Indian Summer"是一位法国籍美国作家1778年在其书中提起的。这里的"Indian"并不是指印度，而是指美洲的土著民族印第安人。整个短语是指秋季出现在美国东海岸中部各州的一段暖和、干燥的天气，通常出现在9月下旬、10月和11月，有时也会出现在8月或12月。本文中，爱伦·坡把它称作"strange interregnum occurring in autumn。中文与这一词相对的特殊表达有"秋老虎""小阳春"。

② 英语中said he一类的语言，位置与汉语不同，而且很多时候并无必要，故此处略而未译。

吃——他会立即服用大量吗啡，然后或是独自出门，或是带上一条狗，在夏洛茨维尔市西南面荒凉的群山中东游西逛。这些小山名字倒很气派，叫凹凸山。

11月底的某一天，天气阴暗，暖和，雾蒙蒙的，正值秋冬之交，美国人叫作“小阳春”的反常时节，贝德洛先生像往常一样到山里去了。一天过去了，他还没有回来。

他迟迟不归让我们着实恐慌，晚上约8点钟的时候，我们正要出门找他去，他却出人意料地回来了，身体和平时一样，精神却好得多。他给我们讲述了自己的出游经过，让他不能脱身的事情，听起来十分独特。

“你们肯定记得我是早上9点钟左右离开夏洛茨维尔市的。我径直进了山，大约10点钟的时候，来到了一个全然陌生的峡谷，峡谷通道蜿蜒曲折，我一路走过，兴致很好。周围的景色虽然说不上壮观，但自有一种难以言状的荒寂，令我心旷神怡。独处此地似乎绝无干扰，我不禁觉得从未有人踏上我脚下这片青青的草地和灰色的岩石。峡谷入口十分隐蔽，要不是那一连串的巧合，根本进不去，因此，我完全有可能是第一个来此探险的人——第一个也是唯一一个进此桃源深处的人。

which I trod, had been trodden never before by the foot of a human being. So entirely secluded, and in fact inaccessible, except through a series of accidents, is the entrance of the ravine, that it is by no means impossible that I was indeed the first adventurer — the very first and sole adventurer who had ever penetrated its recesses[①].

"The thick and peculiar mist, or smoke[②], which distinguishes the Indian Summer, and which now hung heavily over all objects, served, no doubt, to deepen the vague impressions which these objects created. So dense was this pleasant fog, that I could at no time see more than a dozen yards of the path before me. This path was excessively sinuous, and as the sun could not be seen, I soon lost all idea of the direction in which I journeyed. In the meantime the morphine had its customary effect — that of enduing all the external world with an intensity of interest. In the quivering of a leaf — in the hue of a blade of grass — in the shape of a trefoil — in the humming of a bee — in the gleaming of a dew-drop — in the breathing of the wind — in the faint odors that came from the forest — there came a whole universe of suggestion — a gay and motly train of rhapsodical and immethodical thought.

"Busied in this, I walked on for several hours, during which the mist deepened around me to so great an extent, that at length I was reduced to an absolute groping of the way. And now an indescribable uneasiness possessed me — a species of nervous hesitation and tremor. — I feared to tread, lest I should be precipitated into some

① 此处贝得洛描述其偶入峡谷的经历与陶渊明的《桃花源记》中武陵人误入桃花源的经历相似，故将"recesses"译为"桃源深处"。
② 相传在冬天来临之前，印第安人为了把躲藏着的猎物驱逐出来，在其洞口点火熏烧，或者是点火烧尽耕地上的杂草以便来年的春耕，所以才有了"smoke"一词。爱伦·坡在此提到"smoke"一词，增加了这一说法的可信度。

“‘小阳春’特有的浓雾厚厚地笼罩着周围的一切，无疑使他们更加如梦似幻。大雾令我心情愉快，它浓得散不开，我只能看清面前十来码的路。这条路曲曲折折，由于看不见太阳，我很快就迷失了方向。这个时候，吗啡像往常一样起作用了，让我对周围的世界发生了强烈的兴趣。树叶的颤动，小草的颜色，三叶草的模样，蜜蜂的嗡鸣，露珠的闪光，微风的吹拂，树林里飘来的淡淡芬芳，都让我浮想联翩，各种各样令人开怀的奇思怪想纷至沓来。

“我一面沉溺于幻想，一面继续向前，走了几个小时，雾越来越浓，最后只能靠摸索前进。这个时候，一种无法形容的不安，一种令人紧张的犹豫和战栗缠住了我，我不敢迈步，害怕摔下深渊。我还记起了关于凹凸山的那些怪诞的传说，说是有些粗野的人就住在这里的树林和洞穴里。成千上万说不清道不明的想象令我心情沉重、恐慌不已，这些模糊的想象，更加令人痛苦。突然，一阵激昂的鼓声引起了我的注意。

abyss. I remembered, too, strange stories told about these Ragged Hills, and of the uncouth and fierce races of men who tenanted their groves and caverns. A thousand vague fancies oppressed and disconcerted me — fancies the more distressing because vague. Very suddenly my attention was arrested by the loud beating of a drum.

"My amazement was, of course, extreme. A drum in these hills was a thing unknown. I could not have been more surprised at the sound of the trump of the Archangel①. But a new and still more astounding source of interest and perplexity arose. There came a wild rattling or jingling sound, as if of a bunch of large keys — and upon the instant a dusky-visaged and half-naked man rushed past me with a shriek. He came so close to my person that I felt his hot breath upon my face. He bore in one hand an instrument composed of an assemblage of steel rings, and shook them vigorously as he ran. Scarcely had he disappeared in the mist, before, panting after him, with open mouth and glaring eyes, there darted a huge beast. I could not be mistaken in its character. It was a hyena.

"The sight of this monster rather relieved than heightened my terrors — for I now made sure that I dreamed, and endeavored to arouse myself to waking consciousness. I stepped boldly and briskly forward. I rubbed my eyes. I called aloud. I pinched my limbs. A small spring of water presented itself to my view, and here, stooping, I bathed my hands and my head and neck. This seemed to dissipate the equivocal sensations which had hitherto annoyed me. I arose, as I thought, a new man, and proceeded steadily and complacently on my

① 此处"Archangel"指圣经旧约中提及名称的大天使加百列 (Gabriel)，在最后审判中负责鸣喇叭以示死人的复活。

"我当然惊诧至极。这群山之中，鼓从何来，让人不得而知。就算听到了天使长的喇叭声，我也不会更加惊诧。这时，又发生了一件令人好奇、令人困惑的事，比刚才更加令人惊骇。我听到了一阵稀里哗啦的叮当声，像是一串巨大的钥匙发出的，就在此时，一个男人尖叫着从我身边跑过去了，他皮肤黝黑、半裸着身子。他离我如此之近，我都能感受到他呼在我脸上的热气。他一手拿着一个钢圈组成的玩意儿，一边跑，一边拼命地晃动。他刚冲进浓雾，身后就窜出一头巨大的野兽，张着嘴，瞪着眼睛，气喘吁吁的。我绝对不可能搞错，这是一头鬣狗。

"看到这头野兽我反而不如先前那样恐惧了，此时，我确信自己是在做梦，于是努力让自己醒过来。我不管不顾、脚步轻快地往前走去，一边走，一边揉揉眼睛，大声叫喊，又是掐胳膊，又是掐大腿。后来，我看到了一汪清泉，就弯下腰去，洗了洗手，洗了洗头和脖子，原先令我心烦的莫名其妙的感觉似乎消散了。我站起身来，觉得自己换了个人似的，脚步坚定、志满意得，继续走向未知的前方。

unknown way.

"At length, quite overcome by exertion, and by a certain oppressive closeness of the atmosphere, I seated myself beneath a tree. Presently there came a feeble gleam of sunshine, and the shadow of the leaves of the tree fell faintly but definitely upon the grass. At this shadow I gazed wonderingly for many minutes. Its character stupified me with astonishment. I looked upward. The tree was a palm.

"I now arose hurriedly, and in a state of fearful agitation — for the fancy that I dreamed would serve me no longer. I saw — I felt that I had perfect command of my senses — and these senses now brought to my soul a world of novel and singular sensation. The heat became all at once intolerable. A strange odor loaded the breeze. — A low continuous murmur, like that arising from a full, but gently flowing river, came to my ears, intermingled with the peculiar hum of multitudinous human voices.

"While I listened in an extremity of astonishment which I need not attempt to describe, a strong and brief gust of wind bore off the incumbent fog as if by the wand of an enchanter.

"I found myself at the foot of a high mountain, and looking down into a vast plain, through which wound a majestic river. On the margin of this river stood an Eastern-looking city, such as we read of in the Arabian Tales, but of a character even more singular than any there described. From my position, which was far above the level of the town, I could perceive its every nook and corner, as if delineated on a map. The streets seemed innumerable, and crossed each other irregularly in all directions, but were rather long winding alleys than streets, and absolutely swarmed with inhabitants. The houses were

“最后，我筋疲力尽，而且由于天气闷得令人压抑，就在一棵树下坐了下来。不一会儿，一缕微弱的阳光出现了，树叶的影子落在草地上，虽然模糊不清，但却真真切切。我好奇地盯着树叶的影子看了很久，这是什么东西？我十分惊异，抬头一看，原来却是一棵棕榈树。

“我急忙站了起来，深感恐惧，不再觉得自己是在做梦了。我亲眼所见——我觉得自己神志清醒——这让我的心灵经受了许多新奇的感受。天气突然变得酷热难当，微风里弥漫着一种奇怪的味道，我听到一阵阵低沉的声音，就像是来自河水充沛、缓缓流动的河流，夹杂着无数人的嗡嗡声。

“我惊奇万分地侧耳聆听，这无须多说。突然，一阵大风，就像法师的法杖一般，把笼罩一切的大雾吹走了。

“我发现自己在一座山脚下，正在俯视一片宽阔的平原。一条大河横穿其中，河边上坐落着一座城市，看上去颇具东方神韵，类似我们在《天方夜谭》里读到过的，但比这本书里描述的所有城市更加奇特。我所在的位置远远高于这座城市，因而能够看到每个角落，如同画在地图上一样。街道似乎数不胜数，纵横交错，杂乱无章，但与其说是街道，不如说是蜿蜒的长巷，长巷里人山人海。房屋美轮美奂，处处可见各种各样的阳台、回廊、尖塔、神庙和雕刻得奇妙异常的窗子。闹市比比皆是，货物琳琅满目——丝绸、薄棉布、令人眼花缭乱的餐具、华丽无比的珠宝。此外，到处可见旗子和轿子，端庄

wildly picturesque. On every hand was a wilderness of balconies, of verandahs, of minarets, of shrines, and fantastically carved oriels. Bazaars abounded; and in these were displayed rich wares in infinite variety and profusion — silks, muslins, the most dazzling cutlery, the most magnificent jewels and gems. Besides these things, were seen, on all sides, banners and palanquins, litters with stately dames close veiled, elephants gorgeously caparisoned, idols grotesquely hewn, drums, banners and gongs, spears, silver and gilded maces. And amid the crowd, and the clamor, and the general intricacy and confusion — amid the million of black and yellow men, turbaned and robed, and of flowing beard, there roamed a countless multitude of holy filleted bulls, while vast legions of the filthy but sacred ape clambered, chattering and shrieking, about the cornices of the mosques, or clung to the minarets and oriels. From the swarming streets to the banks of the river, there descended innumerable flights of steps leading to bathing places, while the river itself seemed to force a passage with difficulty through the vast fleets of deeply-burthened ships that far and wide encountered its surface. Beyond the limits of the city arose, in frequent majestic groups, the palm and the cocoa, with other gigantic and wierd trees of vast age; and here and there might be seen a field of rice, the thatched hut of a peasant, a tank, a stray temple, a gypsy camp, or a solitary graceful maiden taking her way, with a pitcher upon her head, to the banks of the magnificent river.

"You will say now, of course, that I dreamed; but not so. What I saw — what I heard — what I felt — what I thought — had about it nothing of the unmistakable idiosyncrasy of the dream. All was rigorously self-consistent. At first, doubting that I was really awake, I

的贵妇蒙着严严实实的面纱，坐在轿子上，披着盛装的大象，造型奇特的神像，还有锣鼓、旗帜、长矛、银质或镀金的狼牙棒。熙来攘往，人声鼎沸，一切都纷纷扰扰；上百万黑种人和黄种人包着头巾，身穿长袍，长须飘飘；数不清的牛身披丝带，四处游走；大批浑身污秽却被奉为神圣的猿猴叽叽喳喳，尖叫不断，在清真寺的屋檐上攀来爬去，又或是吊在尖塔或窗子上。从人山人海的街道到河岸，数不清的台阶逐层而低，一直通向沐浴的地方。河面上到处都是满载货物的船只，就好似河水颇费了一番周折才得以穿过。城市四周，不时可见片片壮观的棕榈树林和可可树林，以及其他一些怪异的参天古木。到处都是稻田、农家草屋、池塘、僻静的庙宇、吉普赛人的帐篷，或是优雅的少女头顶水罐，独自走向河岸。

“当然，你们肯定会说我在做梦，但事实并非如此。我所看到的——所听到的——所感受到的——所想的——完全没有梦境那种显而易见的特点。事事前后一致，丝毫不差。起先，我怀疑自己是否完全清醒，就做了一系列测试，使我很快确信自己真的醒着。

entered into a series of tests, which soon convinced me that I really was. Now, when one dreams, and, in the dream, suspects that he dreams, the suspicion never fails to confirm itself, and the sleeper is almost immediately aroused. Thus Novalis, errs not in saying that 'we are near waking when we dream that we dream.' Had the vision occurred to me as I describe it, without my suspecting it as a dream, then a dream it might absolutely have been, but, occurring as it did, and suspected and tested as it was, I am forced to class it among other phenomena."

"In this I am not sure that you are wrong," observed Dr. Templeton, "but proceed. You arose and descended into the city."

"I arose," continued Bedloe, regarding the Doctor with an air of profound astonishment, "I arose, as you say, and descended into the city. On my way, I fell in with an immense populace, crowding through every avenue, all in the same direction, and exhibiting in every action the wildest excitement. Very suddenly, and by some inconceivable impulse, I became intensely imbued with personal interest in what was going on. I seemed to feel that I had an important part to play, without exactly understanding what it was. Against the crowd which environed me, however, I experienced a deep sentiment of animosity. I shrank from amid them, and, swiftly, by a circuitous path, reached and entered the city. Here all was the wildest tumult and contention. A small party of men, clad in garments half-Indian, half European, and officered by gentlemen in a uniform partly British, were engaged, at great odds, with the swarming rabble of the alleys. I joined the weaker party, arming myself with the weapons of a fallen officer, and fighting I knew not whom with the nervous ferocity of despair. We were soon overpowered by numbers, and driven to seek refuge in a species of kiosk. Here we

一个人做梦的时候，如果怀疑他在做梦，这样的怀疑总被证明是正确的，这个人几乎马上就会醒来。这么说来，诺瓦利斯[①]说得没错，‘我们梦见自己在做梦时，就快要醒来了。’如果我所描述的这番景象出现时，我并没有怀疑它是梦，那它很有可能就是梦了，但是，它出现时，我怀疑过，测试过，因此我不得不将它划归梦境以外的现象。”

邓普顿医生说道：“在这一点上，我不敢肯定你是对还是错，请继续说下去。你站了起来，进了城。”

贝德洛十分诧异地看着邓普顿大夫，接着说：“就是像你说的那样，我站了起来，进了城。在路上，我遇到了很多人，每条路上都挤满了人，朝着同一个方向走去，他们无论做什么都十分激动。突然，我心血来潮，不知怎么地就对眼前发生的事产生了强烈的兴趣。我似乎觉得我会起很大的作用，但却并不十分清楚是什么样的作用。然而，对于四周的人群，我感到强烈的憎恨。我躲着他们，绕道而行，迅速进了城。城里骚乱不堪，吵吵嚷嚷，一小队士兵，穿着既有印度风格，又有欧洲风格的衣服，由几名穿着颇像英式制服的军官带领着，正和街上密密麻麻的乱民发生了冲突，双方力量悬殊。我加入了势单力薄的那一方，捡起了一位倒地身亡的军官的武器，不知和谁打了起来，由于绝望变得神经质一般的凶残。很快，我们就寡不敌众，被迫撤退到一间小屋里。我们防守于此，暂无性命之虞，从屋顶的一个洞眼看出去，我发现一大群人，群情激愤，正在围攻一座飞悬河水之上的华丽宫殿。很快，从宫殿一扇高高的窗户里，下来一个看上去像女人似的人，顺着用他的仆人的头巾结成的绳子滑

① 诺瓦利斯 (1772–1801)，德国作家弗里德里希·冯·哈顿伯格的笔名，德国浪漫主义运动的先驱。

barricaded ourselves, and, for the present, were secure. From a loop-hole near the summit of the kiosk, I perceived a vast crowd, in furious agitation, surrounding and assaulting a gay palace that overhung the river. Presently, from an upper window of this palace, there descended an effeminate-looking person, by means of a string made of the turbans of his attendants. A boat was at hand, in which he escaped to the opposite bank of the river.

"And now a new object took possession of my soul. I spoke a few hurried but energetic words to my companions, and, having succeeded in gaining over a few of them to my purpose, made a frantic sally from the kiosk. We rushed amid the crowd that surrounded it. They retreated, at first, before us. They rallied, fought madly, and retreated again. In the meantime we were borne far from the kiosk, and became bewildered and entangled among the narrow streets of tall overhanging houses, into the recesses of which the sun had never been able to shine. The rabble pressed impetuously upon us, harrassing us with their spears, and overwhelming us with flights of arrows. These latter were very remarkable, and resembled in some respects the writhing creese of the Malay. They were made to imitate the body of a creeping serpent, and were long and black, with a poisoned barb. One of them struck me upon the right temple. I reeled and fell. An instantaneous and dreadful sickness seized me. I struggled — I gasped — I died."

"You will hardly persist now," said I, smiling, "that the whole of your adventure was not a dream. You are not prepared to maintain that you are dead?"

When I said these words, I of course expected some lively sally

下。一条小船就在附近，于是他乘船逃到了河对岸。

“这时，我心里有了新的目标。我对着其他人说了几句话，急促但慷慨激昂，争取了几个人的支持后，我们从屋子里亡命突围。我们在包围的人群中左冲右突，他们先是退后，随即又围了上来，拼命反击，然后再一次撤退。与此同时，我们离屋子越来越远，被困在一条条狭窄的街道，不辨东西。街道两旁房屋林立，终年不见阳光。那些乱民逼了上来，气势汹汹，长矛乱刺，箭如雨飞，压得我们抬不起头来。这些箭很不寻常，有点像马来人的曲剑，它们打造得有如蜿蜒前行的毒蛇，箭身修长黝黑，箭簇浸毒。一支箭射中了我的右太阳穴，我踉踉跄跄，倒在地上，旋即难受不已。我挣扎着——上气不接下气——一命呜呼了。”

我笑了笑，说道：“现在你肯定不会坚持说自己的奇遇不是梦吧？你并没有打算说自己已经死了吧？”

我说这些话的时候，当然以为贝德洛会做一些俏皮的答复。但

from Bedloe in reply; but, to my astonishment, he hesitated, trembled, became fearfully pallid, and remained silent. I looked towards Templeton. He sat erect and rigid in his chair — his teeth chattered, and his eyes were starting from their sockets. "Proceed!" he at length said hoarsely to Bedloe.

"For many minutes," continued the latter, "my sole sentiment — my sole feeling — was that of darkness and nonentity, with the consciousness of death. At length, there seemed to pass a violent and sudden shock through my soul, as if of electricity. With it came the sense of elasticity and of light. This latter I felt — not saw. In an instant I seemed to rise from the ground. But I had no bodily, no visible, audible, or palpable presence. The crowd had departed. The tumult had ceased. The city was in comparative repose. Beneath me lay my corpse, with the arrow in my temple, the whole head greatly swollen and disfigured. But all these things I felt — not saw. I took interest in nothing. Even the corpse seemed a matter in which I had no concern. Volition I had none, but appeared to be impelled into motion, and flitted buoyantly out of the city, retracing the circuitous path by which I had entered it. When I had attained that point of the ravine in the mountains, at which I had encountered the hyena, I again experienced a shock as of a galvanic battery; the sense of weight, of volition, of substance, returned. I became my original self, and bent my steps eagerly homewards — but the past had not lost the vividness of the real — and not now, even for an instant, can I compel my understanding to regard it as a dream."

"Nor was it," said Templeton, with an air of deep solemnity, "yet it would be difficult to say how otherwise it should be termed. Let us

令我惊讶的是，他犹豫着，颤抖着，脸色煞白，一言不发。我看着邓普顿，他直挺挺地坐在椅子上，牙齿格格作响，两眼瞪得溜圆。最后，他声音嘶哑地对贝德洛说道：“往下说！”

贝德洛接着说道：“有好一会儿，我唯一的情感、唯一的感觉就是黑暗和虚无，我意识到自己已经死了。最后，我的灵魂像是突然受到强烈的冲击，犹如电击一般，我又能感受到弹性和亮光了。亮光只是能感受到，并不能看到。旋即，我好似从地面上飘了起来，但却没有肉体，看不见，听不见，也摸不着。人群已经散去，骚乱也已平息，整个城市安静多了。我看到自己的尸体就躺在下面，太阳穴上那支箭还在，头部浮肿，已经变形。但这一切，我只是感受到而并未看到，我对一切都无动于衷，连自己的尸体似乎也与我无关。我失去了意识，只似被人推着，轻盈地沿着进城的路飘了出去。我来到山谷间路遇鬣狗的那个地方，仿佛又被电击了一下，重新有了重量和意志，又能感受到世间万物了。我变回了原来的自己，急切地往家里赶，但刚发生的一切还历历在目，即使现在，我还是完全不能把它当作是梦。”

“这本来就不是梦，不过另外给它命名也很难。”邓普顿非常严肃地说道，“我们只能认为，当今人类的灵魂接近于某些了不起的精

suppose only, that the soul of the man of to-day is upon the verge of some stupendous psychal discoveries. Let us content ourselves with this supposition. For the rest I have some explanation to make. Here is a water-color drawing, which I should have shown you before, but which an unaccountable sentiment of horror has hitherto prevented me from showing."

We looked at the picture which he presented. I saw nothing in it of an extraordinary character; but its effect upon Bedloe was prodigious. He nearly fainted as he gazed. And yet it was but a miniature portrait — a miraculously accurate one, to be sure — of his own very remarkable features. At least this was my thought as I regarded it.

"You will perceive," said Templeton, "the date of this picture — it is here, scarcely visible, in this corner — 1780. In this year was the portrait taken. It is the likeness of a dead friend — a Mr. Oldeb — to whom I became much attached at Calcutta, during the administration of Warren Hastings. I was then only twenty years old. When I first saw you, Mr. Bedloe, at Saratoga, it was the miraculous similarity which existed between yourself and the painting, which induced me to accost you, to seek your friendship, and to bring about those arrangements which resulted in my becoming your constant companion. In accomplishing this point, I was urged partly, and perhaps principally, by a regretful memory of the deceased, but also, in part, by an uneasy, and not altogether horrorless curiosity respecting yourself.

"In your detail of the vision which presented itself to you amid the hills, you have described, with the minutest accuracy, the Indian

神发现，先假定如此，聊以自慰吧。其他方面，容我略做解释。这里有一幅水彩画，本来早该给你看看，但由于一种难以形容的恐惧感，我一直也没有这么做。”

我们看了看他那幅画。我看不出任何特别之处，但贝德洛深受震动，几乎晕了过去。不过，这仅仅是一幅小型肖像画啊，相当逼真地描绘了他那独特的五官而已。最起码，我看到这幅画的时候是这么想的。

邓普顿说道：“你们可以看到这幅画作于1780年——日期在这个角落，看不大清楚了。这幅肖像画就是作于这一年，是我一位已故朋友的肖像，他叫娄德贝，我与他在加尔各答[1]时过从甚密，那时还是沃伦·黑斯廷斯[2]主政呢。当时我只有20岁。贝德洛先生，我在萨拉托加第一次见到你的时候，正是因为你和这幅画之间有着惊人的相似，才使我禁不住和你搭话，交朋友，并经过一番巧妙安排，使我们一直不离左右。我这么做，一半是因为，也许主要是因为我对我那位已故朋友深感惋惜，还有一半是因为我对你有一种不安的，甚至带有几分恐惧的好奇。

“你在山中所见幻境的前前后后，丝毫不差地描述了印度恒河

① 加尔各答，印度东部的一座城市，位于恒河三角洲上的胡格利河畔。于公元1690年作为英国东印度公司的商贸据点而建成，是印度最大的城市，主要的港口和工业中心。在臭名昭著的“加尔各答黑洞”中，120名英国士兵被整夜囚禁在狭小憋闷的地牢里然后窒息而死（1756年）。

② 沃伦·黑斯廷斯（1732—1818），英属印度第一位总督，1773—1785年在位。

city of Benares, upon the Holy River. The riots, the combats, the massacre, were the actual events of the insurrection of Cheyte Sing. which took place in 1780, when Hastings was put in imminent peril of his life. The man escaping by the string of turbans, was Cheyte Sing himself. The party in the kiosk were sepoys and British officers, headed by Hastings. Of this party I was one, and did all I could to prevent the rash and fatal sally of the officer who fell, in the crowded alleys, by the poisoned arrow of a Bengalee. That officer was my dearest friend. It was Oldeb. You will perceive by these manuscripts," (here the speaker produced a note-book in which several pages appeared to have been freshly written) "that at the very period in which you fancied these things amid the hills, I was engaged in detailing them upon paper here at home."

In about a week after this conversation, the following paragraphs appeared in a Charlottesville paper:

"We have the painful duty of announcing the death of Mr. AUGUSTUS BEDLO, a gentleman whose amiable manners and many virtues have long endeared him to the citizens of Charlottesville.

"Mr. B., for some years past, has been subject to neuralgia, which has often threatened to terminate fatally; but this can be regarded only as the mediate cause of his decease. The proximate cause was one of especial singularity. In an excursion to the Ragged Mountains, a few days since, a slight cold and fever were contracted, attended with great determination of blood to the head. To relieve this, Dr. Templeton resorted to topical bleeding. Leeches were applied to the temples. In a fearfully brief period the patient died, when it appeared that, in the jar containing the leeches, had been introduced, by accident, one of the

边上的贝拿勒斯城。那些暴乱、战斗、杀戮，都是1780年切特·辛[1]起义时发生的真实事件，当时黑斯廷斯几乎丧命。用头巾连成绳子逃命的那个人，正是切特·辛本人。那间屋子里的人，是黑斯廷斯率领的印度士兵和英国军官，我当时也是其中一员，还曾极力劝阻那位军官莽撞的亡命突围。后来他中了孟加拉人的毒箭，命丧暴民蚁聚的小巷。这位军官是我最好的朋友，他就是娄德贝。”说到这里，他拿出一个笔记本，翻倒几页新近写成的文字，说：“通过这个手稿，你们可以看到，你在山中见到这些幻境时，我正在家里详细地描述这一切呢！”

这次谈话之后过了大约一个星期，夏洛茨维尔市一家报纸刊登了如下文章：

“我们不得不沉痛地宣布奥古斯塔斯·贝德娄先生已经辞世，他和蔼可亲、道德高尚，一直深受本市市民的喜爱。

数年以来，贝德娄先生一直深受神经痛之苦，常有性命之虞，然而，这只能被当作是他与世长辞的间接原因，其直接原因相当离奇。几天前他去凹凸山郊游，偶感风寒，引起发烧，同时头部严重充血。为了缓解充血症状，邓普敦大夫采用了局部放血法，将水蛭放在病人的太阳穴上。病人很快就去世了，原因似乎是在盛水蛭的瓶子里，一不留神混进了一条有毒的水蛭，这种水蛭在附近的池塘里

① 切特·辛，当时是贝拿勒斯的国王。1778年，英法在印度开战。为了支付军费，黑斯廷斯加重了对切特·辛的盘剥。1780年，不堪重负的切特·辛向黑斯廷斯行贿，后者接受了贿赂，但后来又将其上交，并对切特·辛步步紧逼，甚至亲临贝拿勒斯，将他逮捕，终于激起民变。作者在这里描述的起义经过，与史实基本吻合。

venomous vermicular sangsues[①] which are now and then found in the neighboring ponds. This creature fastened itself upon a small artery in the right temple. Its close resemblance to the medicinal leech caused the mistake to be overlooked until too late.

"N. B. The poisonous sangsue of Charlottesville may always be distinguished from the medicinal leech by its blackness, and especially by its writhing or vermicular motions, which very nearly resemble those of a snake."

I was speaking with the editor of the paper in question, upon the topic of this remarkable accident, when it occurred to me to ask how it happened that the name of the deceased had been given as Bedlo.

"I presume," I said, "you have authority for this spelling, but I have always supposed the name to be written with an e at the end."

"Authority? —no," he replied. "It is a mere typographical error. The name is Bedlo [Bedloe] with an e, all the world over, and I never knew it to be spelt otherwise in my life."

"Then," said I mutteringly, as I turned upon my heel, "then indeed has it come to pass that one truth is stranger than any fiction — for Bedlo, without the e, what is it but Oldeb conversed? And this man tells me it is a typographical error."

① 此处疑为作者故弄玄虚。英语中并无 sangsue 一词，它是法语单词，与英文中的 leech 同义。

时有发现。这个畜生叮住病人右太阳穴上一根小小的动脉，由于它和医用水蛭极为相似，人们发现这个失误时，为时已晚。

注意：夏洛茨维尔市的有毒水蛭和医用水蛭的区别在于，它很黑，蠕动前行，与蛇甚为相似。”

有一次，我正和该报编辑谈论这桩离奇的事，突然想到应该问问死者的名字为何变成了“贝德娄”。

“虽然我觉得你把名字写成这个自有道理，但我一直以为最后一个字是‘洛’。”我说道。

“道理？没有的事，只是排版错误而已。”他回答道，“名字的确是贝德洛，全世界都一样，我从来都不知道它还可以有另外的写法。”

我转身离开时，喃喃自语道：“这么说，事实果然比小说还要离奇？贝德洛错写成了贝德娄，不就是娄德贝倒过来吗？这个人却跟我说，这是个印刷错误。”

The Oblong Box
长方形的箱子

《长方形的箱子》(*The Oblong Box,* 1844) 引领我们追踪了一只神秘的长方形箱子，成功地给后世树立了设置悬念的典范。从爱伦·坡开创侦探小说，经过威尔基·柯林斯、柯南·道尔、阿尔弗莱德·希区柯克及斯蒂芬·金等一代代作家的开拓发展，至今，侦探小说已经成为人们喜闻乐见的一种文化读物。而侦探小说的核心部分——悬念的设置，便成为众多艺术家们绞尽脑汁、耗费心力去攻克的难题。爱伦·坡在《长方形的箱子》中所使用的设置悬念的技巧和手段成为后世侦探小说家们广为模仿的对象，并继而演化为侦探小说的特定模式之一。

希区柯克曾经给"悬念"下过这样一个定义：如果你要表现一群人围着一张桌子玩牌，然后突然一声爆炸，那么你便只能拍到一个十分呆板的场面；另一种情况，虽然你表现的是同一场面，但在打牌开始之前，先表现桌子下面的定时炸弹，那么，你就造成了悬念，并牵动了读者的心。由此，我们可以窥见悬念的定义和悬念所能造成的奇特效果，也就是它带给读者的那种紧张、焦虑与迫切想知道下文的心情。从心理学的角度来说，只有那些奇异事件才能够强烈刺激人的感官，从而引起人的阅读兴趣。这类事件不外乎两类：一类是自然事件，如一场莫名其妙的大火，或是一只奇怪的动物；另一类就是社会事件，例如一桩谋杀案、一次奇特的经历，或是一个奇怪物件的出现。《长方形的箱子》一文中出现的那只箱子就具备这种功能。为了渲染这只箱子的神秘和重要，作者不惜笔墨介绍故事背景和相关人物的信息，并提前设置了悬念。故事直到最后才道出了整个事件的来龙去脉：那只长方形的箱子里装的是怀亚特太太被做过防腐处理的尸体，而船上的那位怀亚特太太只是一个女仆。我们回头再看那些悬念：为什么怀亚特一家四人要订三个房间；为什么"及仆人"三个字被画掉了；为什么怀亚特先生深夜打开那只箱子；为什么怀亚特最后不顾一切地与箱子一起沉海；为什么哈代船长说要等盐化掉等。这些悬念既是作者为引发读者兴趣设置的障碍，也是逻辑发展的必然体现，更是走向通往真相之路的台阶。悬念的意义和魅力也因此彰显得淋漓尽致。从小说第一句话开始，爱伦·坡就费尽心思地玩起了悬念游戏；接下来的每一个词、每一句话都将这个游戏渲染得轰轰烈烈，从而将整个故事从一个高潮推向另一个高潮。这也使得爱伦·坡无愧于“悬念大师”的美名。

Some years ago, I engaged passage from Charleston, S. C., to the city of New York, in the fine packet-ship "Independence," Captain Hardy. We were to sail on the fifteenth of the month (June,) weather permitting; and, on the fourteenth, I went on board to arrange some matters in my state-room.

I found that we were to have a great many passengers, including a more than usual number of ladies. On the list were several of my acquaintances; and among other names, I was rejoiced to see that of Mr. Cornelius Wyatt, a young artist, for whom I entertained feelings of warm friendship. He had been with me a fellow-student at C-University, where we were very much together. He had the ordinary temperament of genius, and was a compound of misanthropy, sensibility, and enthusiasm. To these qualities he united the warmest and truest heart which ever beat in a human bosom.

I observed that his name was carded upon *three* state-rooms; and, upon again referring to the list of passengers, I found that he had engaged passage for himself, wife, and two sisters — his own. The state-rooms were sufficiently roomy, and each had two berths, one above the other. These berths, to be sure, were so exceedingly narrow as to be insufficient for more than one person; still, I could not comprehend why there were *three* state-rooms for these four persons. I was, just at that epoch, in one of those moody frames of mind which make a man abnormally inquisitive about trifles; and I confess, with shame, that I busied myself in a variety of ill-bred and preposterous conjectures about this matter of the supernumerary state-room. It was no business of mine, to be sure; but with none the less pertinacity did I occupy myself in attempts to resolve the enigma. At last I reached a

几年前，我订了从南卡罗来纳州的查尔斯顿到纽约的船票，船是一艘名为“独立号”的豪华邮轮，船长叫哈代。如果天公作美，我们将于当月（6月）15日出发；所以在14日那天，我就上船将自己预订的包间整理了一下。

我发现同船的乘客相当多，女客的数量更是比平常多出许多。乘客名单上有我的一些熟人，并且我欣喜地发现，还有科尼利厄斯·怀亚特先生的名字。他是一位年轻的画家，被我引为知己。我们曾是C大学的同学，那时我们总是形影不离。他具有天才身上所具备的一切特质：孤傲、敏感和狂热。此外，他还有一颗世上最温暖、最真诚的心。

我注意到有三个包间的门卡上写着他的名字；再对照乘客名单，我发现那是他为自己、妻子和他的两个妹妹订的。包间都很宽敞，内设上下两个铺位。当然，每个铺位异常狭窄，只能容下一个人。可即便如此，我还是想不通为什么这四个人要订三个包间。彼时彼刻，我心血来潮，对琐事异常好奇；虽然有些羞愧，但我得承认，当时我确实对那个多余的包间做了种种荒唐而又拙劣的猜测。很明显，这不关我的事，可我依然一门心思想解开这个谜。最终，我得出了一个结论，并且我很诧异自己为什么没有早些想到这一点。“肯定是为仆人准备的，”我说道，“我真傻，这么显而易见的答案，怎么早没想到！”然而，当我再次对照乘客名单，我清楚地看到他们并没有带仆人，虽然他们原本确实打算带一个的——因为名单上原来写着的“及仆人”三个字被画掉了。“哦，一定是额外的行李，”我自言自语道，“某件他不想放在货舱，而想摆在眼皮底下的东西——

conclusion which wrought in me great wonder why I had not arrived at it before. "It is a servant, of course," I said; "what a fool I am, not sooner to have thought of so obvious a solution!" And then I again repaired to the list — but here I saw distinctly that *no* servant was to come with the party; although, in fact, it had been the original design to bring one — for the words "and servant" had been first written and then overscored. "Oh, extra baggage to be sure," I now said to myself — "something he wishes not to be put in the hold — something to be kept under his own eye — ah, I have it — a painting or so — and this is what he has been bargaining about with Nicolino, the Italian Jew." This idea satisfied me, and I dismissed my curiosity for the nonce.

Wyatt's two sisters I knew very well, and most amiable and clever girls they were. His wife he had newly married, and I had never yet seen her. He had often talked about her in my presence, however, and in his usual style of enthusiasm. He described her as of surpassing beauty, wit, and accomplishment. I was, therefore, quite anxious to make her acquaintance.

On the day in which I visited the ship, (the fourteenth,) Wyatt and party were also to visit it — so the captain informed me — and I waited on board an hour longer than I had designed, in hope of being presented to the bride; but then an apology came. "Mrs. W. was a little indisposed, and would decline coming on board until to-morrow, at the hour of sailing."

The morrow having arrived, I was going from my hotel to the wharf, when Captain Hardy met me and said that, "owing to circumstances," (a stupid but convenient phrase,) "he rather thought the 'Independence' would not sail for a day or two, and that when all

哈，我明白了——八成是油画之类的东西——就是那幅他一直和那个意大利犹太人尼可雷诺讨价还价的画。”这个想法令我感到很满意，于是我暂时打消了好奇心。

我对怀亚特先生的两个妹妹非常熟悉，她们和蔼可亲、聪明伶俐，而他的新婚妻子我尚未见过。他曾多次以惯常的狂热口吻在我面前描述她那非同寻常的美丽、智慧和多才多艺，因此我极其渴望能够与她结识。

在我上船的那天(14号)，怀亚特一行也要过来——船长是这么告诉我的——于是我在船上多逗留了一个小时，希望能见到那位新娘；可结果盼来的却是一份抱歉：“怀亚特夫人有点儿不舒服，所以明天起航时她才会上船。”

第二天一早，就在我从旅馆赶往码头的时候，我碰到了哈代船长。他说，因为“一些情况”(愚蠢却省事的托词)，他认为“独立号”在一两天内都不会起航；当一切准备就绪后，他会派人通知我。这让我觉得不可思议，因为当时正刮着强劲的南风；不过，尽管我一再

was ready, he would send up and let me know." This I thought strange, for there was a stiff southerly breeze; but as "the circumstances" were not forthcoming, although I pumped for them with much perseverance, I had nothing to do but to return home and digest my impatience at leisure.

I did not receive the expected message from the captain for nearly a week. It came at length, however, and I immediately went on board. The ship was crowded with passengers, and everything was in the bustle attendant upon making sail. Wyatt's party arrived in about ten minutes after myself. There were the two sisters, the bride, and the artist — the latter in one of his customary fits of moody misanthropy. I was too well used to these, however, to pay them any special attention. He did not even introduce me to his wife; — this courtesy devolving, per force, upon his sister Marian — a very sweet and intelligent girl, who, in a few hurried words, made us acquainted.

Mrs. Wyatt had been closely veiled; and when she raised her veil, in acknowledging my bow, I confess that I was very profoundly astonished. I should have been much more so, however, had not long experience advised me not to trust, with too implicit a reliance, the enthusiastic descriptions of my friend, the artist, when indulging in comments upon the loveliness of women. When beauty was the theme, I well knew with what facility he soared into the regions of the purely ideal.

The truth is, I could not help regarding Mrs. Wyatt as a decidedly plain-looking woman. If not positively ugly, she was not, I think, very far from it. She was dressed, however, in exquisite taste — and then I had no doubt that she had captivated my friend's heart by the more

追问，他也不肯透露那“一些情况”到底是什么。我无可奈何，只好回到旅馆，慢慢地打发心中的焦躁。

差不多一个星期过去了，我却迟迟没等到船长的通知。不过最后总算是等来了，于是我立即赶上了船。船上挤满了乘客，船一起航，四处便陷入纷乱嘈杂。怀亚特一行比我晚到了十来分钟。两姐妹、新娘和画家本人都到了——画家还是一贯孤傲的样子。可我对此再熟悉不过了，也就没放在心上。他甚至没把我介绍给他的妻子——所以这一礼节自然就落在了他的妹妹玛利安身上——她是一个聪明可爱的女孩，只三言两语，我和新娘就彼此相识了。

怀亚特夫人严严实实地裹着面纱，我朝她鞠了一躬，她揭开面纱还礼，我得承认自己当时深感意外。多年的经验早已告诉我，在我这位画家朋友纵情称颂女性的可爱时，不能盲目相信他的热烈赞扬，否则我会感到更加意外。我很清楚，话题一旦牵涉到“美”，他总是很容易陷入理想化的完美境地。

说真的，我打心底里认为怀亚特夫人绝对只是一个相貌平平的女人。虽然不能肯定地说她长相丑陋，可我觉得也差不多。不过，她穿衣打扮的品位倒很高雅——于是我确信，她必定是凭着智慧和灵魂这种更持久的魅力俘获了我朋友的心。她几乎没说什么话，很

enduring graces of the intellect and soul. She said very few words, and passed at once into her state-room with Mr. W.

My old inquisitiveness now returned. There was no servant — *that* was a settled point. I looked, therefore, for the extra baggage. After some delay, a cart arrived at the wharf, with an oblong pine box, which was everything that seemed to be expected. Immediately upon its arrival we made sail, and in a short time were safely over the bar[①] and standing out to sea.

The box in question was, as I say, oblong. It was about six feet in length by two and a half in breadth; — I observed it attentively, and like to be precise. Now this shape was *peculiar*; and no sooner had I seen it, than I took credit to myself for the accuracy of my guessing. I had reached the conclusion, it will be remembered, that the extra baggage of my friend, the artist, would prove to be pictures, or at least a picture; for I knew he had been for several weeks in conference with Nicolino: — and now here was a box which, from its shape, *could* possibly contain nothing in the world but a copy of Leonardo's "Last Supper;" and a copy of this very "Last Supper," done by Rubini the younger, at Florence, I had known, for some time, to be in the possession of Nicolino. This point, therefore, I considered as sufficiently settled. I chuckled excessively when I thought of my acumen. It was the first time I had ever known Wyatt to keep from me any of his artistical secrets; but here he evidently intended to steal a march upon me, and smuggle a fine picture to New York, under my very nose; expecting me to know nothing of the matter. I resolved to quiz him *well,* now and hereafter.

① 此处指的是航海中碰到的沙洲，即 sand bar。

快就和怀亚特先生一起进了包间。

这时，我原先的好奇心又犯了。没有仆人——这一点确定无疑。所以，我就看看有没有额外的行李。过了一会儿，码头上来了一辆马车，载着一只长方形的松木箱子，大家在等的似乎就是这件东西了。箱子一到，我们就起航了，并且很快就安全地穿过沙洲，驶向大海。

如我所言，那只箱子是长方形的，大约有六英尺长、两英尺半宽——我当时仔细打量过，在此也想描述得更准确些。箱子的形状很特别，我一看见它就相信自己先前猜得没错。你可能还记得，我曾断言我那位画家朋友额外的行李应该是些画作，起码是一幅画作。因为我知道，他已经和尼可雷诺谈了几个星期——而现在这只箱子就在眼前，从外观看，里面装的很可能就是达·芬奇[①]《最后的晚餐》的复制品。我早就知道，这幅《最后的晚餐》是由小鲁比尼于佛罗伦萨[②]仿绘的，一度为尼可雷诺所有。我认为关于箱子的疑问已得到充分的解释，想到自己如此聪明，我不禁窃笑不已。这还是怀亚特头一次对我隐瞒他的艺术秘密。他显然是想出其不意，在我的眼皮底下偷运一幅好画去纽约，还指望我对此一无所知。我决定从今往后，要好好地盘问他。

① 达·芬奇(1452—1519)，“意大利文艺复兴三杰”之一，多才多艺，集画家、雕塑家、发明家、哲学家、音乐家、医学家、建筑工程师等身份于一身。画作《最后的晚餐》《安吉里之战》和《蒙娜丽莎》是他一生的三大杰作。

② 佛罗伦萨，意大利中部的一座城市，托斯卡纳区首府，是15至16世纪欧洲最著名的艺术中心，以美术工艺品和纺织品驰名全欧。

One thing, however, annoyed me not a little. The box did not go into the extra state-room. It was deposited in Wyatt's own; and there, too, it remained, occupying very nearly the whole of the floor — no doubt to the exceeding discomfort of the artist and his wife; — this the more especially as the tar or paint with which it was lettered in sprawling capitals, emitted a strong, disagreeable, and, to *my* fancy, a peculiarly disgusting odor. On the lid were painted the words — "*Mrs. Adelaide Curtis, Albany, New York. Charge of Cornelius Wyatt, Esq. This side up. To be handled with care.*"

Now, I was aware that Mrs. Adelaide Curtis, of Albany, was the artist's wife's mother; — but then I looked upon the whole address as a mystification, intended especially for myself. I made up my mind, of course, that the box and contents would never get farther north than the studio of my misanthropic friend, in Chambers Street, New York.

For the first three or four days we had fine weather, although the wind was dead ahead; having chopped round to the northward, immediately upon our losing sight of the coast. The passengers were, consequently, in high spirits, and disposed to be social. I *must* except, however, Wyatt and his sisters, who behaved stiffly, and, I could not help thinking, uncourteously to the rest of the party. *Wyatt's* conduct I did not so much regard. He was gloomy, even beyond his usual habit — in fact he was *morose* — but in him I was prepared for eccentricity. For the sisters, however, I could make no excuse. They secluded themselves in their state-rooms during the greater part of the passage, and absolutely refused, although I repeatedly urged them, to hold communication with any person on board.

Mrs. Wyatt herself was far more agreeable. That is to say, she

不过，有一件事让我很心烦。这箱子没有放到多余的包间里，而是放在了怀亚特自己的房间里，并且一直都放在那里，几乎把地板都占满了——这无疑会让画家和他的妻子很不舒服——尤其是箱子上还用大写字母龙飞凤舞地写了些字，这些字不知是用柏油还是油漆写的，散发出一股浓烈、刺鼻的味道，在我看来，这股味道特别令人恶心。盖子上写着如下字句——“纽约州阿尔巴尼市阿德莱得·柯蒂斯夫人收。科尼利厄斯·怀亚特先生押运。此面向上，小心轻放。”

现在我才明白，这位阿尔巴尼市的阿德莱得·柯蒂斯夫人是画家的岳母——不过当时我把这个地址看作是画家用来故弄玄虚的，尤其是用来迷惑我的。很自然地，我认定当箱子和里面的东西抵达我那孤傲的画家朋友在纽约市钱伯斯街的工作室后，就绝不会再向北行了。

开始的三四天，天气很不错，只是顶着风；而当我们一驶出海岸线，就刮起了北风。由于天气很好，乘客们兴致都很高，乐于彼此交往。不过怀亚特和他的两个妹妹必须除外，他们举止拘谨，这使我不由得觉得他们对其他乘客很不礼貌。对于怀亚特的行为我不以为然，他平时就总是闷闷不乐，现在更甚——简直可以说是哭丧着脸——不过我对他怪异的行为早就习以为常了。可他的两个妹妹也这样，实在让我捉摸不透。旅途的大部分时间里，她们都把自己关在包间里，尽管我一再力劝，她们仍拒绝同船上的任何人打交道。

怀亚特夫人则随和得多。我是说，她挺爱聊天的，而在海上，

was *chatty;* and to be chatty is no slight recommendation at sea. She became *excessively* intimate with most of the ladies; and, to my profound astonishment, evinced no equivocal disposition to coquet with the men. She amused us all very much. I say "*amused*" — and scarcely know how to explain myself. The truth is, I soon found that Mrs. W. was far oftener laughed *at* than *with*. The gentlemen said little about her; but the ladies, in a little while, pronounced her "a good-hearted thing, rather indifferent-looking ①, totally uneducated, and decidedly vulgar." The great wonder was, how Wyatt had been entrapped into such a match. Wealth was the general solution — but this I knew to be no solution at all; for Wyatt had told me that she neither brought him a dollar nor had any expectations from any source whatever. "He had married," he said, "for love, and for love only; and his bride was far more than worthy of his love." When I thought of these expressions, on the part of my friend, I confess that I felt indescribably puzzled. Could it be possible that he was taking leave of his senses? What else could I think? *He,* so refined, so intellectual, so fastidious, with so exquisite a perception of the faulty, and so keen an appreciation of the beautiful! To be sure, the lady seemed especially fond of him — particularly so in his absence — when she made herself ridiculous by frequent quotations of what had been said by her "beloved husband, Mr. Wyatt." The word "husband" seemed forever — to use one of her own delicate expressions — forever "on the tip of her tongue." In the meantime, it was observed by all on board, that he avoided *her* in the most pointed manner, and, for the most part, shut himself up alone in his state-room, where, in fact, he might have been

① indifferent-looking, (相貌)一般的，相当于 plain-looking。

这一点可是值得大力推荐的。她同大多数女士打成一片，显得异常亲昵；而且让我大为惊讶的是，她显然生性风骚，尽向男士们卖弄风情。她总能把大伙逗乐，我所说的“逗乐”——真不知道怎么才能自圆其说。事实上，我很快发现，大伙更常讥笑怀亚特夫人，而不是同她一起欢笑。男士们对她几乎不置一词，而女士们很快就断言她是个“好心肠的家伙，但相貌平平，毫无教养，粗俗不堪”。最让人费解的是，怀亚特先生怎么会和她结婚，简直像是被骗进了圈套。一般来说都是因为钱——但我知道，这并非答案，因为怀亚特跟我说过，她既没带给他一个子儿，也不指望能通过其他任何渠道发财。他说，他是“为了爱情而结婚的，且只为爱情，他的新娘非常值得他爱”。想到我朋友的这番表白，站在他的立场看，我承认我感到难以名状的困惑：他会不会是脑子出了问题？除此之外我还能怎么想呢？他是如此优雅、聪明和讲究，对缺陷异常敏感，对美无比狂热！当然，她看起来很喜欢他——尤其是当他不在场的时候——她一再引用她那“心爱的丈夫怀亚特先生”的话，这使她显得特别可笑。“丈夫”这个词似乎永远——套用一句她本人的妙语——永远“挂在她嘴边”。同时，全船的人都看得出，他毫不掩饰地回避着她，大多数时间都把自己独自关在包间里。事实上，他就是完全待在自己的包间里，放任妻子自由自在地在主舱中同乘客们肆意取乐。

said to live altogether, leaving his wife at full liberty to amuse herself as she thought best, in the public society of the main cabin.

My conclusion, from what I saw and heard, was, that, the artist, by some unaccountable freak of fate, or perhaps in some fit of enthusiastic and fanciful passion, had been induced to unite himself with a person altogether beneath him, and that the natural result, entire and speedy disgust, had ensued. I pitied him from the bottom of my heart — but could not, for that reason, quite forgive his incommunicativeness in the matter of the "Last Supper." For this I resolved to have my revenge. ①

One day he came upon deck, and, taking his arm as had been my wont, I sauntered with him backwards and forwards. His gloom, however, (which I considered quite natural under the circumstances,) seemed entirely unabated. He said little, and that moodily, and with evident effort. I ventured a jest or two, and he made a sickening attempt at a smile. Poor fellow! — as I thought of *his wife,* I wondered that he could have heart to put on even the semblance of mirth. At last I ventured a home thrust. I determined to commence a series of covert insinuations, or innuendoes, about the oblong box — just to let him perceive, gradually, that I was *not* altogether the butt, or victim, of his little bit of pleasant mystification. My first observation was by way of opening a masked battery. I said something about the "peculiar shape of *that* box;" and, as I spoke the words, I smiled knowingly, winked, and touched him gently with my fore-finger in the ribs.

The manner in which Wyatt received this harmless pleasantry,

① revenge 按惯例译为“复仇”，但“复仇”语气过重，故此处处理为“不会善罢甘休”。

根据我的所见所闻，我得出了这样的结论：由于某种难以解释的无常命运，或是因为一时的狂热，画家头脑发热，突发奇想地娶了一个完全配不上他的人；至于之后的结果，自然是他很快就开始彻底地厌恶起这个女人。我打心底里同情他——但却无法因此而完全原谅他对我隐瞒《最后的晚餐》那桩事。关于这件事，我是不会善罢甘休的。

一天，他来到了甲板上，我像往常那样挽着他的胳膊，和他一起来来回回地闲逛。然而，他的忧郁看起来一点都未消退（我觉得在他现在的处境中，这是最自然不过的了）。他的话很少，即便硬挤出几句来，也抑郁得很。我斗胆说了一两个笑话，他勉强笑了一下，可是比哭还难看。可怜的家伙！想到他的妻子，我奇怪他怎么还能强颜欢笑。最后，我大胆出击要害，决定针对那个长方形箱子展开一连串旁敲侧击的盘问——好让他慢慢明白，他那点诙谐打趣的故弄玄虚，根本难不倒我。第一步是要揭开他的伪装。我说了一些关于“那个箱子的特殊形状”的话，说话时脸上挂着心照不宣的微笑，眨了眨眼，还用食指轻轻捅了捅他的肋骨。

怀亚特对我那无伤大雅的玩笑的反应，让我立刻确信他疯了。

convinced me, at once, that he was mad. At first he stared at me as if he found it impossible to comprehend the witticism of my remark; but as its point seemed slowly to make its way into his brain, his eyes in the same proportion, seemed protruding from their sockets. Then he grew very red — then hideously pale — then, as if highly amused with what I had insinuated, he began a loud and boisterous laugh, which, to my astonishment, he kept up, with gradually increasing vigor, for ten minutes or more. In conclusion, he fell flat and heavily upon the deck. When I ran to uplift him, to all appearance he was *dead.*

I called assistance, and, with much difficulty, we brought him to himself. Upon reviving he spoke incoherently for some time. At length we bled him and put him to bed. The next morning he was quite recovered, so far as regarded his mere bodily health. Of his mind I say nothing, of course. I avoided him during the rest of the passage, by advice of the captain, who seemed to coincide with me altogether in my views of his insanity, but cautioned me to say nothing on this head to any person on board.

Several circumstances occurred immediately after this fit of Wyatt's, which contributed to heighten the curiosity with which I was already possessed. Among other things, this: I had been nervous — drank too much strong green tea, and slept ill at night — in fact, for two nights I could not be properly said to sleep at all. Now, my state-room opened into the main cabin, or dining-room, as did those of all the single men on board. Wyatt's three rooms were in the after-cabin, which was separated from the main one by a slight sliding door, never locked even at night. As we were almost constantly on a wind, and the breeze was not a little stiff, the ship heeled to leeward very considerably; and

起初，他只是瞪着我，好像根本听不懂我的俏皮话；但随着他似乎慢慢领会了我的言外之意，他的眼睛像是要突出眼眶。紧接着，他满面通红——之后又苍白得吓人——然后，他又像是被我暗示的东西给逗乐了似的，放声狂笑起来。令我不解的是，他就这么笑着，越笑越厉害，一直持续了十多分钟。最后，他一下子直挺挺地重重摔倒在甲板上。我奔过去扶起他时，发现他已同死了差不多。

我赶紧呼救，大家好不容易把他弄醒了。苏醒后，有那么一会儿，他一直语无伦次地说着什么。最后，我们给他放了血[①]，将他抬到床上。第二天早上，他就完全恢复了。当然，这只是对于他的身体而言，至于他的精神健康，我无话可说。我听从了船长的建议，在接下来的旅途中避免与他见面。船长同我一样，认为他精神错乱了，不过他提醒我不要对船上的任何人说起这事。

怀亚特的这次发病过后，紧接着又发生了几件事，更加重了我的好奇心。其中一件是这样的：我一直心神不宁——喝多了浓茶，晚上睡不着——实际上，有两个晚上，我可以说是彻夜难眠。同船上其他单身男子的房间一样，我的房门也正对着主舱，即餐厅。怀亚特的三个房间所在的后舱，与主舱隔着一道小滑门，这道门即便在晚上也不上锁。因为是迎风行驶，而且风很强劲，所以船向下风方向倾斜得厉害。每当右舷倾向下风方向时，两个船舱之间的滑门就会自动滑开，并且之后就一直这么开着，因为没人愿意爬起来把

① 给病人放血是一种直到 19 世纪晚期才被弃用的疗法，现代医学证明其害处远远大于好处。

whenever her starboard side was to leeward, the sliding door between the cabins slid open, and so remained, nobody taking the trouble to get up and shut it. But my berth was in such a position, that when my own state-room door was open, as well as the sliding door in question, (and my own door was *always* open on account of the heat,) I could see into the after-cabin quite distinctly, and just at that portion of it, too, where were situated the state-rooms of Mr. Wyatt. Well, during two nights (*not* consecutive) while I lay awake, I clearly saw Mrs. W., about eleven o'clock upon each night, steal cautiously from the state-room of Mr. W., and enter the extra room, where she remained until daybreak, when she was called by her husband and went back. That they were virtually separated was clear. They had separate apartments — no doubt in contemplation of a more permanent divorce; and here, after all, I thought, was the mystery of the extra state-room.

There was another circumstance, too, which interested me much. During the two wakeful nights in question, and immediately after the disappearance of Mrs. Wyatt into the extra state-room, I was attracted by certain singular, cautious, subdued noises in that of her husband. After listening to them for some time, with thoughtful attention, I at length succeeded perfectly in translating their import ①. They were sounds occasioned by the artist in prying open the oblong box, by means of a chisel ② and mallet ③ — the latter being apparently muffled, or deadened, by some soft woollen or cotton substance in which its head was enveloped.

① 在这里，import 并不解释为“进口”，而是“含义”的意思。
② chisel, 名词，凿子，一种用来切削或雕刻石头、木头、金属的有锋利斜刃的金属工具。
③ mallet, 名词，木槌，一种手柄较短的锤子，通常带有木制的圆头，主要用来敲击凿子或钎子。

它关上。巧的是，当滑门和我的房门同时敞开时（因为天热，我自己的房门总是开着），从我的铺位刚好能清楚地看到后舱，而且看到的部分，恰恰是怀亚特先生的几个包间。在我无法入睡的那两天夜里（不是连着的两天），我分明看到，怀亚特夫人每晚11点左右都会偷偷溜出怀亚特先生的房间，走进那个空着的包间，一直待到黎明，等她丈夫来叫她的时候才回去。显然，他们两个事实上已经分居了。他们有各自的房间——毫无疑问是在计划着离婚，永远井水不犯河水。我想，原来那间一直让我好奇的包间有着这样的秘密。

还有一件事让我很感兴趣。在那两个不眠之夜，怀亚特夫人一溜进另外那间包房，她丈夫的房间就会传出一阵奇怪而异常小心、压得很低的声响，这引起了我的注意。经过仔细聆听和反复寻思后，我终于成功地破解了那声音的含义。那是画家在用凿子和木槌之类的工具撬开那只长方形箱子的声音——木槌的响声闷闷的，显然是用羊毛或者棉花之类的东西蒙住了槌头。

In this manner I fancied I could distinguish the precise moment when he fairly disengaged the lid — also, that I could determine when he removed it altogether, and when he deposited it upon the lower berth in his room; this latter point I knew, for example, by certain slight taps which the lid made in striking against the wooden edges of the berth, as he endeavored to lay it down *very* gently — there being no room for it on the floor. After this there was a dead stillness, and I heard nothing more, upon either occasion, until nearly daybreak; unless, perhaps, I may mention a low sobbing, or murmuring sound, so very much suppressed as to be nearly inaudible — if, indeed, the whole of this latter noise were not rather produced by my own imagination. I say it seemed to *resemble* sobbing or sighing — but, of course, it could not have been either. I rather think it was a ringing in my own ears. Mr. Wyatt, no doubt, according to custom, was merely giving the rein to one of his hobbies — indulging in one of his fits of artistic enthusiasm. He had opened his oblong box, in order to feast his eyes on the pictorial treasure within. There was nothing in this however, to make him *sob*. I repeat, therefore, that it must have been simply a freak of my own fancy, distempered by good Captain Hardy's green tea. Just before dawn, on each of the two nights of which I speak, I distinctly heard Mr. Wyatt replace the lid upon the oblong box, and force the nails into their old places, by means of the muffled mallet. Having done this, he issued from his state-room, fully dressed, and proceeded to call Mrs. W. from hers.

We had been at sea seven days, and were now off Cape Hatteras, when there came a tremendously heavy blow from the southwest. We were, in a measure, prepared for it, however, as the weather had been

我想，就这样倾听着，我就可以准确地分辨出他何时把盖子撬开——也可以判断出他何时把盖子移开，何时把它放到房间的下铺上。举例来说，由于箱盖碰到木头床沿就会发出轻微的声音，这样我就知道他正非常小心地把盖子放到床上——因为地板上没处可放。这之后是一片死寂，直到黎明，我再也没听到任何动静，两天夜里都是如此。或许我听到了低声的哭泣或是喃喃细语声，但声音压得很低，几乎听不见——当然，或许这些声音都只是我的想象。我说它像啜泣或是叹息——不过当然了，它也可能什么都不是，我更觉得那是我的耳鸣。毫无疑问，怀亚特先生只是一如既往地沉浸在自己的嗜好中——猛然一头扎进对艺术的狂热中。他打开长方形箱子，是为了饱览里面那幅珍贵的画作。然而，这里面并没有什么能让他哭泣的东西呀。因此，我再次声明，那一定是我自己的幻觉，是好心的哈代船长的绿茶让我有点不对劲了。在我提到的这两个夜晚，就在黎明前，我清楚地听到怀亚特先生重新盖好箱盖，用蒙住布的木槌把钉子照原样钉好。做完这些，他就穿戴整齐，走出房间，去怀亚特夫人的房间里把她叫出来。

我们已经在海上航行了七天，离开哈特拉斯角[1]时，刮起了一场猛烈的西南风。不过我们在一定程度上已经对此做好了准备，因为

① 哈特拉斯角，也译作哈特勒斯角。美国北卡罗来纳州外滩群岛 (Outer Banks) 哈特拉斯岛上一狭长、弯曲的沙洲形成的岬角，长 113 千米。其东南方的浅滩暗流长期以来对大西洋航行构成危险。

holding out threats for some time. Everything was made snug, alow and aloft; and as the wind steadily freshened, we lay to, at length, under spanker and foretopsail, both double-reefed.

In this trim, we rode safely enough for forty-eight hours — the ship proving herself an excellent sea-boat, in many respects, and shipping no water of any consequence. At the end of this period, however, the gale had freshened into a hurricane, and our after-sail split into ribbons, bringing us so much in the trough of the water that we shipped several prodigious seas, one immediately after the other. By this accident we lost three men overboard, with the caboose, and nearly the whole of the larboard bulwarks. Scarcely had we recovered our senses, before the foretopsail went into shreds, when we got up a storm stay-sail, and with this did pretty well for some hours, the ship heading the sea much more steadily than before.

The gale still held on, however, and we saw no signs of its abating. The rigging was found to be ill-fitted, and greatly strained; and on the third day of the blow, about five in the afternoon, our mizzen-mast, in a heavy lurch to windward, went by the board. For an hour or more, we tried in vain to get rid of it, on account of the prodigious rolling of the ship; and, before we had succeeded, the carpenter came aft and announced four feet of water in the hold. To add to our dilemma, we found the pumps choked and nearly useless.

All was now confusion and despair — but an effort was made to lighten the ship by throwing overboard as much of her cargo as could be reached, and by cutting away the two masts that remained. This we at last accomplished — but we were still unable to do anything at the pumps; and, in the meantime, the leak gained on us very fast.

这段时间的天气一直是山雨欲来。船上，上上下下每样东西都放置妥当了；可由于风越刮越猛，我们最终无法继续前行，后桅纵帆和前桅帆都折叠了起来。

就这样，我们安全地漂行了48小时——事实证明，这艘船在许多方面都称得上是一艘出色的海船，越舷而入的海水始终没给船什么大碍。但后来，大风演变成了飓风，我们的后帆被撕得一条一条的，这使得我们的船置身浪尖风口，接连遭受了几个大浪的袭击。在这场事故里，有三个人和舱面厨房一起被卷入大海，差不多整个左舷的舷墙都不见了。还没等我们缓过神来，前桅帆又被撕成了碎片。我们撑起了抵挡风暴的支索帆，船这才在海面上顺利航行了几个小时，比之前稳当了许多。

然而，飓风仍未平息，看不出一点减弱的迹象。我们发现，船上的索具装得不大好，绷得太紧了。起大风的第三天，大约下午五点钟时，船的后桅迎风倾斜得很厉害，已经越过船舷了。我们花了一个多小时想把它拆除，但因为船身摇晃得厉害，最终无功而返。而且，这边还没弄好，船匠就奔到船尾来，嚷嚷着说船舱里积了四英尺深的水。雪上加霜的是，水泵阻塞了，几乎没法再用。

眼下，一切都混乱不堪，令人绝望——我们设法减轻船的重量，拿到什么货物就把它往海里扔，还把剩下的两根桅杆也砍掉了。后来，我们终于把这些干完了——但还是没能修好水泵，而与此同时，漏进来的水正以极快的速度上涨。

At sundown, the gale had sensibly diminished in violence, and, as the sea went down with it, we still entertained faint hopes of saving ourselves in the boats. At eight, P. M., the clouds broke away to windward, and we had the advantage of a full moon — a piece of good fortune which served wonderfully to cheer our drooping spirits.

After incredible labor we succeeded, at length, in getting the long-boat over the side without material accident, and into this we crowded the whole of the crew and most of the passengers. This party made off immediately, and, after undergoing much suffering, finally arrived, in safety, at Ocracoke Inlet, on the third day after the wreck.

Fourteen passengers, with the Captain, remained on board, resolving to trust their fortunes to the jolly-boat at the stern. We lowered it without difficulty, although it was only by a miracle that we prevented it from swamping as it touched the water. It contained, when afloat, the captain and his wife, Mr. Wyatt and party, a Mexican officer, wife, four children, and myself, with a negro valet.

We had no room, of course, for anything except a few positively necessary instruments, some provisions, and the clothes upon our backs. No one had thought of even attempting to save anything more. What must have been the astonishment of all then, when having proceeded a few fathoms[①] from the ship, Mr. Wyatt stood up in the stern-sheets, and coolly demanded of Captain Hardy that the boat should be put back for the purpose of taking in his oblong box!

"Sit down, Mr. Wyatt," replied the captain, somewhat sternly; "you will capsize us if you do not sit quite still. Our gunwale is almost in the water now."

① fathom 意为"英寻"，测水深单位，1 英寻约合 1.8 米。

日落时分，肆虐的狂风明显减弱，海面上也平静了下来，我们还抱着渺茫的希望，想利用救生艇自救。到了晚上8点，云层随风散去，显出一轮满月——这真是个好兆头，我们萎靡的精神顿时为之大振。

最后，我们费了九牛二虎之力，终于顺利地把船边的大救生艇放了下去，所有船员和大部分乘客都挤上了救生艇。这批人立刻出发，他们历经艰险，终于在船只失事后的第三天安全抵达了奥克拉科克港①。

船长和14名乘客留在了船上，他们决定把希望寄托在船尾的小救生艇上。我们没花什么力气就把小艇放了下去，下水时它竟然没有翻船，这简直算得上是个奇迹。艇上坐的是船长夫妇、怀亚特先生一行、一名墨西哥官员、他的妻子和四个孩子、我和一个黑人男仆。

当然，除了一些绝对必需的装备、食物和身上的衣服，小船上再没多余的地方可以放东西了，也没人想到要再去抢救些别的东西。可是小船刚划出不远，让所有人吃惊不已的事情发生了。只见怀亚特先生从船尾的船板上站起来，冷冷地要求哈代船长把船划回去，他要去取他的长方形箱子！

“坐下，怀亚特先生，”船长有些严厉地回应道，“你要是不老老实实坐着会把船弄翻的。现在我们的舷缘已经差不多在水里了。”

① 奥克拉科克港，位于美国北卡罗来纳州外滩群岛河口，连接大西洋和帕姆利科湾 (Pamlico)。

"The box!" vociferated Mr. Wyatt, still standing — "the box, I say! Captain Hardy, you cannot, you *will* not refuse me. Its weight will be but a trifle — it is nothing — mere nothing. By the mother who bore you — for the love of Heaven — by your hope of salvation, I *implore* you to put back for the box!"

The captain, for a moment, seemed touched by the earnest appeal of the artist, but he regained his stern composure, and merely said —

"Mr. Wyatt, you are *mad*. I cannot listen to you. Sit down, I say, or you will swamp the boat. Stay — hold him — seize him! — he is about to spring overboard! There — I knew it — he is over!"

As the captain said this, Mr. Wyatt, in fact, sprang from the boat, and, as we were yet in the lee of the wreck, succeeded, by almost superhuman exertion, in getting hold of a rope which hung from the fore-chains. In another moment he was on board, and rushing frantically down into the cabin.

In the meantime, we had been swept astern of the ship, and being quite out of her lee, were at the mercy of the tremendous sea which was still running. We made a determined effort to put back, but our little boat was like a feather in the breath of the tempest. We saw at a glance that the doom of the unfortunate artist was sealed.

As our distance from the wreck rapidly increased, the madman (for as such only could we regard him) was seen to emerge from the companion-way, up which by dint of a strength that appeared gigantic, he dragged, bodily, the oblong box. While we gazed in the extremity of astonishment, he passed, rapidly, several turns of a three-inch rope, first around the box and then around his body. In another instant both body and box were in the sea — disappearing suddenly, at once and forever.

“那箱子！”怀亚特先生仍站在那儿大声嚷道，“那箱子，听见没！哈代船长，您不能，您不会拒绝我的。它的重量微不足道——几乎没有重量——根本没重量。看在生您的母亲的份上——为了上帝的爱——看在您的灵魂希望得到救赎的份上，我恳求您，把小艇划回去，取那只箱子吧！”

有那么一会儿，船长似乎被画家真诚的请求打动了，但他很快便恢复了之前严厉而镇定的态度，只是说道：

“怀亚特先生，你疯了。我不能听你的。坐下，听到没？否则你会把船打翻的。别动——抱住他——抓住他！他要跳海了！瞧——我就知道——他完蛋了！”

就在船长说这话时，怀亚特先生实际上已经跳下了船。因为我们还处在失事船只的避风一侧，所以他以超人般的力量抓住从前索条上垂下的一根绳子，不一会儿便爬上了甲板，发疯似的冲进船舱。

与此同时，我们已被刮到船尾，远远出了避风区，只得任凭波涛汹涌的大海摆布。我们竭力想要划回去，然而我们的小船像是暴风中的一片羽毛般不受控制。我们瞥了一眼，那不幸的画家看来是在劫难逃了。

我们离失事的船只越来越远。这时，那个疯子（我们只能这么看待他）出现在升降梯上，一个人把那只长方形箱子拖了上来，力气大得惊人。我们目瞪口呆地看着他，只见他飞快地用一根手腕粗的绳子在箱子上绕了几圈，然后在自己身上也绕了几圈。很快，他和箱子都沉入海里，并且突然就消失了，再也没有出现。

We lingered awhile sadly upon our oars, with our eyes riveted upon the spot. At length we pulled away. The silence remained unbroken for an hour. Finally, I hazarded a remark.

"Did you observe, Captain, how suddenly they sank? Was not that an exceedingly singular thing? I confess that I entertained some feeble hope of his final deliverance, when I saw him lash himself to the box, and commit himself to the sea."

"They sank as a matter of course," replied the Captain, "and that like a shot. They will soon rise again, however — *but not till the salt melts*."

"The salt!" I ejaculated.

"Hush!" said the Captain, pointing to the wife and sisters of the deceased. "We must talk of these things at some more appropriate time."

We suffered much, and made a narrow escape; but fortune befriended us, as well as our mates in the long-boat. We landed, in fine, more dead than alive, after four days of intense distress, upon the beach opposite Roanoke Island. We remained here a week, were not ill-treated by the wreckers, and at length obtained a passage to New York.

About a month after the loss of the "Independence," I happened to meet Captain Hardy in Broadway. Our conversation turned, naturally, upon the disaster, and especially upon the sad fate of poor Wyatt. I thus learned the following particulars.

The artist had engaged passage for himself, wife, two sisters and a servant. His wife was, indeed, as she had been represented, a most lovely, and most accomplished woman. On the morning of the fourteenth of June, (the day in which I first visited the ship,) the lady suddenly sickened and died. The young husband was frantic with grief — but circumstances imperatively forbade the deferring his voyage

我们悲哀地停下了桨，久久凝视着他和箱子沉没的地方。最终，我们离开了。在一个小时的时间里，大家都没说话。最后，我斗胆说道：

"船长，你注意到他们是怎么一下子就沉下去的吗？那不是十分奇怪吗？坦白说，当我看到他把自己和箱子捆在一起跳进海里时，我还以为他有一丝脱险的希望呢。"

"他们当然会沉下去，"船长回答道，"而且会立刻沉下去。但很快他们就会浮上来——不过要等到盐溶化了以后。"

"盐！"我喊了出来。

"安静！"船长说道，指着死者的妻子和两个妹妹。"等到了比较合适的时候，我们再谈这些事。"

我们历经磨难，九死一生，不过幸好上天保佑了我们，就像它庇护我们在大救生艇上的同伴一样。经过四天的痛苦挣扎，我们最终在罗阿诺克岛[1]对面的海滩登陆了，上岸时已经半死不活。我们在那里待了一个星期，打捞沉船的人对我们不错，最终，我们搭船去了纽约。

"独立号"失事后大约一个月，我在百老汇邂逅了哈代船长。我们很自然地谈到了那场海难，还特别讲到了可怜的怀亚特的悲惨命运。我因此得知了以下的详情。

画家为他自己、妻子、两个妹妹和一个仆人订了舱位。正像画家所描述的那样，他的妻子是一位非常可爱、多才多艺的女子。6月14日早晨（我第一次上船的那天），那位女士突发疾病去世了。年轻的丈夫伤心得快要发疯了——可是当时的情况不允许他推迟

① 罗阿诺克岛，北卡罗来纳海岸附近。在历史上，因沃尔特·雷利 (Walter Raleigh) 想在此建立新的殖民地而出名。

to New York. It was necessary to take to her mother the corpse of his adored wife, and on the other hand, the universal prejudice which would prevent his doing so openly, was well known. Nine-tenths of the passengers would have abandoned the ship rather than take passage with a dead body.

In this dilemma, Captain Hardy arranged that the corpse, being first partially embalmed, and packed, with a large quantity of salt, in a box of suitable dimensions, should be conveyed on board as merchandise. Nothing was to be said of the lady's decease; and, as it was well understood that Mr. Wyatt had engaged passage for his wife, it became necessary that some person should personate her during the voyage. This the deceased's lady's-maid was easily prevailed on to do. The extra state-room, originally engaged for this girl, during her mistress' life, was now merely retained. In this state-room the pseudo-wife ① slept, of course, every night. In the day-time she performed, to the best of her ability, the part of her mistress — whose person, it had been carefully ascertained, was unknown to any of the passengers on board.

My own mistake arose, naturally enough, through too careless, too inquisitive, and too impulsive a temperament. But of late, it is a rare thing that I sleep soundly at night. There is a countenance which haunts me, turn as I will. There is an hysterical laugh which will forever ring within my ears.

① 这是作者自己创造的合成词，其前缀 pseudo- 表示“假的”。其他类似的词还有 pseudo-science(伪科学)，pseudo-intellectual(假知识分子) 等。

去纽约的行程。他必须要把爱妻的尸体运给她的母亲，而另一方面，谁都知道，世人的偏见不允许他公开这么做。乘客十有八九肯定宁愿弃船而去，也不会愿意和一具死尸同船而行。

进退两难之际，哈代船长做了这样的安排：给尸体的一部分涂上防腐香油，和大量的盐一起打包放在大小合适的箱子里，然后作为货物运上了船，而对于女士的死只字不提。因为大家都知道怀亚特先生已经为妻子订了舱位，所以就必须有人在旅程中假扮她，于是已故女士的女仆就很容易地被说服了来做这件事。在女主人活着的时候，那间多订的包房就是给这个女孩的，后来也就那么保留着。当然，每天晚上，这名假冒的妻子就睡在那间房里。白天，她则尽己所能地扮演她的女主人——事先已仔细查明，船上的乘客中没有人见过真正的女主人。

我的错误自然是由于过于粗心、爱管闲事、脾气冲动造成的。不过，最近我夜里总是睡不安稳。无论怎样翻来覆去，总有一张面容在我眼前晃动，总有一串歇斯底里的笑声在我耳边久久回响。

Diddling Considered as One of the Exact Sciences
欺骗是一门精密的科学

本篇小说最初以《招揽钱财；或欺骗是一门精密的科学》(*Raising the Wind; or Diddling Considered as One of the Exact Sciences*) 于 1843 年 10 月 14 日刊登在《费城周六信使报》上，并于 1845 年 9 月 13 日以《欺骗是一门精密的科学》刊登在《百老汇杂志》上。综观整篇小说，爱伦·坡以其幽默讽刺的语言和严谨细致的逻辑，让读者在轻松愉快的阅读体验中感受了幽默大师犀利的文笔和充满睿智的叙事技巧。此外，这篇小说还反映了美国 19 世纪上半叶的社会现实，具有深刻的现实意义。爱伦·坡创作这篇小说的灵感和动机来源于当时十分流行的功利主义 (utilitarianism) 哲学，以英国经济学家、哲学家杰里米·边沁 (Jeremy Bentham, 1748—1832) 为代表的功利主义思想家在 19 世纪上半叶的欧美国家大放光彩。对功利主义者来说，一切事物只要产生快乐的结果就是好的，应该提倡；反之则是坏的，要予以取缔。爱伦·坡反对这些片面的学说，但是他并没有直接对其进行批判，而是以幽默讽刺的形式来针砭其中的弊病。同时，爱伦·坡借用了伦敦当时上演的一出介绍骗子杰里米 (Jeremy Diddler) 行骗生活的笑剧作为该小说的题材。小说的题记“嘿，骗人啦骗人啦，猫儿把提琴拉”让熟悉爱伦·坡短篇小说的读者立刻想到了他的另一部短篇小说《黑猫》。那只叫普鲁托的黑猫给故事的主人公带来了毁灭性的灾难，然而这篇小说中的猫却是一只精明的、擅长骗术的动物，与《格林童话》里那只穿着靴子欺骗国王和民众的猫如出一辙，为该篇以幽默和讽刺为特征的众多骗局故事做好了铺垫。与其他短篇小说不同的是，这篇小说包含了许多关于骗术的小故事，但作者以其天才般的叙事技巧把这些小故事串联起来，层层递进，娓娓道来，使其整体看起来像是一篇科学论文。表面看来，作者似乎是以科学的叙述方法来提倡骗术的科学性，但如果联想本篇小说的创作动因，我们就不难看出，爱伦·坡其实是在使用反讽的手法讽刺功利主义学说。他把骗术和科学联系在一起，表达了对科学的某种成见。在诗歌《十四行诗——致科学》(Sonnet—To Science, 1829) 中，诗人对“科学‘蹂躏’艺术想象力”的说法提出了批判。在本篇小说中，作者用科学和理性的叙述手法来展示骗术的合理性，其根本目的是用这种理性思维达到反讽的效果，讥讽以边沁为代表的功利主义思想家。综观整篇小说，作者尽其所能地展示了骗子的作案才华和他们的心理状态，但却未给予受害者任何同情的笔墨，这与爱伦·坡的创作理念是分不开的。同说教式的传统小说不同，爱伦·坡从作品中隐退出来，把重心放在故事的叙述方面，而不像传统小说的作者那样，以上帝的身份把自己的价值观和世界观融入作品中。对人物的行为和思想他并不给予道德评价，也未提出任何解决办法，他甚至刻意表现一些潜意识和违反道德的行为。这种对人性阴暗面的揭露反映出他对人性的关注，法国著名诗人波德莱尔就对他这种独特的道德观推崇备至，他在《埃德加·爱伦·坡的生平及其作品》中这样写道：“一个经常把一切社会制度看作是违反常理、看作是骗局的人……这样设想也是很自然的。”因此我们有理由说，这篇小说不仅在当时有着积极的意义，而且还穿越时空，影响了后世作家的创作。

Hey, diddle diddle,
The cat and the fiddle.[1]

SINCE the world began there have been two Jeremys. The one wrote a Jeremiad about usury, and was called Jeremy Bentham. He has been much admired by Mr. John Neal, and was a great man in a small way. The other gave name to the most important of the Exact Sciences, and was a great man in a great way — I may say, indeed, in the very greatest of ways.

Diddling — or the abstract idea conveyed by the verb to diddle — is sufficiently well understood. Yet the fact, the deed, the thing diddling, is somewhat difficult to define. We may get, however, at a tolerably distinct conception of the matter in hand, by defining — not the thing, diddling, in itself — but man, as an animal that diddles. Had Plato but hit upon this, he would have been spared the affront of the picked chicken.

Very pertinently it was demanded of Plato, why a picked chicken, which was clearly "a biped without feathers," was not, according to his own definition, a man? But I am not to be bothered by any similar query. Man is an animal that diddles, and there is no animal that diddles but man. It will take an entire hen-coop of picked chickens to get over that.

① 节选自一首英语童谣，全文是：Hey diddle diddle, /The cat and the fiddle, /The cow jumped over the moon. /The little dog laughed to see such fun, /And the dish ran away with the spoon. 这首童谣荒诞有趣，音乐感强，符合一般童谣的特点。爱伦·坡首次发表本文时，曾嘲讽地注明它是取自美国诗人 Flaccus(即汤姆斯·沃德)的史诗，后来的版本则取消了这一附注。

嘿，骗人啦骗人啦，

猫儿把提琴拉。

自从开天辟地以来，就有两个杰里米。一位是写了《为高利贷辩护》哀史的杰里米·边沁[①]，可这位被约翰·尼尔[②]先生大加赞赏的杰里米虽然伟大，所事毕竟微不足道。至于另一位杰里米[③]，最重要的精密科学就是因他而得名的，而且他不光伟大，所事亦不平凡——事实上，可以说是极不平凡。

骗术——或是由欺骗这一动作所表达的抽象意义——是人们相当了解的。然而，欺骗这一事实、这种行为、这种事情却多少难以定义。但如果不是从欺骗本身，而是从“人是一种会欺骗的动物”这一角度来定义，我们对于上述问题，或许就能有较为明了的认识。如果当初柏拉图能这样思考，就不会因一只被拔光毛的鸡[④]而遭人奚落了。

一只被拔光毛的鸡显然是“无羽毛的两足动物”，但依据柏拉图自己下的定义，它为什么不是人？这么质问他可谓恰当。但是，我绝不会被类似的问题所难倒。人是会欺骗的动物，除了人以外，没有别的动物有此本领。要想推翻这个定义，想必就需要整整一笼被拔光毛的鸡。

① 杰里米·边沁(1748—1832)，英国功利主义哲学家、法学家、社会改革家。他认为，痛苦和快乐是人类的两大主宰，追求快乐、回避痛苦是人的天性，并因此提出，判断国家制度和法律好与坏的唯一标准，就在于它们能否使绝大多数人幸福。爱伦·坡认为他一无是处，故在此加以嘲讽。

② 约翰·尼尔，美国作家、文艺评论家。成就不高，但兴趣广泛，是美国第一个用方言写作的作家、早期女权主义者之一、禁酒运动的拥护者、律师、拳击手、建筑师。事实上，约翰·尼尔与爱伦·坡是朋友关系，作者为何在此捎带着讽刺他，原因不详。

③ 这里指的是19世纪初英国一部不太出名的戏剧中的主人公，名叫Jeremy Diddler，专门骗人。

④ 柏拉图曾把人定义为“无羽毛的两足动物”。第欧根尼(Diogenes)听说后，就带着一只羽毛被拔光的鸡，来到柏拉图讲学的地方，说：“这儿有个柏拉图所谓的人。”柏拉图后来就把自己的定义修正为“无羽毛的、指甲宽而平的两足动物”。

What constitutes the essence, the nare, the principle of diddling is, in fact, peculiar to the class of creatures that wear coats and pantaloons. A crow thieves; a fox cheats; a weasel outwits; a man diddles. To diddle is his destiny. "Man was made to mourn," says the poet. But not so: — he was made to diddle. This is his aim — his object — his end. And for this reason when a man's diddled we say he's "done."

Diddling, rightly considered, is a compound, of which the ingredients are minuteness, interest, perseverance, ingenuity, audacity, nonchalance, originality, impertinence, and grin.

Minuteness: — Your diddler is minute. His operations are upon a small scale. His business is retail, for cash, or approved paper at sight. Should he ever be tempted into magnificent speculation, he then, at once, loses his distinctive features, and becomes what we term "financier." This latter word conveys the diddling idea in every respect except that of magnitude. A diddler may thus be regarded as a banker *in petto* — a "financial operation," as a diddle at Brobdingnag. The one is to the other, as Homer to "Flaccus" — as a Mastodon to a mouse — as the tail of a comet to that of a pig.

Interest: — Your diddler is guided by self-interest. He scorns to diddle for the mere sake of the diddle. He has an object in view — his pocket — and yours. He regards always the main chance. He looks to Number One. You are Number Two, and must look to yourself.

Perseverance: — Your diddler perseveres. He is not readily discouraged. Should even the banks break, he cares nothing about it. He steadily pursues his end, and

事实上，构成骗术的精髓、本质和原则的那些因素，是身着华袍衮服的某类动物所特有的。乌鸦会偷窃，狐狸会欺诈，黄鼠狼聪明过人，但唯有人类懂得欺骗。欺骗就是人的宿命。诗人[①]说，"上帝造人，使其哀悼"，倒不如说是"上帝造人，旨在行骗"。这是人的目的，人的目标，人的归宿。正因为如此，当一个人行骗之后，我们就会说他"大功告成"了。

如果我们实事求是地想一想，就会发现骗术糅合了多种元素：小打小闹、唯利是图、坚持不懈、长于创造、胆大妄为、泰然自若、独具匠心、傲慢自大、沾沾自喜。

小打小闹——骗子只是小打小闹而已。他们经营规模不大，干的是小买卖，交货后，要么付现，要么见票即付。一旦他们受到诱惑，扩大投机规模，就会立即失去自身的特点，成为我们所谓的"金融家"。这个词除了规模之外，在其他各方面都可传达欺骗的意义。因此，骗子可以被认为是小型的金融家，而金融运作则可以被认为是巨人国[②]里的欺骗行为。金融运作相比于欺骗，如同荷马与"弗拉库斯"[③]相比——亦如乳齿象与老鼠相比——彗星之尾与猪的尾巴相比。

唯利是图——骗子是自私自利的。他们鄙视为欺骗而欺骗的行径，他们眼里只有一个目标——自己的口袋，当然还有你们的口袋。他们总是留意着赚钱的机会，将自身的利益视为头等重要的事情，而你们的利益则位在其次，所以你们要自己照看好自己。

坚持不懈——骗子都是坚持不懈的人，不太容易气馁。即便银行破产，他们也毫不在乎。他们执着地追求自己的目标，

---

① 此处指的是英国诗人彭斯及他的诗作《人生来是为了哀悼》。
② 《格列佛游记》中的巨人国。
③ 指与爱伦·坡同时代的美国诗人汤姆斯·沃德。爱伦·坡曾撰文评价他的诗作，语言十分尖刻。

Ut canis a corio nunquam absterrebitur uncto,

so he never lets go of his game.

Ingenuity: — Your diddler is ingenious. He has constructiveness large. He understands plot. He invents and circumvents. Were he not Alexander he would be Diogenes. Were he not a diddler, he would be a maker of patent rat-traps or an angler for trout.

Audacity: — Your diddler is audacious. — He is a bold man. He carries the war into Africa. He conquers all by assault. He would not fear the daggers of Frey Herren. With a little more prudence Dick Turpin would have made a good diddler; with a trifle less blarney, Daniel O'Connell; with a pound or two more brains, Charles the Twelfth.

Nonchalance: — Your diddler is nonchalant. He is not at all nervous. He never had any nerves. He is never seduced into a flurry. He is never put out — unless put out of doors. He is cool — cool as a cucumber. He is calm — "calm as a smile from Lady Bury." He is easy — easy as an old glove, or the damsels of ancient Baiæ.

Originality: — Your diddler is original — conscientiously so. His thoughts are his own. He would scorn to employ those of another. A stale trick is his aversion. He would return a purse, I am sure, upon discovering that he had obtained it by an unoriginal diddle.

Impertinence: — Your diddler is impertinent. He swaggers. He sets his arms a-kimbo. He thrusts his hands in his trousers' pockets. He sneers in your face. He treads on your corns. He eats your dinner, he drinks your wine, he borrows your money, he pulls your nose, he kicks your poodle, and he kisses your wife.

就像无法从油腻腻的肉皮前赶走的狗一样，

从不放走自己的猎物。

长于创造——骗子都是足智多谋的。他们极富创造能力，懂得运筹帷幄、无中生有、左右腾挪。如果他做不了亚历山大，就做第欧根尼[①]。如果他没成为骗子，就该是捕鼠利器的发明者或钓鱼能手。

胆大妄为——骗子都是胆大妄为之人。他们无所畏惧，把战火烧至非洲，主动出击，征服一切。他们不怕弗雷·赫伦[②]的匕首。如果大盗迪克·特平[③]再多几分审慎，丹尼尔·奥康乃尔[④]再少几分花言巧语，查理十二世[⑤]再多几分头脑，他们也许都能成为个中高手。

泰然自若——骗子都是泰然自若的。他们根本不会神经紧张，因为他们从来就没有过神经。没有什么能使他们惊慌失措。他们从不会颜面扫地——除非被扫地出门。他们很冷静——冷静得像块石头，镇定自若似伯丽夫人[⑥]的微笑。他们很自在——自在得有如戴惯了的手套，又有如古比亚村[⑦]的少女。

独具匠心——骗子都饶有独创性，并且他们是刻意为之。他们只用自己的点子，不屑于盗用他人的想法，更厌恶老调重弹。我敢肯定，如果他们发现自己骗人钱财的伎俩早已有人用过，他们一定会物归原主的。

傲慢自大——骗子都十分傲慢。他们趾高气扬，两手叉腰，有

① 第欧根尼为古希腊哲学家，犬儒主义的创始人。据传，有次他晒太阳时，亚历山大大帝来看他，并问他可以为他做些什么。他回答道：“别挡我阳光就可以了。”亚历山大大帝听后感慨地说：“如果我不是亚历山大大帝，那么我就要做第欧根尼。”

② 弗雷·赫伦，所指不明。Frey 有可能指的是北欧神话中的和平丰饶农耕之神，他的剑可以自动作战，后为恋人放弃此剑，终遭杀害。

③ 迪克·特平，英国强盗，死后在民间传说和文学作品中多被美化。

④ 丹尼尔·奥康乃尔，爱尔兰政治家，从政生涯中，长期为天主教徒的权益和爱尔兰的独立奔走。

⑤ 查理十二世，瑞典国王，1697—1718年在位，生性好战。

⑥ 伯丽夫人，与爱伦·坡同时代的英国贵妇，以甜美著称。

⑦ 古比亚村，古罗马旅游胜地，由于火山运动，该村现已位于海平面以下。

Grin: — Your true diddler winds up all with a grin[①]. But this nobody sees but himself. He grins when his daily work is done — when his allotted labors are accomplished — at night in his own closet, and altogether for his own private entertainment. He goes home. He locks his door. He divests himself of his clothes. He puts out his candle. He gets into bed. He places his head upon the pillow. All this done, and your diddler grins. This is no hypothesis. It is a matter of course. I reason *à priori*, and a diddle would be no diddle without a grin.

The origin of the diddle is referrable to the infancy of the Human Race. Perhaps the first diddler was Adam. At all events, we can trace the science back to a very remote period of antiquity. The moderns, however, have brought it to a perfection never dreamed of by our thick-headed progenitors. Without pausing to speak of the "old saws," therefore, I shall content myself with a compendious account of some of the more "modern instances."

A very good diddle is this. A housekeeper in want of a sofa, for instance, is seen to go in and out of several cabinet warehouses. At length she arrives at one offering an excellent variety. She is accosted, and invited to enter, by a polite and voluble individual at the door. She finds a sofa well adapted to her views, and, upon inquiring the price, is surprised and delighted to hear a sum named at least twenty per cent lower than her expectations. She hastens to make the purchase, gets a bill and receipt, leaves her address, with a request that the article be sent home as speedily as possible, and retires amid a profusion of

① grin，名词，露齿而笑。

时将双手放在裤子口袋里，对你冷嘲热讽，惹你生气。他们吃你的饭，喝你的酒，借你的钱，拧你的鼻子，踹你的狗，还要吻你的老婆。

沾沾自喜——真正的骗子大功告成时，定会笑得合不拢嘴。但这一点，他们只能孤芳自赏。当一天的差事完成时，即分配给他们的活儿干完后，骗子就会笑逐颜开。晚上回到自己的房间后，他们满面春风，完全是自娱自乐。他们回到家，锁好门，脱衣就寝，吹灭蜡烛，惬意地枕着枕头。做完这些事后，骗子就会沾沾自喜。这并非假设，而是顺理成章的事，是从本质到表象推演出来的。如果没有洋洋自得，欺骗就不能算是欺骗。

欺骗的起源可以追溯到人类的婴幼儿时期。亚当[①]有可能就是第一个骗子。无论如何，骗术都可以追溯到极其遥远的古代。然而，现代人的行骗术登峰造极，这是我们的祖先民智未开，根本无法想象的。因此，我没必要翻“老黄历”，简明扼要地讲几件“时新事”就可以了。

以下是一次精彩的骗局。比如，一个家庭主妇想要买一把沙发，有人看见她进出了好几家家具店。最后，她到了一家沙发款式多样、质量颇佳的店，门口的人彬彬有礼、滔滔不绝，迎上前来，邀她进店。她看到一款十分中意的沙发，一问价钱，发现比自己预想的低了两成，不禁喜出望外。她很爽快地买下沙发，拿了账单和收据，留下自己的地址，并要求尽快把货送到家里，然后在店主的频频鞠躬中离开了。到了晚上，沙发还没送到。她派了一个用人去打听延误的原因，可对方却根本不承认有这笔买卖。他们没有出售过沙发——没人收到过钱——当然这不包括那个临时冒充店主的骗子。

① 根据《圣经》，亚当是上帝造就的第一个人。

bows from the shop-keeper. The night arrives and no sofa. A servant is sent to make inquiry about the delay. The whole transaction is denied. No sofa has been sold — no money received — except by the diddler, who played shop-keeper for the nonce.

Our cabinet warehouses are left entirely unattended, and thus afford every facility for a trick of this kind. Visiters enter, look at furniture, and depart unheeded and unseen. Should any one wish to purchase, or to inquire the price of an article, a bell is at hand, and this is considered amply sufficient.

Again, quite a respectable diddle is this. A well-dressed individual enters a shop, makes a purchase to the value of a dollar; finds, much to his vexation, that he has left his pocket-book in another coat pocket; and so says to the shop-keeper —

"My dear sir, never mind! — just oblige me, will you, by sending the bundle home? But stay! I really believe that I have nothing less than a five-dollar bill, even there. However, you can send four dollars in change with the bundle, you know."

"Very good, sir," replies the shop-keeper, who entertains, at once, a lofty opinion of the high-mindedness of his customer. "I know fellows," he says to himself, "who would just have put the goods under their arm, and walked off with a promise to call and pay the dollar as they came by in the afternoon."

A boy is sent with the parcel and change. On the route, quite accidentally, he is met by the purchaser, who exclaims:

"Ah! This is my bundle, I see — I thought you had been home with it, long ago. Well, go on! My wife, Mrs. Trotter, will give you the five dollars — I left instructions with her to that effect. The change

家具店根本无人看管，因此给这种骗局提供了无穷的便利。顾客进来，看家具，然后离开，整个过程都无人理睬。如果有人想购买家具或是询问价格，可以摇摇手边的铃铛，人们觉得这样安排就够了。

以下是一次体面的骗局。一个穿着体面的人进了一家商店，买了价值一美元的东西，结果却懊丧地发现自己把钱包忘在了另一件大衣的口袋里，于是他对店主说——

“亲爱的先生，请别介意！——您能帮个忙，把东西送到我家吗？先等等！我觉得我家里的钞票也都是五元以上的。不过，你可以把货物和四元的找零一起送来。”

“好的，先生，”店主答道，立刻对这位顾客的高尚品德有了很高的评价。他心里想，要是别人，肯定会答应下午路过时再来付款，然后把东西夹在腋下匆匆离去。

店主派一个伙计去送货物，并带着找零。伙计在路上恰巧遇见了那位顾客，顾客嚷道：

“啊！这是我的东西——我以为你很早就送到我家了。去吧，我的太太乔特夫人会给你五元钱的——我已经吩咐过她了。找零你最好还是给我吧——我去邮局需要些零钱。很好！一块、两块，

you might as well give to me — I shall want some silver for the Post Office. Very good! One, two, is this a good quarter? — three, four — quite right! Say to Mrs. Trotter that you met me, and be sure now and do not loiter on the way."

The boy doesn't loiter at all — but he is a very long time in getting back from his errand — for no lady of the precise name of Mrs. Trotter is to be discovered. He consoles himself, however, that he has not been such a fool as to leave the goods without the money, and re-entering his shop with a self-satisfied air, feels sensibly hurt and indignant when his master asks him what has become of the change.

A very simple diddle, indeed, is this. The captain of a ship which is about to sail, is presented by an official looking person with an unusually moderate bill of city charges. Glad to get off so easily, and confused by a hundred duties pressing upon him all at once, he discharges the claim forthwith. In about fifteen minutes, another and less reasonable bill is handed him by one who soon makes it evident that the first collector was a diddler, and the original collection a diddle.

And here, too, is a somewhat similar thing. A steamboat is casting loose from the wharf. A traveller, portmanteau in hand, is discovered running towards the wharf at full speed. Suddenly, he makes a dead halt, stoops, and picks up something from the ground in a very agitated manner. It is a pocket-book, and — "Has any gentleman lost a pocket-book?" he cries. No one can say that he has exactly lost a pocket-book; but a great excitement ensues, when the treasure trove is found to be of value. The boat, however, must not be detained.

"Time and tide wait for no man," says the captain.

这不是假币吧？——三块、四块——正好！和我太太说你遇到我了，现在就去，别在路上闲逛。”

那伙计根本就没有闲逛——但他却在这趟差使上费了很长时间——因为他没找到所谓的乔特夫人。然而，他自我安慰道，毕竟自己还没傻到没拿钱就把东西留下。他回到店里，看上去倒挺得意的。当老板问他找零哪儿去了时，他还觉得愤愤不平，显然内心很受伤。

以下是一次简单的骗局。一艘船即将起航，船长接见了一个官员模样的人，并收到了一份异常合理的市政收费单据。船长喜于能如此容易地了结此事，且因诸事缠身、头昏脑涨，他立即付清了账单。15分钟后，他收到了另一张不太合理的账单。递单人很快证实了前者是个骗子，前一次收款是骗局。

这里还有一个类似的情况。轮船即将离开码头，这时，一个手拿行李箱的旅客飞奔过来。突然，他停住了，俯下身，烦躁不安地从地上拾起一样东西。那是一个钱包，于是他喊道：“哪位先生遗失了钱包？”没有人会说自己正好掉了钱包。但当那位旅客发现钱包里的钱款数额不小时，人群一阵骚动。然而，船不可能就此滞留。

“时间不等人。”船长说。

"For God's sake, stay only a few minutes," says the finder of the book — "the true claimant will presently appear."

"Can't wait!" replies the man in authority; "cast off there, d'ye hear?"

"What am I to do?" asks the finder, in great tribulation. "I am about to leave the country for some years, and I cannot conscientiously retain this large amount in my possession. I beg your pardon, sir," [here he addresses a gentleman on shore,] "but you have the air of an honest man. Will you confer upon me the favor of taking charge of this pocket-book — I know I can trust you — and of advertising it? The notes, you see, amount to a very considerable sum. The owner will, no doubt, insist upon rewarding you for your trouble —"

"Me! — no, you! — it was you who found the book."

"Well, if you must have it so — I will take a small reward — just to satisfy your scruples. Let me see — why these notes are all hundreds — bless my soul! a hundred is too much to take — fifty would be quite enough, I am sure —"

"Cast off there!" says the captain.

"But then I have no change for a hundred, and upon the whole, you had better —"

"Cast off there!" says the captain.

"Never mind!" cries the gentleman on shore, who has been examining his own pocket-book for the last minute or so — "never mind! I can fix it — here is a fifty on the Bank of North America — throw me the book."

And the over-conscientious finder takes the fifty with marked reluctance, and throws the gentleman the book, as desired, while

"看在上帝的分上，等几分钟吧，"那位旅客说，"真正的失主很快就会出现的。"

"不能等！"大权在握的船长回答道，"准备开船，听到了吗？"

"那我该怎么办？"这位旅客十分为难地问道，"我要出国好几年呢，私吞这笔巨款，我于心不安啊。我恳求您，先生，"（这时，他对岸上的一位先生说）"你一看就像是个老实人。你可不可以帮我保管这个钱包——我知道我可以信任你——并为此登一则失物招领广告吗？你看这钱是一笔相当可观的数目了。失主无疑会为此酬谢你的——"

"谢我？——不，该谢的是你！——是你发现钱包的。"

"好吧，如果你执意如此，我就拿点酬劳吧，免得你心里不安。让我看看——为什么都是百元大钞——天啊，拿100美元太多了——我觉得50美元差不多了——"

"开船！"船长下令道。

"可我找不开100美元啊，想来想去，你最好——"

"开船！"船长喊道。

"不要紧！"岸上的那位先生喊道，他刚翻看了自己的钱包。"不要紧，我有办法。我这儿有一张北美银行发行的50美元钞票——把钱包给我吧。"

那位过分正直的旅客很不情愿地收下了50美元，然后按岸上那位先生的要求，把钱包扔给了他。轮船嘶嘶作响地冒着浓烟起航

the steamboat fumes and fizzes on her way. In about half an hour after her departure, the "large amount" is seen to be a "counterfeit presentment," and the whole thing a capital diddle.

A bold diddle is this. A camp-meeting, or something similar, is to be held at a certain spot which is accessible only by means of a free bridge. A diddler stations himself upon this bridge, respectfully informs all passers-by of the new county law, which establishes a toll of one cent for foot passengers, two for horses and donkeys, and so forth, and so forth. Some grumble but all submit, and the diddler goes home a wealthier man by some fifty or sixty dollars well earned. This taking a toll from a great crowd of people is an excessively troublesome thing.

A neat diddle is this. A friend holds one of the diddler's promises to pay, filled up and signed in due form, upon the ordinary blanks printed in red ink. The diddler purchases one or two dozen of these blanks, and every day dips one of them in his soup, makes his dog jump for it, and finally gives it to him as a *bonne bouche*① . The note arriving at maturity, the diddler, with the diddler's dog, calls upon the friend, and the promise to pay is made the topic of discussion. The friend produces it from his *escritoire*, and is in the act of reaching it to the diddler, when up jumps the diddler's dog and devours it forthwith. The diddler is not only surprised but vexed and incensed at the absurd behavior of his dog, and expresses his entire readiness to cancel the obligation at any moment when the evidence of the obligation shall be forthcoming.

A very minute diddle is this. A lady is insulted in the street by a diddler's accomplice. The diddler himself flies to her assistance, and, giving his friend a comfortable thrashing, insists upon attending the

① 法语，意思是"美味可口的食物"，此处译为"美食"。

了。大约半小时后，岸上那位先生就发现这所谓的"一大笔钱"都是假的，整件事情不过是一场绝佳的骗局。

以下是一次大胆的骗局。一次野营会或类似的聚会，举办场地只有通过一座不用收费的桥才能抵达。一个骗子站在这座桥上，恭敬地告知每位路过的人该县新公布的法律规定，即每个步行过桥的人要收一美分，马匹或驴子经过，要收两美分等。虽然有人抱怨，但无人拒缴。骗子回家后，身家一下子多了五六十美元。不过诸如此类的骗局，要收取一大群人的钱，也是件麻烦事。

以下是一次干净利落的骗局。骗子的一位朋友持有他许诺还款的字据，字据是用红墨水印制的普通表格，已填写妥当并签字。那骗子买了几十张这种票据，每天取一张浸在汤里，训练他的狗跳跃扑食，最后再把它当美食赏给这条狗。还款的日子到了，骗子带着他的狗一起拜访了他的那位朋友，那张他许诺还款的字据就是他们谈论的主要话题。当朋友从写字台中取出字据，递给骗子时，那条狗立即跳起，将字据扑食。骗子不仅大为吃惊，且对狗的荒唐行为十分恼怒，他向朋友表示，一旦有了他欠款的字据，他随时准备前来还款。

以下是一次小打小闹的骗局。一位女士在大街上被骗子的同伙侮辱，骗子飞身相救，在不痛不痒地打了他同伙一顿之后，坚持要送这位女士回家。到家后，他把手放在胸口，鞠了个躬，非常恭敬地与她道别。那位女士邀请他，以她救命恩人的身份，进屋小坐，并将

lady to her own door. He bows, with his hand upon his heart, and most respectfully bids her adieu. She entreats him, as her deliverer, to walk in and be introduced to her big brother and her papa. With a sigh, he declines to do so. "Is there no way, then, sir," she murmurs, "in which I may be permitted to testify my gratitude?"

"Why, yes, madam, there is. Will you be kind enough to lend me a couple of shillings?"

In the first excitement of the moment the lady decides upon fainting outright. Upon second thought, however, she opens her purse-strings and delivers the specie. Now this, I say, is a diddle minute — for one entire moiety of the sum borrowed has to be paid to the gentleman who had the trouble of performing the insult, and who had then to stand still and be thrashed for performing it.

Rather a small, but still a scientific diddle is this. The diddler approaches the bar of a tavern, and demands a couple of twists of tobacco. These are handed to him, when, having slightly examined them, he says:

"I don't much like this tobacco. Here, take it back, and give me a glass of brandy and water in its place."

The brandy and water is furnished and imbibed, and the diddler makes his way to the door. But the voice of the tavern-keeper arrests him.

"I believe, sir, you have forgotten to pay for your brandy and water."

"Pay for my brandy and water! — didn't I give you the tobacco for the brandy and water? What more would you have?"

"But, sir, if you please, I don't remember that you paid me for

他介绍给她的哥哥和爸爸。他叹了口气，拒绝了邀请。她低声说："先生，有什么方法可以让我表达一下我的感激之情吗？"

"有啊，小姐，有的。请问你可以借我几个先令吗？"

起初，这位女士感到一阵不安，宁愿晕过去。但转念一想后，她打开了钱包，将钱递给他。我说这是一次小打小闹的骗局——因为借来的钱有整整一半要付给那个扮演侮辱女士、随后还得一动不动地站着被暴打一顿的人。

以下是一个不大却毫无破绽的骗局。骗子来到一家酒馆的吧台，点了几根卷烟。东西送来后，他扫了一眼，说道：

"我不太喜欢这种烟。拿回去吧，给我换杯兑水的白兰地。"

兑水的白兰地送来了。骗子喝光后，朝门口走去，但是店主叫住了他。

"先生，我想你忘了付兑水白兰地的钱了。"

"付兑水白兰地的钱！——我不是用烟换的兑水白兰地吗？你还想要什么呢？"

"但是先生，我记得你没付过烟钱。"

the tobacco."

"What do you mean by that, you scoundrel? — Didn't I give you back your tobacco? Isn't that your tobacco lying there? Do you expect me to pay for what I did not take?"

"But, sir," says the publican, now rather at a loss what to say, "but sir —"

"But me no buts, sir," interrupts the diddler, apparently in very high dudgeon, and slamming the door after him, as he makes his escape. — "But me no buts, sir, and none of your tricks upon travellers."

Here again is a very clever diddle, of which the simplicity is not its least recommendation. A purse, or pocket-book, being really lost, the loser inserts in one of the daily papers of a large city a fully descriptive advertisement.

Whereupon our diddler copies the facts of this advertisement, with a change of heading, of general phraseology and address. The original, for instance, is long, and verbose, is headed "A Pocket-Book Lost!" and requires the treasure, when found, to be left at No. 1 Tom Street. The copy is brief, and being headed with "Lost" only, indicates No. 2 Dick, or No. 3 Harry Street, as the locality at which the owner may be seen. Moreover, it is inserted in at least five or six of the daily papers of the day, while in point of time, it makes its appearance only a few hours after the original. Should it be read by the loser of the purse, he would hardly suspect it to have any reference to his own misfortune. But, of course, the chances are five or six to one, that the finder will repair to the address given by the diddler, rather than to that pointed out by the rightful proprietor. The former pays the reward, pockets the treasure and decamps.

“你这个无赖，你这是什么意思啊？——我不是把烟还给你了吗？你的烟不就在那儿吗？难道你想让我为我没买的东西付钱？”

“但是，先生，”酒店老板一下子不知该说什么才好，“但是，先生——”

“先生，别和我说那么多‘但是’。”骗子打断了他，神情异常气愤。他摔门而去，末了还说了句：“先生，别和我说那么多‘但是’，别用你的把戏愚弄我们这些旅客。”

以下又是一次十分聪明的骗局，其简便易行颇值得推荐。某人真的丢了钱包，于是他在某大城市的一份日报上登了一则寻物启事，详细描述了所丢的钱包。

骗子抄录了那条寻物启事中提及的事实，但对标题、用词和地址做了修改。例如，原来的寻物启事冗长啰唆，标题是：“钱包遗失！”要求拾到者把钱包送到汤姆街一号。骗子抄录的版本则十分简单，标题仅为“遗失”两字，并请拾到者把钱包送到诸如迪克街二号或是哈利街三号之类的地方，即可见到失主。不仅如此，这份寻物启事当天至少刊登在五六份日报上，刊登时间也只比原来的那份晚了几小时。就算真正的失主看到了这则寻物启事，他也不太可能由此联想到自己的不幸遭遇。但是，拾到者把钱包交给骗子的概率与交给真正失主的概率之比是5 ∶ 1或6 ∶ 1。骗子只需付点酬金，便可拿好钱包，溜之大吉。

Quite an analogous diddle is this. A lady of ton has dropped, somewhere in the street, a diamond ring of very unusual value. For its recovery, she offers some forty or fifty dollars reward — giving, in her advertisement, a very minute description of the gem, and of its settings, and declaring that, on its restoration at No. so and so, in such and such Avenue, the reward would be paid instanter, without a single question being asked. During the lady's absence from home, a day or two afterwards, a ring is heard at the door of No. so and so, in such and such Avenue; a servant appears; the lady of the house is asked for and is declared to be out, at which astounding information, the visitor expresses the most poignant regret. His business is of importance and concerns the lady herself. In fact, he had the good fortune to find her diamond ring. But perhaps it would be as well that he should call again. "By no means!" says the servant; and "By no means!" says the lady's sister and the lady's sister-in-law, who are summoned forthwith. The ring is clamorously identified, the reward is paid, and the finder nearly thrust out of doors. The lady returns, and expresses some little dissatisfaction with her sister and sister-in-law, because they happen to have paid forty or fifty dollars for a fac-simile[①] of her diamond ring — a fac-simile made out of real pinchbeck and unquestionable paste.

But as there is really no end to diddling, so there would be none to this essay, were I even to hint at half the variations, or inflections, of which this science is susceptible. I must bring this paper, perforce, to a conclusion, and this I cannot do better than by a summary notice[②] of a very decent, but rather elaborate diddle, of which our own city

① 源自拉丁语，意思是"相似、仿真"。
② notice，名词，此处意思是"回顾"。

以下是一次与之极为相似的骗局。一位时尚女郎在大街上遗失了一枚价值不菲的钻戒。为了找到它，她将悬赏拾到者四五十美元。在寻物启事中，她非常详尽地描述了那件宝贝和它上面的镶嵌物，并宣称，若有人将其归还到某街某号，酬金马上支付，绝无半句啰唆。一两天后，趁该女士外出时，有人按响了某街某号家的门铃，用人应声而出。来者求见该女士，却被告知她并不在家。惊闻这个消息后，来访者深表遗憾，因为他有要事求见，而这要事与这位女士本人有关，事实上他有幸找到了那枚钻戒。也许他下次再来，也是一样吧。“绝对不行！”用人说。该女士的妹妹和妹夫闻讯赶来，也异口同声地说道：“绝对不行！”大家吵吵嚷嚷地验明了戒指正身，付了酬金，将来者几乎是推出门去。可女士回到家后，却对妹妹和妹夫略表不满，因为他们花了四五十美元换了一枚假的钻戒——那其实是一枚用正宗的仿金合金和地道的人造宝石制成的假钻戒。

然而，骗术是无止境的。即便我只是枚举这门学问诸多变化中的一半，这篇文章也收不了尾。但文章总得结尾，我想简要地回顾某次体面而周密的骗局并就此搁笔是最好不过的了。这个骗局不久前在本市上演，之后又在合众国某些更易行骗的地方一再发生。一位中年绅士从一个不为人知的地方来到这座城市。他为人严谨，绝不鲁莽，相当沉稳，三思而后行。他衣着整洁，但朴实无华，打着白色领结，穿着只求舒服的宽松背心和没有吊带的裤子，脚上是一

was made the theatre, not very long ago, and which was subsequently repeated with success, in other still more verdant localities of the Union. A middle-aged gentleman arrives in town from parts unknown. He is remarkably precise, cautious, staid, and deliberate in his demeanor. His dress is scrupulously neat, but plain, unostentatious. He wears a white cravat, an ample waistcoat, made with an eye to comfort alone; thick-soled cosy-looking shoes, and pantaloons without straps. He has the whole air, in fact, of your well-to-do, sober-sided, exact, and respectable "man of business," *par excellence* — one of the stern and outwardly hard, internally soft, sort of people that we see in the crack high comedies — fellows whose words are so many bonds, and who are noted for giving away guineas, in charity, with the one hand, while, in the way of mere bargain, they exact the uttermost fraction of a farthing with the other.

He makes much ado before he can get suited with a boarding-house. He dislikes children. He has been accustomed to quiet. His habits are methodical — and then he would prefer getting into a private and respectable small family, piously inclined. Terms, however, are no object — only he must insist upon settling his bill on the first of every month, (it is now the second) and begs his landlady, when he finally obtains one to his mind, not on any account to forget his instructions upon this point — but to send in a bill, and receipt, precisely at ten o'clock, on the first day of every month, and under no circumstances to put it off to the second.

These arrangements made, our man of business rents an office in a reputable rather than a fashionable quarter of the town. There is nothing he more despises than pretence. "Where there is much

双看起来很舒服的厚底鞋。事实上，他看上去完全就是那种富有、沉稳、严谨、令人尊敬的“商人”，堪称表率——他就像我们在一流喜剧中常看到的某类人一样，外表严厉而内心温柔；他们言出必行，而且，如您所知，行善时一掷千金，讨价还价时锱铢必较。

他大费周折之后才找到一个寄宿处。习惯了安静生活的他不喜欢孩子，他的生活习惯有条不紊——因此他更想入住一个不吵不闹、受人尊敬、一心信教的小家庭。费用什么的倒不是问题——不过他坚持要在每月的第一天支付账单（今天是二号了）。当他终于找到一户中意的人家时，他叮嘱女主人，无论如何不可忘记这一点——每月一号的十点整，把账单和收条给他送去，无论如何都不能拖到第二天。

安排完这些事后，这位生意人在城里一块体面但并不时尚的地方租了一间办公室。他最看不起矫揉造作，他说：“外表光鲜亮丽之处，背后定是虚无肤浅。”女房东对他的这席话感触颇深，于是立即

show," he says, "there is seldom anything very solid behind" — an observation which so profoundly impresses his landlady's fancy, that she makes a pencil memorandum of it forthwith, in her great family Bible, on the broad margin of the Proverbs of Solomon.

The next step is to advertise, after some such fashion as this, in the principal business sixpennies ① of the city — the pennies are eschewed as not "respectable" — and as demanding payment for all advertisements in advance. Our man of business holds it as a point of his faith that work should never be paid for until done.

WANTED — The advertisers, being about to commence extensive business operations in this city, will require the services of three or four intelligent and competent clerks, to whom a liberal salary will be paid. The very best recommendations, not so much for capacity, as for integrity, will be expected. Indeed, as the duties to be performed, involve high responsibilities, and large amounts of money must necessarily pass through the hands of those engaged, it is deemed advisable to demand a deposit of fifty dollars from each clerk employed. No person need apply, therefore, who is not prepared to leave this sum in the possession of the advertisers, and who cannot furnish the most satisfactory testimonials of morality. Young gentlemen piously inclined will be preferred. Application should be made between the hours of ten and eleven A. M., and four and five P. M., of Messrs.

BOGS, HOGS, LOGS, FROGS, & Co.

No. 110 Dog Street

① 当时许多比较贵的报纸杂志定价都是六便士。此处的 business sixpennies 指的就是 business/mercantile sixpenny papers/magazines。

用铅笔记在家用圣经中《所罗门箴言》[1] 边缘的空白处。

下一步是刊登广告。依照时新的做法，广告得登在本市主要的高价商业性刊物上，而且需要提前支付广告的费用——但我们的这位生意人对费用避而不谈，因为这“有辱斯文”。他秉持的一条信念是，只有事情做成了才该付款。

招聘——本公司将在本市大力发展业务，诚招三四位有头脑、有才干的员工，待遇优厚。本公司并不特别注重能力，而看重品行端正。事实上，由于该工作责任重大、涉及经手大笔钱款，因此，每位雇员最好先交纳50美元押金。如不打算向本公司交纳押金或者无法提供有效道德品质证明，请勿应聘。优先考虑虔诚信奉教规的年轻绅士。请于上午10点至11点或下午4点至5点间将申请表送至本公司。

布格斯、豪格斯、罗格斯、弗洛格斯公司

道格街110号

① 圣经的《所罗门箴言》，所载多为睿智之语，教人如何持身守节、行善避恶等。

By the thirty-first day of the month, this advertisement has brought to the office of Messrs. Bogs, Hogs, Logs, Frogs and Company, some fifteen or twenty young gentlemen piously inclined. But our man of business is in no hurry to conclude a contract with any — no man of business is ever precipitate — and it is not until the most rigid catechism in respect to the piety of each young gentleman's inclination, that his services are engaged and his fifty dollars receipted for, just by way of proper precaution, on the part of the respectable firm of Bogs, Hogs, Logs, Frogs, and Company. On the morning of the first day of the next month, the landlady does not present her bill, according to promise — a piece of neglect for which the comfortable head of the house ending in *ogs*, would no doubt have chided her severely, could he have been prevailed upon to remain in town a day or two for that purpose.

As it is, the constables have had a sad time of it, running hither and thither, and all they can do is to declare the man of business most emphatically, a "hen knee high"① — by which some persons imagine them to imply that, in fact, he is n. e. i.② — by which again the very classical phrase *non est inventus*, is supposed to be understood. In the meantime the young gentlemen, one and all, are somewhat less piously inclined than before, while the landlady purchases a shilling's worth of the best Indian rubber, and very carefully obliterates the pencil memorandum that some fool has made in her great family Bible, on the broad margin of the Proverbs of Solomon.

① 这个词组无处可查，疑为作者自创，所以按字面意思翻译成“高脚鸡”。
② 此处的 n. e. i. 显然无所指，故结合上下文译为“溜得快”。

到了当月的31号，这则广告已为布格斯、豪格斯、罗格斯、弗洛格斯公司招揽了15至20位虔诚信奉教规的年轻绅士。但是我们的这位生意人并不急于和他们中的任何一位签合同——生意人从不草率——直到他们通过关于是否虔诚信奉教规的严格的教义问答后，这些年轻人才得以录用并交纳50美元押金。这是这家体面的布格斯、豪格斯、罗格斯、弗洛格斯公司采取的正当预防措施。第二个月的第一天早上，女房东并没有像之前答应的那样，把账单给这位生意人——那家格斯公司的头头无疑会因这个小疏忽而严厉批评她——可前提是，如果人们能说服他为了这一目的，继续在本市待上一两天。

事实上，警方正为到处寻找此人而忙得焦头烂额，可他们所能做的，只不过是郑重其事地宣布那位生意人实则一只"高脚鸡"——有人认为，警方的这一说法事实上是在暗示他"溜得快"——也有人认为，这就是古话说的：此人下落不明。与此同时，那些年轻绅士们通通都不像从前一样虔诚了，而那位女房东则花了一先令买了块最好的印度橡皮，非常小心地擦掉了某个蠢货当初用铅笔在她的家用圣经中《所罗门箴言》边缘的空白处所做的记录。